MORTGAGE MYTHS

77 Secrets That Will Save You Thousands on Home Financing

RALPH ROBERTS, CRS, GRI

CHIP CUMMINGS, CMC

BICENTENNIAL
1807
WILEY
2007
BICENTENNIAL

John Wiley & Sons, Inc.

Published by John Wiley & Sons, Inc., Hoboken, New Jersey.
Published simultaneously in Canada.

Wiley Bicentennial Logo: Richard J. Pacifico.

For general information on our other products and services or for technical support, please contact our Customer Care Department within the United States at (800) 762-2974, outside the United States at (317) 572-3993 or fax (317) 572-4002.

Wiley also publishes its books in a variety of electronic formats. Some content that appears in print may not be available in electronic formats. For more information about Wiley products, visit our web site at www.wiley.com.

Library of Congress Cataloging-in-Publication Data:

Roberts, Ralph.
    Mortgage myths: 77 secrets that will save you thousands on home financing / Ralph Roberts, Chip Cummings.
        p. cm.
    Includes index.
    ISBN 978-0-470-19587-1 (pbk.)
    1. House buying.   2. Mortgage loans.   3. Residential real estate—Purchasing.
    I. Cummings, Chip.   II. Title.
HD1390.5.R63 2008
332.7′22–dc22

                                                                                    2007026269

Printed in the United States of America.

10 9 8 7 6 5 4 3 2 1

What Others Are Saying...

"The whole process starts by dealing with people you can trust. You can trust your first step with Chip and Ralph, as they have put together an incredible collection of 'truths' brought to you by the biggest names in the business. *Mortgage Myths* tears down the wall between you and the home buying process, exposes the real secrets to building equity, and gets you on the Road to Homeownership—the right way!"

—Eric Weinstein, CEO, Carteret Mortgage Corporation

"Never has there been a time when borrowers have needed more solid, dependable information, and that's what Chip and Ralph deliver in *Mortgage Myths*. This should be in the hands of every borrower out there!"

—Joe Falk, past president, National Association of Mortgage Brokers

"Consumers today need to arm themselves with the best tools available. *Mortgage Myths* gives borrowers a sledgehammer! It provides straight answers that will allow even a first-time homebuyer to deal like a pro. This book is a must-read for anyone serious about saving money on home financing!"

—Barry Habib, CEO, Mortgage Market Guide, and frequent guest on CNBC

"Every consumer needs to read this book! *Mortgage Myths* shows you exactly how to go about the home-buying process—without losing your shirt!"

—Tim Wooding, president, Executive Mortgage Group; president, Kansas Association of Mortgage Brokers

"With so many new mortgage programs available, it really has become a world of 'buyer beware!' Chip and Ralph have sorted through all the 'hype,' and provided a clear view of the basics you need to know when buying a home. I plan on giving this to every consumer that walks through our door!"

—Pam Bennett, vice president, Benchmark Mortgage

"If you're even thinking about buying a house, you can use this book. It even includes key forms and booklets no home buyer should be without."

—Ruth Faynor, National Education Consultant for the National Association of Mortgage Brokers (NAMB)

"Home ownership is the American dream. Too many times I've seen this dream go sour. We are in the business of making those dreams a reality, and Chip and Ralph have opened the doors! If you're a first-time homebuyer, REALTOR®, or loan officer, you've gotta have this book."

—Aaron Metaj, CEO, Apollo Mortgage Corp.

"Owning a home is the best thing you can ever do—it ties you to the community and makes you feel a part of things. This book will give you a running start so you can do it knowledgeably and without fear."

—Patrice Yamato, president, Florida Association of Mortgage Brokers

"Borrowers need to understand how the system works, and deal with professionals who know what they're doing. Read *Mortgage Myths* before you get started—it'll save you thousands in the long run."

—Sue Woodard, Vice President, Mortgage Market Guide

"The mortgage marketplace can be confusing and intimidating. In *Mortgage Myths*, Chip and Ralph cut to the heart of how to save money as a homebuyer, and what to look for in a mortgage planning professional. This is a must-have for anyone looking to build wealth and strategically utilize equity in real estate!"

—Steven Marshall, best-selling author of *The Millionaire Mortgage Planner*

For Debbie Forth and Lois Maljak—our incredible personal assistants, who have helped us touch the lives of thousands of homebuyers over the years, and devotes countless hours to helping our customers—and always with a smile!

To the millions of hard-working Americans who are pursuing the American Dream of Homeownership, building vibrant communities, and investing in the future of our great country, and to the thousands of loan officers, processors, underwriters, closers, real estate agents, and others who work hard every day to help people to do just that!

—Ralph & Chip

Contents

Foreword   xiii

Acknowledgments   xv

About the Authors   xvII

Introduction   xix

1   Where Do I Start?   1

MYTH #1   Renting Is Better than Buying.   2
MYTH #2   I Can't Qualify for a Loan.   7
MYTH #3   Only U.S. Citizens Can Qualify for a Mortgage.   11
MYTH #4   I Should Look at Some Houses First.   12
MYTH #5   I Need a Down Payment—But I Don't Have
           the Funds.   16
MYTH #6   I Should Make the Biggest Down Payment I Can.   18
MYTH #7   All Mortgage Companies and Loan Officers Are
           Licensed and Regulated.   21
MYTH #8   Big Lenders and Major Banks Are Always Better.   24
MYTH #9   My Best Bet Is to Use a Friend (or Someone Local).   26
MYTH #10   I'll Find a Better Deal on the Internet.   29
MYTH #11   I Can Get a Higher Return by Investing in Stocks.   33

2   Playing the Mortgage Game   37

MYTH #12   My Main Goal Is to Snag the Lowest Interest Rate.   37
MYTH #13   The Federal Reserve Controls Interest Rates.   42

MYTH #**14** Stay with Fixed Rates—ARMs Are Just Too Risky. 43
MYTH #**15** A Shorter Term Always Beats a 30- or 40-Year Term. 47
MYTH #**16** My Credit History Needs to be Perfect. 50
MYTH #**17** My Credit Score Determines My Loan's Approval. 55
MYTH #**18** Be Conservative—Don't Stretch Yourself. 61
MYTH #**19** I'm Divorced or Declared Bankruptcy, So I'll Never Qualify. 63
MYTH #**20** Special Financing Programs Aren't Available to Me. 66
MYTH #**21** I Should Avoid Mortgage Insurance. 68
MYTH #**22** The Good Faith Estimate Guarantees My Closing Costs. 71
MYTH #**23** I Have to Use the REALTOR®/Builder's Loan Officer. 73

3 Selecting the Right Home **77**

MYTH #**24** I'll Save Big Money Buying FSBO. 77
MYTH #**25** I Have to Shop Within a Certain Price Range. 80
MYTH #**26** Everything Is Included in the Sales Price. 82
MYTH #**27** The Appraiser Will Specify the Value and Any Required Repairs. 83
MYTH #**28** The Real Estate Agent Will Protect Us. 86
MYTH #**29** Condos Are Bad Investments and Hard to Finance. 90
MYTH #**30** Seller Disclosures Are Complete and Accurate. 92
MYTH #**31** I Should Buy the Biggest House at a Bargain Price. 95
MYTH #**32** I Should Always Use an Attorney. 96
MYTH #**33** I Don't Need an Inspection—It Looks Great to Me! 97
MYTH #**34** I've Seen Enough, I've Found the Home I Love! 100
MYTH #**35** It's Okay to Buy—This Area Is Booming. 101
MYTH #**36** All Sales Agreements and EMD Requirements Are Standard. 103
MYTH #**37** I Can't Withdraw My Offer—It's Too Late. 106
MYTH #**38** Beware of Foreclosures—They're a Headache. 107

MYTH **#39** I Make Money When I Sell—Not When I Buy. 114

MYTH **#40** My Tenants Will Finance My Investment Property. 116

4 The Mortgage Process 119

MYTH **#41** The Loan Process Takes a Long Time. 119

MYTH **#42** All Applications and Disclosure Forms Are
Standard. 122

MYTH **#43** We're Approved. Our Worries Are Over! 125

MYTH **#44** My Interest Rate Is Locked In *and* Guaranteed. 128

MYTH **#45** A Preapproval Is a Preapproval. 131

MYTH **#46** I Have to Let My Lender Escrow Taxes and
Insurance. 132

MYTH **#47** I'm Self Employed   Getting Approved Will
Be Tough. 133

MYTH **#48** The House Needs Repairs—We'll Do Them Later. 135

MYTH **#49** Personal Profiling Is Part of the Approval Process. 137

5 It's Closing Time 139

MYTH **#50** Someone Else Decides the Closing Date and
Location. 139

MYTH **#51** Why Do I Need Title Insurance—I Can't Even
Select the Provider. 140

MYTH **#52** It's Cheaper to Close at the End of the Month. 143

MYTH **#53** I Can't Review Documents in Advance. 144

MYTH **#54** The Seller's Home Warranty Protects Us. 146

MYTH **#55** The House Will Be in Move-In Condition. 149

MYTH **#56** It's All Triple-Checked and Ready to Go! 150

MYTH **#57** I Need Homeowners Insurance to Cover the Entire
Purchase Price. 152

MYTH **#58** I Need Credit Life Insurance to Protect Myself. 153

MYTH **#59** My House Payment Will Never Change. 154

6   The Refinance Game   157

MYTH #60   Never Refinance Until the Rate Is 2% Lower.   157

MYTH #61   I Should Never Refinance Into a Higher
Interest Rate.   161

MYTH #62   I'm Not Allowed to Pay Extra—There's a
Prepayment Penalty.   164

MYTH #63   Reverse Mortgages Are a Bad Idea.   166

MYTH #64   My Terms May Change If the Loan Is Sold.   169

MYTH #65   Refinancing Is Easy—I Already Qualify.   170

MYTH #66   Refinancing: Better than Home Equity or
Construction Loans.   172

MYTH #67   Low Inflation Means Low Appreciation.   173

MYTH #68   I Have to Live There at Least Three Years
to Break Even.   175

MYTH #69   Refinancing Is a Cheap Way to Get Cash.   177

MYTH #70   My Escrows Are Already Set Up.   179

7   Short of Cash? Creative Financing Solutions   181

MYTH #71   I Can't Use a Gift for a Down Payment.   181

MYTH #72   A Biweekly Mortgage Simply Changes My
Payment Schedule.   183

MYTH #73   Seller Financing Is Risky and Expensive.   185

MYTH #74   Government Loans Are Only for Low-Income
Borrowers.   189

MYTH #75   No Bank Will Finance Us.   190

MYTH #76   A Lease-Option Plan Is Always a Bad Idea.   197

MYTH #77   I Can't Make My Payments, So I'll Lose
My Home.   200

Appendix   207

Consumer Handbook on Adjustable Rate
   Mortgages   209
Buying Your Home   223
Mortgage Application—Form 1003   245
Sample Good Faith Estimate   249
Sample Truth in Lending Disclosure   250
Sample HUD-1 Closing Statement   251
Homebuyer Checklist   253
Home Financing Checklist   259
Personal Qualification Form   260
National/State Associations and Regulatory
   Agencies   260
Additional Resources   269
   Homebuyer Education Classes   269
   Other Web Site Resources   269
Terms You Need to Know   270

Index   273

Foreword

You may not be happy with your financial position, even though where you are today is the direct result of decisions you've made in the past.

The problem is that you made those decisions based on the information you had available—that's all any of us can do. To increase your wealth, you must increase your knowledge and then put what you learn into action. This book is a crucial tool for your future financial success!

We believe real estate is the greatest wealth-building vehicle available to the average person. Real estate gives us places to live, places to conduct business, and places for all of us to educate and entertain ourselves. Because of the enormous expense of installing the infrastructure to support a large population, real estate in the most desirable areas is somewhat limited in supply. With the population of the United States currently at over 300 million people (with projections to reach 400 million in less than 40 years), there is no doubt that the demand for real estate will continue to grow. As any economics student knows, when supply is limited and demand is growing, conditions are ripe for price increases—as long as buyers have the ability to pay.

Enter the mortgage. A mortgage is a powerful tool for helping people, including homeowners, businesses, and investors, to acquire and control real estate. With only a relatively small payment each month, a buyer can service a large mortgage and therefore control and enjoy the use of a piece of real estate. Over time, as the value of the real estate rises, equity happens and enriches the owner!

One of the most important keys to successful real estate ownership is the proper use of financing. In *Mortgage Myths—77 Insider Secrets to Saving Thousands on Home Financing*, mortgage expert and dynamic teacher Chip Cummings, and one of the biggest names in real estate in the nation, Ralph Roberts, do a fabulous job of revealing the insider secrets every borrower must know before obtaining a mortgage or a home. Chip and Ralph don't just teach theory. Instead, they draw upon years of first-hand experience as borrowers, mortgage brokers, real estate brokers, instructors, and industry insiders. Chip and Ralph pull together the knowledge of many other industry experts to create a useful resource to help people make informed choices when they borrow. Most importantly, they "get it"! They understand that mortgages aren't a disease to be avoided, but a powerful tool to be used strategically to build your real estate wealth.

Whether you are a first-time home buyer or an avid investor with dozens of properties, we are sure you will enjoy *Mortgage Myths* and the easy reading style. By dispelling the myths, you can put these great ideas into action and find the financing that is right for building your financial future. Remember: Equity Happens! And mortgages can help more of it happen to you.

To your success!

> —Robert Helms and Russell Gray
> Hosts of *The Real Estate Guys* Radio and TV Shows
> Authors of *Equity Happens—Building Lifelong Wealth with Real Estate*

Acknowledgments

Wow, incredible! Little did we realize when we started this project, how much support would pour in! Professionals and friends from across the country in every industry got excited and had a story to share.

There are so many people and organizations that assisted us during this project, but we would especially like to thank our dedicated staff at Northwind and Roberts Realty, especially our personal assistants Debbie Forth and Lois Maljak, assistant Jeff Haden, and our editor Laurie Harting. Others who made this possible.

Tim Kleyla, president, The Mortgage House; past president—Michigan Mortgage Brokers Assn.

David Pearson, CRMS, Division Manager, Bank of America; former Chair, National Education Committee, National Assn. of Mortgage Brokers

David Acquisti, president, M Source Financial; past president, Michigan Mortgage Brokers Assn.

Audrey Acquisti, president, M Source Training

Aaron Metaj, president, Apollo Mortgage

George Carroll, senior loan officer, The Home Loan Center

Jay Capozzoli, loan originator, The Home Loan Center

Matt Gibson, loan originator, The Home Loan Center

David Rodriquez, loan officer, The Home Loan Center

Pam Bennett, vice-president, Benchmark Mortgage

Paco Torch, CEO of Torch Mortgage Corp.; director of Georgia Assn. of Mortgage Brokers Education Foundation

Atare E. Agbamu, CRMS, president of *ThinkReverse LLC*

ACKNOWLEDGMENTS

Patrice Yamato, CMC, president of Florida Assn. of Mortgage Brokers

Joe Falk, CMC, past president of National Assn. of Mortgage Brokers

Lorenzo Wooten, regional director, Fannie Mae

Eric Weinstein, president, Carteret Mortgage Corporation

Amy Tierce, CEO, Fairway New England Mortgage

Ginny Ferguson, President, Heritage Valley Mortgage, Board member of NAMB

Tim Wooding, president of Executive Mortgage Group; past president of Kansas Assn. of Mortgage Brokers

Terri Murphy, real estate agent, US Learning Center

Barry Habib, CEO of Mortgage Market Guide

Sue Woodard, VP of Mortgage Market Guide

A big thanks to Bob Naperalski, Kristi Dockter, Greg Rau, of Greatland Corporation (www.Greatland.com) for contributing the forms and consumer guides.

We also wish to express our appreciation to the National Association of Mortgage Brokers, National Association of REALTORS®, the Mortgage Bankers Association of America, and the Michigan Mortgage Brokers Association for their support and assistance.

If you have a personal real estate experience or financing story to share, and want to contribute to future editions, go to www.TheMortgageMyths.com/stories.

About the Authors

Ralph Roberts, CRS, GRI

Ralph R. Roberts is the official spokesman for Guthy-Renker Home, a company dedicated to equipping homebuyers, sellers, and real estate professionals with the tools, information, and community setting they need to achieve mutual success. Visit www.HurryHome.com and www.RealtyTracker.com to experience the exciting innovations that Guthy-Renker Home offers now and is planning for the future.

Ralph has been profiled by the Associated Press, CNN, and *Time* magazine, and has done hundreds of radio interviews. He is a seasoned professional in all areas of real estate, including buying and selling homes, investing in real estate, and building and managing real estate agent teams. He is the author of several successful titles, including *Sell It Yourself: Sell Your Home Faster and for More Money without Using a Broker* (Adams Media Corporation); *Walk Like a Giant, Sell Like a Madman: America's #1 Salesman Shows You How to Sell Anything* (Collins); *52 Weeks of Sales Success: America's #1 Salesman Shows You How to Close Every Deal!* (Collins); *Real Wealth by Investing in Real Estate* (Prentice Hall); *Protect Yourself Against Real Estate and Mortgage Fraud: Preserving the American Dream of Homeownership* (Kaplan); *Flipping Houses for Dummies* (John Wiley & Sons); *Foreclosure Investing for Dummies* (John Wiley & Sons); and *Advanced Selling for Dummies* (John Wiley & Sons).

To find out more about Ralph Roberts and what he can offer you and your organization as a speaker and coach, visit AboutRalph.com. For details on how to protect yourself and your home from real estate and mortgage fraud, check out Ralph's blog at FlippingFrenzy.com. And don't miss the latest addition to his family of web sites and blogs, GetFlipping.com, where he offers additional information and tips on the art of flipping houses. You can contact Ralph by e-mailing him at RalphRoberts@RalphRoberts.com or calling 586-751-0000.

Chip Cummings, CMC

Chip Cummings is a recognized expert in the areas of real estate lending and e-marketing, and is a Certified Mortgage Consultant with over 24 years in the mortgage industry and over a billion dollars in sales volume.

Chip has written hundreds of articles and appeared numerous times on radio, on television, and in various magazines, including *Entrepreneur*, *Mortgage Originator*, *Real Estate Banker/Broker*, and *The Mortgage Press*. An experienced professional in all areas of real estate financing, including residential and commercial mortgages, government lending, and regulatory and compliance issues, he is past president of the Michigan Mortgage Brokers Association (MMBA), and is a licensed mortgage broker in Michigan.

As an international speaker, he has addressed groups and organizations of all types, and trains thousands of mortgage professionals from around the country every year. Chip is a certified national trainer for continuing education in more than 35 states, and has served as an expert witness in state and federal courts. He is also the author of *ABC's of FHA Lending* (Northwind) and *Stop Selling and Start Listening!—Marketing Strategies That Create Top Producers* (Northwind).

Chip lives in Rockford, Michigan, with his wife Lisa and three children, Katelyn, CJ, and Joe.

To learn more about Chip Cummings, his many success products, or how he can help your organization as a speaker or business consultant, visit www.ChipCummings.com. To receive a complimentary subscription to his multimedia e-newsletter "The Marketing Minute," check out www.TheMarketingMinute.com, and don't miss him on 24/7 Internet radio at www.PersonalPowerRadio.com. You can also reach Chip by e-mailing him at info@ChipCummings.com or by calling 616–977-7900.

Introduction

Ralph Roberts

I graduated high school with a 1.8 grade point average and $900 in the bank. (The $900 was a graduation gift.) I used it as a down payment on a fixer-upper in my neighborhood. I bought other investment properties with money I borrowed from my grandmother, with conventional loans (when banks would loan me money), and even with credit cards. One of my mentors taught me that the cost of borrowing money isn't something to worry too much about—the access to money is what's important.

I moved 19 times in 23 years, before marriage slowed me down. Over the course of 25 years, I earned hundreds of thousands of dollars buying and selling residential real estate. I've bought and sold thousands of properties and helped other people buy and sell thousands more through my real estate business. With my personal investment properties, I made most of my money using other people's money.

That's right, I borrowed it.

Far too many people are averse to taking on debt and the risk that often accompanies it. Our society has unleashed a mythological beast that scares us into believing that debt is evil and risky. Many people talk themselves out of buying an "expensive" house, even when that house would cost less than what they would pay in rent for a smaller home.

Most people are also convinced that borrowing money to invest in real estate is too risky, never realizing that by not taking a risk, they're increasing their financial burden.

In the *Mortgage Myths*, Chip Cummings and I blast away at the 77 myths that prevent would-be homeowners and real estate investors from pursuing their dreams of homeownership and wealth building. We distinguish between good debt and bad debt, reveal just how easy it is to obtain approval for a mortgage loan, and unveil the power of using other people's money to leverage your own personal investments.

If mortgage myths are holding you back from achieving your dream of owning your own home or from building wealth in real estate, let us liberate you as we blast away every single myth that's getting in your way.

—Ralph Roberts

December, 2007

Chip Cummings

I'm a very lucky man. I've had the privilege of helping thousands of people—from all walks of life—own their own home. To me, there's no bigger thrill—or privilege.

All of us want a place to call our own. In addition to providing shelter, as an added bonus, real estate creates more millionaires than any other form of investment. (How many other great investment vehicles can you live in?)

Closing on a new home should be a time for celebration and happiness. The process of buying a new home should be *fun*.

Unfortunately, for many, it's not.

The average person only buys a few homes over the course of a lifetime, and as a result, doesn't have a wealth of real estate and mortgage financing experience to draw from. The consequence for many Americans is that the process is more painful, time-consuming, and considerably more expensive than it needs to be. I've seen simple mistakes cost people thousands of dollars, hurt feelings, lost friendships, and stress levels reach so high that they've resulted in divorce.

Why? Because of the Mortgage Myths. Misinformation, misconceptions, and missteps—sometimes directly from well-meaning friends and family.

My goal is to expose the Mortgage Myths—and in the process help you save thousands on your next mortgage. You'll learn the secrets—directly from mortgage and real estate insiders—that will save you time, money, heartache, and possibly your sanity! You'll discover negotiating strategies, how to find the best loan for you, how to protect your investment, what to look for in selecting a home, and how to leverage the knowledge of experts to create your own real estate team.

To start, here's a key point. Do you see a mortgage as simply a debt or a bill that has to be paid every month? While it must be repaid, *a mortgage isn't just a debt*—it's actually a wealth-building tool. A mortgage helps you purchase a place to live and it secures a long-term investment, an investment that for many will be the most profitable one they'll ever make. But the investment isn't just in the real estate itself—it's in the financing. Smart homebuyers know that their mortgage is an integral part of their overall financial plan rather than just another debt.

While mortgage financing can be complicated, don't worry; I'll make it simple. I've drawn from my own experiences as well as those from acknowledged experts around the country to give you the inside secrets to how the mortgage industry works. And I've included plenty of real-world examples of home buying and mortgage mistakes—and successes—from homebuyers across the country. Many of these may sound all too familiar. That's because they all involve real people, in real situations! In fact, if you have a story you'd like to share with our readers, we'd love to hear from you! Tell us about your "myth" at www.TheMortgageMyth.com/stories.

Let me be the first to welcome you into the world of homeownership—from behind the scenes. I hope you enjoy reading this as much as I've enjoyed living it. Best of all, you'll learn how to be a knowledgeable and informed consumer because the more you know, the more you'll save!

—Chip Cummings, CMC

December, 2007

Important Disclosure Notice

This book may have been provided to you as part of a loan application package. As such, there are certain disclosures that are included in the Appendix section of this book. Please take the time to read these, and if you have any questions, discuss them with your loan officer, attorney or real estate agent. These comply with federal disclosure requirements, as of the date of printing, but may not be all the disclosures you are entitled to receive.

This publication is designed to provide accurate and authoritative information with regard to the subject matter covered. It is sold with the understanding that the publisher, author, and individual contributors are not engaged in rendering professional services. If professional advice or other expert assistance is required, the services of a competent professional should be sought.

As with any type of printed material, information is subject to change. All reference items, web sites, addresses, phone numbers, and program requirements were current as of date of publishing, but may change from time to time. For current updated information and releases, go to www.TheMortgageMyths.com.

Bulk quantities of this publication are available at a reduced cost for educational, nonprofit, corporate, or association distribution. Contact the publisher toll-free at (866) 977-7900, or go to www.TheMortgage Myths.com for more details.

Throughout this book, icons are used to illustrate important points— specific tips or strategies that can make, or cost, you thousands! They are:

STOP! This message is a warning, that, left unheeded, could wind up costing you extra time, money, or aggravation—or all three!

GO! This message is a tip or strategy that can save you time, money, and probably a lot of headaches!

SECTION 1

Where Do I Start?

For most people, that's the $200,000 question. Should I buy? Should I rent? How much cash do I need? Does house hunting or mortgage application come first? Asking one question just leads to three more questions.

Chip clearly remembers the day he first met Bruce and Mary. Bruce was 19, covered in sweat and grease from a local tool and die shop, and Mary was 18—fresh out of school and seven months pregnant.

With no extra money, and seemingly starting life with one hand tied behind their backs, they were given one simple instruction—go see Chip. The forceful directive came from her father, with whom Chip had worked on several mortgages over the years. "Go see Chip, and do exactly what he says," was the order.

Chip feels working with first-time home buyers has been a privilege over the years, but this case was a little different. Dad was a wealthy businessman, but was only willing to help the couple if they helped themselves.

Chip took extra time explaining the home buying process, the power of creating wealth through owning real estate—and more importantly, the concept of "mortgage management." With a REALTOR® by their side, they found a small two-bedroom cottage north of town, and once Dad was convinced they understood the plan, he chipped in the $1,400 gift to get them started. They nervously joined the ranks of millions of other first-time homeowners. *But they had a plan!*

"I remember the closing very well," says Chip, "We actually had to postpone it by a few days, since Mary had just given birth to a beautiful baby girl—the youngest person I've ever had attend a closing!"

Fast-forward 15 years. Chip is standing in a closing room with Bruce and Mary, admiring their now 15-year-old daughter, and reviewing their closing statement for the refinance on their four-family rental property. The property is just one of eight properties that they now own, many of which are free-and-clear of any debt. We're leveraging the property to invest in another multi-family unit. Needless to say, Bruce doesn't work at the tool and die shop any longer!

Simple? Yes. Easy? No. They made plenty of sacrifices over the years, but Chip gave them a plan. They listened, they learned, they executed. You can do the same thing yourself!

So where do we start? At the beginning, of course!

MYTH # **1**

Renting Is Better than Buying.

Fact: Owning Real Estate Is the Fastest Way to Build Wealth

Buying a home offers most families a sense of belonging, a sense of putting down roots, and a sense of shared community with neighbors. As a home-owner you can make improvements, decorate, and modify your home to match your lifestyle and your decorating tastes. The financial rewards are significant, too; let's look at just a few of the reasons that buying instead of renting is a great financial move.

You Pay Your Own Mortgage; Not Your Landlord's. When you rent, you're in effect helping your landlord make his or her mortgage payments. Let's compare the financial impact on a renter to that of you as a home-owner.

To make the comparison fair, we'll assume you both earn $60,000 per year, putting you in the 25% tax bracket. We'll also assume a rent payment of $1,000 and a house payment (principal and interest at 7%) of $1,000; as a homeowner, we'll also assume that you pay the national average of $3,000 per year in property taxes. (How far can a $1,000 per month mortgage payment go? You can get a $150,000 loan at 7% for 30 years!) Here's what happens to your rent payments (see Figure 1.1):

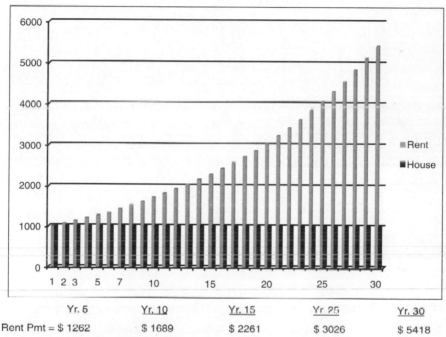

	Yr. 5	Yr. 10	Yr. 15	Yr 25	Yr. 30
Rent Pmt =	$ 1262	$ 1689	$ 2261	$ 3026	$ 5418

Figure 1.1 Monthly Payments. 30-year fixed mortgage payment of $1000 per month versus a $1000 per month rent payment. Assumes a rental increase of 6% per year.

Ouch! But wait, it gets better.... When it's time to pay income taxes, the renter pays $15,000 in taxes on the $60,000 income. You, however, only pay $11,507 in taxes because you can deduct your interest payments and your personal property tax. Your savings are $3,493 per year, or almost $291 per month. Those tax benefits make an $1100 house payment *feel* like a $850 rent payment! Take a look at how much farther your money will go (see Figure 1.2).

There's one other benefit to buying instead of renting; as long as you have a fixed-rate mortgage, your base mortgage payment will never go up — your landlord can increase the rent whenever your current lease expires!

Monthly Rent	15%	25%	28%	33%	35%
$ 600	$ 690	$ 768	$ 794	$ 843	$ 864
750	863	959	992	1,053	1,080
900	1,036	1,152	1,191	1,264	1,296
1,200	1,381	1,536	1,588	1,685	1,728
1,500	1,726	1,919	1,985	2,107	2,160
1,800	2,071	2,304	2,382	2,528	2,592
2,000	2,301	2,560	2,647	2,809	2,880
2,500	2,877	3,200	3,308	3,511	3,600
2,800	3,222	3,584	3,705	3,933	4,032

Figure 1.2 Monthly Rent-Equivalent Payments. Select your monthly rent in the left column. Select your tax bracket at the top to find your monthly mortgage payment-equivalent. Numbers assume year-1 P/I payment at 7% 30-year amortization. For example, if you are in the 28% tax bracket, paying $1500 per month—you could spend an equivalent of $1985 per month on your mortgage principal and interest payment—and it would feel the same.

You Take Advantage of a Great Long-Term Investment. Each year the U.S. government publishes statistics regarding median home prices. If you started with an average home with a value of $23,000 in 1970, take a look at how rapidly the median home price, including land, has appreciated over the past 35 years:

1970	$23,600
1975	$37,200
1980	$62,900
1985	$82,500
1990	$125,500
1995	$127,900
2000	$163,500
2005	$223,100
2007	$249,400 (1st quarter)

What's interesting to note is that while prices have certainly boomed in the past five years, prices have risen at double digit levels in nearly every five-year period! Very few investments can match that level of appreciation over the long term, and when you look at any 20-year stretch in history, real estate values have always gone up.

Although some markets around the country suffer some short-term hardships, real estate prices are likely to continue to rise, at least over the long term. Looking out over the next 20 years, the following is likely to happen:

- The U.S. population is expected to grow to over 400 million people.
- The U.S. median income is expected to increase by over 50%.
- Ten million people will choose to buy vacation homes in the United States.
- More than 60 million children and grandchildren of baby boomers will enter the housing market.
- Environmental restrictions and land shortages will tighten property development in popular areas, causing a decrease in supply and an increase in housing prices.
- More than 60 million baby boomers will seek retirement income, and many will sensibly turn to real estate investments.
- Minorities and immigrants will continue to buy homes in record numbers. Currently 75% of whites live in their own homes, while only 40% of Hispanics and Asians own their homes. As their rate of home ownership increases, demand for housing will increase.

So what's the end result? Real estate investing, like any other form of investing, is cyclical: As we write this, the United States is in the middle of the worst downturn in real estate values since the 1990s. In the future, values will continue to rise and fall—but over the long term, real estate prices will continue to rise, making smart real estate investing one of the best ways to grow wealth.

You Build Wealth—Tax-Free. Not only is the mortgage interest you pay tax-deductible, but so is the profit you make when you sell your home.

Let's take a $100,000 house, and compare renting it at $850 per month *(with 6% annual increase)* vs. purchasing it with a 5% down payment:

Year	0	1	5	10	15	20
Rental cost	$850	$10,200	$56,361	$128,294	$220,101	$337,272
Equity	0	0	0	0	0	0
Home value	$100,000	$105,000	$127,628	$484,987	$2,131,390	$4,052,194
Own (equity)*	$5,000	$ (34)	$24,832	$131,030	$574,994	$1,582,051

*Includes 8% maintenance and 3% tax expenses; reinvestment of equity every 5 years with 10% down in years 5–10 and 20% down in year 15.

Figure 1.3 Building Equity

When you sell your personal residence (defined as a home where you lived for at least two of the past five years), up to $250,000 in profits for an individual and $500,000 for a couple is tax free. You can buy and sell your personal residences every two years and continue to avoid taxes on your gains! But let's look at how the numbers work together (see Figure 1.3).

As you can see from the example, by simply upgrading your home every five years, and reinvesting the equity—in just 10 years you've increased your net worth by over $126,000! In 20 years, you've built a personal fortune of over $1.5 million—*and* you got to live in it!

We can't state this more strongly: You need to own your own home—unless you plan on moving in the next six months! Owning real estate should be the foundation of everyone's financial plan—if you don't already own a home, get started *today*.

(STOP) Although owning a home is one of the safest investments you can make, beware of buying into areas where property values are increasing at rates of 15–20% a year or more. If the area is growing in popularity, the rising rates may be justified, but soaring rates may be a sign of speculative investing or even illegal house flipping. Before you buy—know your market.

MYTH # **2**

I Can't Qualify for a Loan.

Fact: There Are Hundreds of Programs for Almost Any Conceivable Situation

What is one of the most creative and innovative industries today? You may be surprised, but the answer is the mortgage lending business. Seemingly every week, new loan programs are introduced—credit is no longer "one size fits all"; it's customized to the individual. Even though it sounds like programs are being eliminated or investors are going under, new ones step in to take their place. There are programs for first-timers, retirees, self-employed, zero-down, good credit, bad credit, even special programs for teachers, firefighters, police and medical workers!

Or you may be concerned you won't be able to obtain financing for a home in a "bad" neighborhood. Think again.

"Many consumers think they won't be able to get a loan in certain neighborhoods or areas," says Lorenzo Wooten, regional manager for the Federal National Mortgage Association (Fannie Mae). "We have programs specifically designed for under-served neighborhoods and communities. Our My Community mortgage program was created to help people finance homes in what some might consider 'bad' neighborhoods."

Even if you've experienced major credit problems like bankruptcy or foreclosure it's likely you can qualify for a mortgage. While it may be a mortgage with a higher interest rate or additional points and fees, if you want it—chances are that a subprime loan is out there waiting for you.

While "subprime" may sound a little rough, and many subprime lenders have taken a beating in the market and the media, they are vital to serving the interests of homeowners, buyers, and investors from all walks of life.

Subprime, by definition, refers to a category of loans that are not sold through the government-sponsored-agencies or GSEs such as Fannie Mae and Freddie Mac, and are made available to borrowers who have damaged credit or other extenuating circumstances. What is damaged credit? It could entail mortgage credit problems, consumer credit problems, collections, or public record postings. Mortgage credit refers to problems with past mortgages; consumer credit refers to problems with credit cards, car loans, or other nonmortgage credit; and public record postings refer to foreclosures or judgments against you.

Some lenders even specialize in making these subprime loans. Some mortgage brokers, for instance, have dozens of established relationships with a network of financial institutions willing to make subprime loans, and they work hard on behalf of their customers to help them qualify for financing in spite of their challenging situations.

But you may not need a subprime mortgage. "Say you're worried about having money for a down payment or closing costs," continues Lorenzo Wooten. "Or you're worried about bad credit or a bankruptcy. We've introduced a product called My Community mortgage: there's no minimum credit score, up to one hundred percent financing, seller concessions to help with closing costs, and private mortgage insurance (PMI) at roughly half the rate required for traditional loans. Overall the monthly payment will tend to be lower with a My Community mortgage than on subprime or even FHA loans."

"Anybody can get a mortgage," states Pam Bennett of Benchmark Mortgage, a 23-year industry veteran, who has underwritten more than 14,000 loans. "It's just a question of whether or not the mortgage they can get makes sense. Borrowers have to decide if they're willing to pay that rate . . . but there's a loan out there for anyone."

Subprime borrowers fall into different categories. An "A-minus" borrower might be someone who had a 30-day late mortgage payment in the past year, while a "D" borrower may have recently declared bankruptcy.

What level of subprime borrower you are isn't important (at least to you); what is important is what the loan will cost you. If you have a poor credit history, you'll pay more for a mortgage than a borrower with an outstanding credit history. (That may not seem fair, but think about it from the lender's perspective: the greater the level of risk they face in making a loan, the more they should be compensated for taking on that risk—otherwise why take the risk?) If you're an "A" borrower and qualify for a standard "conforming" loan, you'll get the best rates and terms. If you're a

"D" borrower, you may pay an interest rate premium that's between 2 and 10% higher than the rate available to "A" borrowers—until you can prove yourself!

If you have damaged credit, some lenders will offer better terms if you make a significant down payment. If you can put 10 to 20% down on the purchase, the lender faces less risk if you default on the loan and can offer better terms. For example, a borrower with a previous bankruptcy who can make a substantial down payment could conceivably qualify for a better rate than someone who was late a few times on their mortgage payments but has less equity!

Ginny Ferguson is a broker and co-owner of Heritage Valley Mortgage, and is a recognized expert on credit and credit scoring. "Many people think they'll only qualify for a loan if their credit score is above 620 or some other magic number," she said. "A few years ago a couple came to me seeking mortgage financing; his score was a 408, and hers was a 654. While at first glance you may think their cause was hopeless, but with a little effort we found an 'A' grade loan because they had brought delinquent obligations up to date and they had three years' worth of reserves in the bank.

"Many people think credit scores have made it harder for individuals to qualify for loans," she continued. "In fact the opposite is true: we can put more people—with weaker profiles—into homes than we did in the old underwriting days. Automated systems utilize technology and guidelines that are actually more flexible today because credit scoring has proven to be an extremely useful tool in predicting how a particular loan will perform. Credit scoring hasn't been a bad thing for consumers—far from it."

The key is to make sure you're up front with the loan officer when you apply for a loan. "Customers should always tell the lender or mortgage broker everything about their financial position," Pam states. "Hiding debts or inflating income will always come back to haunt you, and may kill your chance of approval. If I know everything I need to know about your financial situation I can work with you to overcome hurdles. Don't exaggerate how much cash you'll have to close, and don't hide debts or financial problems—most of the time we can overcome those problems if we know about them ahead of time."

Mortgage lending is customized and based on individual circumstances and conditions—if you look, there's a loan out there for you. Talk to several mortgage brokers—don't take no for an answer!

And besides making sure you provide honest and factual information, steer clear of loan officers or agents who advise you to make misleading or incorrect statements. "If someone asks you to say you make more than you do, or asks you to lie about something, or to do anything fraudulent, don't," says Ralph Roberts, president of Roberts Realty and recognized by *Time* magazine as one of America's top producing REALTOR®s. "Fraud for housing is when you manipulate or misrepresent facts, with the intent of helping you qualify for or purchase a property. It's a crime—owning a home is important, but don't do anything to break the law. It's not worth it. Never sign blank docs, never sign someone else's name, and never do anything unethical. And if a real estate "professional" asks you to, find another person to work with."

Also make sure you sense-check any advice you're given. In recent months the foreclosure and bankruptcy rates have risen, in large part due to subprime loans. (Subprime loans are loans made to "riskier" borrowers; some lenders will even lend you more than you can reasonably afford.) How much can you reasonably afford? Everyone's situation is different, but our advice is to stay within 50% of your "back ratio." Your back ratio is the ratio of long- and short-term debt you have compared to your monthly income. If the total of your debt (including your new house payment) will add up to more than 50% of your gross monthly income, you're biting off more than you can probably chew.

Don't become so desperate to qualify for a loan that you become an unwitting accomplice to mortgage fraud. Fudging the numbers on a loan application—Form 1003—is committing fraud. Having a relative with better credit than you sign the loan indicating that he will be residing in the home when he has no intention of doing so is another example of fraud. When you apply for a loan, enter only true and accurate information—and *never* sign a blank application.

MYTH # **3**

Only U.S. Citizens Can Qualify for a Mortgage.

Fact: You Don't Even Have to Be a Permanent Resident Alien to Get a Loan

If you've got a job, and you're in this country legally—we want to give you a loan! Mortgages are made to nonresident aliens every day. If you're a lawful U.S. resident, you qualify under the same terms and conditions that a U.S. citizen would. You'll simply have to prove residency by providing a green card or Certificate of Resident Alien status.

If you're a nonpermanent resident alien, you can still qualify. If you will occupy the property as your permanent residence, and if you can document a two-year history of employment, have a two-year credit history, and can verify your assets, you can qualify for a mortgage.

Foreign nationals can also qualify! As Chip speaks to groups across the country, he sometimes tells the story of two Vietnamese brothers he met many years ago. Having no money or possessions, they were sponsored by a church to come to the United States. They worked the midnight shift as janitors in a book bindery, and while they spoke no English, they had worked incredibly hard and saved about $17,000 in cash. They paid cash for all their needs, so they had no bank accounts and no credit history. Using documents from their employers and taking advantage of the sizeable down payment they could make, he helped them qualify for an FHA loan. After only one year in this country they owned their own home!

As long as you show a good loan officer that you have the means to repay the loan, he or she can find a home mortgage for you.

Eric Weinstein, the president of Carteret Mortgage Corporation based in Centreville, Virginia, agrees. (He founded Carteret in 1995; today there are over 300 locations with over 2,000 loan officers across the country doing over $4 billion in loan volume per year.) He shared this story:

"A few years ago I met a lady from Guatemala who never thought she could buy a house. It just wasn't done in her country, as only the very wealthy or those associated with royal families owned homes. She had been in the country only eighteen months and had an entry-level job and no real savings. We talked about the low- and no-down payment loans that were available in this country, but she was very skeptical and didn't believe it was possible for her.

"The REALTOR®s, the sellers, the processors—everybody said it would never work! They were wrong: I was able to find a no-down-payment, adjustable-rate loan with almost no money out of her pocket. Best of all the mortgage payment was lower than her current rent payment.

"It took time, I must admit. I spent a lot of time with her, and did the deal for nothing, simply because it was the right thing to do. My philosophy has always been that this business is not about making money—it's about helping people. And that attitude comes from the top down. That's what I try to teach my thousands of team members every day.

"And what happened to that great lady from Guatemala? She's not only a happy homeowner—she referred over $10 million in new customers to me within six months. The mortgage business is actually pretty simple—it comes down to doing the right thing."

 If you're a noncitizen you can qualify for a mortgage loan, but don't be tempted to lie on your loan application. Providing a false Social Security number or counterfeit pay stubs to prove that you're someone you're not, or that you earn more than you really do, misleads the lender and is therefore illegal.

MYTH # **4**

I Should Look at Some Houses First.

Fact: You'll Save Time and Money Setting Up Your *Financing* First

If you've spent any time with a real estate agent before, you're probably familiar with a scenario like this one.

You meet the agent at the property. As you're walking through, the agent describes some of the features of the home. The agent also casually asks you questions about yourself: where you work, how long you've worked there, where you currently live, if you're renting or own your own home.

Your agent is, naturally, trying to get to know you. After all, an agent wants to try to build a relationship, even if it's just a business relationship. But the agent is also trying to determine if you're a serious buyer and if you'll be able to qualify for a loan for the home you're visiting—or for *any* home at all, for that matter. (If you've noticed, the same thing happens when you visit a car dealership—it's called "qualifying" a potential buyer.) Every agent is looking for serious, qualified buyers for the properties they show, and they'll work harder for serious buyers.

An easy way to show you're a serious buyer, and to improve your power in negotiations, is to get preapproved for a loan. You'll immediately establish credibility as a serious buyer, and in a bidding contest between other buyers, your offer will carry more weight.

Two happy clients, Sam and Betty, called Chip with the good news— their offer had just been accepted over three other offers! In his follow-up call with a REALTOR®, he learned that their offer wasn't even the highest—but was accepted simply because their financing was already in place! Although the other offers were for more money, the seller wasn't about to waste time with an unqualified borrower.

Many people get prequalified, but *prequalified* is not the same thing as *preapproved*. Let's look at each.

- *Prequalified* simply means you have described your financial situation with a lender, and the lender is rendering an opinion about whether or not you will qualify for a loan. Prequalification is a lender's opinion based on information received; it does not mean the lender has reviewed your credit report, verified your information, and so forth.

  In simple terms, a prequalification letter can be translated as saying: "I, the lender, feel this individual is probably qualified for a loan of this size if everything he told me about his financial situation is accurate. I have not tried to make sure the individual truly *does* qualify, however . . . so who knows how it will all turn out in the end."

- *Preapproved* means you have provided documentation proving income, assets, and liabilities . . . you've provided everything the lender needs to evaluate your creditworthiness. The lender has checked your credit report, and most of the paperwork needed for your loan has been prepared. Sellers and agents can be as certain as possible that a preapproved buyer will be able to close on the home they're selling.

A preapproval letter can be translated as saying: "I, the lender, have reviewed all necessary documentation and have run appropriate credit checks to ensure the individual will qualify for a loan of this size . . . I'll happily make the loan."

Obviously there's a big difference between *prequalified* and *preapproved*. Real estate agents know the difference, and some home sellers know it, too. Getting a preapproval letter provides several advantages that can save you time and money—and it only takes minutes.

If you've been preapproved:

◆ The sellers can feel comfortable accepting your offer and taking their home off the market. In many cases sellers accept an offer only to find out, sometimes weeks later, the buyer could not qualify for financing. They then have to put their home back on the market, losing valuable weeks of time and possibly having missed a qualified buyer.

◆ A seller reviewing several offers will look more favorably upon your offer because she is confident you will be able to obtain financing. If an owner needs to sell his home quickly, for instance, many times he will accept a lower-priced contract from a buyer he knows can get financing.

◆ Completing the home purchase can be quicker. If you're preapproved, much of the loan application work has already been done, allowing your closing to possibly take place sooner. Motivated sellers may also further discount their home price if they know they can close quickly.

Here's the bottom line: you should always shop for a loan and get preapproved for financing before you start seriously looking at homes. At the very least get preapproved before you decide to make an offer on a property.

Why do we recommend getting preapproved before you start seriously looking at new homes? Here are the advantages to you:

♦ You'll know exactly how much house you can afford, which will keep you from getting stretched too far when you are shown that house that you just have to have.

♦ You'll be in a better negotiating position when you do find the house you want.

♦ You won't be caught in the trap of hurriedly searching for a loan after you've found the house you want. Most home sales are contingent on your getting financing, and you're typically allowed only 30 days or so to get financing in place. It can be tough to shop around properly during that time do it ahead of time, and you can find the best financing deal possible. Here's an easy rule of thumb that's fairly accurate: the bigger hurry you're in, the more you'll probably spend on your mortgage.

Keep in mind that getting preapproved doesn't lock you into any one type of loan, or even to working with a certain lender: it just lets sellers know that you can get financing if you make an offer on their house. You can still choose the right lender and the right loan later on. When you begin looking for a home, it's important that you know exactly what you can afford, and can make an offer on a home with the confidence that comes from knowing you have financing in place. You'll be in a better position to negotiate with the seller, and you'll know exactly what price range of homes you should be looking for.

Take a few minutes, and prequalify yourself by using the "Prequalification" form in the Appendix, or visit our online resource at www.The MortgageMyths.com; that way, you'll know exactly what you can afford—but don't start shopping until you know you've got the money to spend!

In fact, put together your team before you start looking seriously at houses. "Find a great agent and a great loan officer first," Ralph Roberts recommends. "It's the best way to ensure you'll have the greatest success and the fewest problems."

Make sure you're comfortable with your REALTOR® and your loan officer. "Many first-time buyers simply call the number on the sign on the lawn," continues Ralph. "I think you should approach it a different way: go into it thinking your agent and loan officer will be your agent and loan officer *for life*. If you approach it that way, you should spend more time finding the people you're most comfortable with. And don't just go for the "top" person: the "top" agent or loan officer may not be the right person for you. Some agents specialize in selling or financing luxury homes, for example, and if you're looking for a starter home, they may not know your market as well as someone who does."

"The most valuable thing you need for the home-buying process is trust," says Eric Weinstein, president of Carteret Mortgage. "Trust in your loan officer, trust in your REALTOR®, trust in your title company, trust in your inspection company . . . trust is the key in real estate as in any business. Before you go too far, put together a team you trust—then the rest will be easy."

Preapproval is especially important for real estate investors. When you find a great deal on a property, move on that deal as quickly as possible to prevent another investor from swooping in.

MYTH # **5**

I Need a Down Payment—But I Don't Have the Funds.

Fact: You Can Buy a Home without Putting a Single Dollar Down

As recently as the 1980s, the average down payment for a home loan was approximately 20%. Mortgage lenders were much more conservative and protected their investments by requiring significant down payments in almost every case. Today the average down payment is approximately 5%; some borrowers still put down more cash at closing, but many make no down payment at all on a new home purchase—in some cases avoiding paying cash for closing costs, too. In effect you're financing 100% of the value of the home. There are even loans for 105% or 125% or more of the value of the home!

Mortgage lenders typically call these types of loans "zero-down" or "no down payment" mortgages. While it's a riskier loan for a lender to make, if your credit profile is positive and the lender is confident in your ability to repay the loan, you could easily qualify. This allows you to leverage your money, increase your investment power—and your return.

If you're a veteran of the armed services you may qualify for a VA loan. A VA loan requires no down payment as long as the house appraisal meets VA specifications; the house can't appraise for less than the purchase price, and must not need any major repairs. Keep in mind that if your credit is damaged and the lender would have required a down payment if you *weren't* seeking VA financing, you may not be strong enough to qualify for a zero-down VA loan.

Is a zero-down mortgage right for you? It depends on your circumstances. If you don't have the funds to make a down payment, getting a zero-down loan is possibly the only way you can buy a home. Or you may want to save your cash to make improvements or buy furniture. Or you could have the money available but don't wish to dip into your savings, investments, or retirement account.

Whether a zero-down loan is right for you depends on your individual circumstances and needs. Some home buyers need the money they save for paying off debt. (In some cases consolidating debt by using available funds to pay off other credit obligations is a good move, because mortgage interest paid is tax-deductible while "consumer" interest paid is not.) Or you may need the cash to fund a child's tuition or to fund other investments.

Another way to finance the down-payment is through the seller! Called "seller-seconds," or seller "take-backs," these second mortgages may be very attractive. If the seller of the property doesn't need all her money right away, a second mortgage can be a great investment! She gets a solid return on her money, and it's secured by an asset she knows well—her own real estate!

Also increasingly popular, but getting harder to find are "piggy-back seconds." In this case, the lender (or another financial institution) carries a second mortgage for a portion of the total. For example, an 80/20 would include an 80% first mortgage, and a 20% second mortgage. Although the interest rate on the second will likely be higher, the "blended" rate at 100% will make for a sweet return on your investment—of zero!

If your financial situation allows you to choose whether to make a down payment or not, make sure to discuss the terms of the loans available to you with your mortgage broker. The interest rate or costs you'll be charged are typically higher on zero-down loans; make sure you understand the options available to you so that you make the right choice for your needs. But if you don't have the cash available, take heart: there are dozens of zero-down loan options available. All you have to do is ask your lender or mortgage broker.

"In America you *can* buy a house with no money down," says Ralph. "There are loans available for almost any potential homeowner. A good loan officer can help you find the right package. It may take a little time and effort—but it's definitely worth it."

 Down-payment assistance funds (DPA's) are available nationwide, and so are state and local grants. Check with your state Housing Finance Authority. Gift funds can be used from family members or nonprofits too!

 Don't let anyone "assist" you in creating a paper trail for a creative gift or depositing money in your account. Doing so is almost always considered fraud!

MYTH # **6**

I Should Make the Biggest Down Payment I Can.

Fact: Your Down Payment Should Be Appropriate to Your Financial Situation

In general, a large down payment is a good thing: qualifying for a loan may be easier because the lender carries less risk, your monthly payments will be lower, you may avoid paying private mortgage insurance (PMI) if you put down more than 20% of the purchase price, and you're less likely to owe more than the house is worth if property values decline. A basic rule of thumb is the larger the down payment, the weaker the borrower's credit can be.

On the other hand, putting all your available cash into a down payment could backfire. Emergencies can and do occur, or you may simply need or want cash for another purpose.

There's no single best amount to put down, and the best amount varies based on your situation. Twenty years ago the average down payment was 20% of the purchase price; as we write this book, the national average has dropped to approximately 5% of the purchase price!

Mortgage lenders typically like to have you pay 20% or more down (which means you're only financing 80% of your purchase price), but some special loan plans allow you to qualify for 10%, 5%, or even zero down payment loans. If you put down less than 20%, you'll probably have to pay PMI, which can cost, for example, around $220 for a $285,000 loan.

However, even if you can make a large down payment, you may not want to. You may wish to put the extra money toward some other goal like home improvements, retirement, or college expenses.

Here are a few questions to consider when deciding how large a down payment to make:

- What is your personal financial situation? Do you have short-term and long-term savings? Do you have funds set aside for emergencies?
- Do you have high-interest debt? You may want to use available cash to pay off credit cards or auto loans with high interest rates.
- Is a lower monthly mortgage payment important to you? Are you more concerned about paying off your home as quickly as possible than investing funds elsewhere, such as in the stock market?

Amy Tierce, a top originator with Fairway New England Mortgage in the Boston area, shares this advice: "I always suggest that people take mortgage insurance if they intend to do a lot of work on the house, and save some of their cash for those improvements. That way they can use cash to improve the house and have the PMI removed after the house is re-appraised."

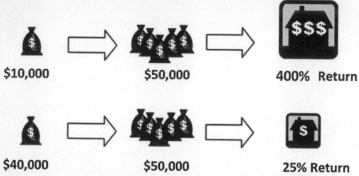

$10,000 $50,000   400% Return

$40,000 $50,000   25% Return

Figure 1.4 Leveraging Equity. Lower down payments will result in greater returns on your investment.

Many homebuyers take advantage of the principal of leverage: the less money they put down, the greater their investment return. For example, if you put down $10,000 on a home and sell it two years later for a $50,000 profit, you've turned that $10,000 investment into $50,000. If you put down $40,000 and sell for the same $50,000 your rate of return on investment is lower (see Figure 1.4).

If safety is your main concern, a larger down payment lowers your monthly payment and makes it more likely you'll still have equity in your home even if property values decline. Making as large a down payment as possible can be comforting, but it will be small comfort if you lose your job or have a medical emergency with no cash reserves to fall back on.

Remember, a mortgage isn't a debt. It's a financial planning tool. Make sure your down payment fits within your overall financial plan. Don't stretch yourself too thin, as it can be expensive to get that cash back out if you need it later on!

 If you do put down a large down payment on your property, consider taking out a home equity line of credit on the property. With a home equity line of credit you don't pay interest until you actually borrow money, so the money is available in the event of an emergency. (For more information about home equity lines of credit, see Myth #69.)

MYTH # **7**

All Mortgage Companies and Loan Officers Are Licensed and Regulated.

Fact: In Most Areas, the Loan Officer could be Moonlighting from Burger King

Here's the good news:

- ◆ Licensed mortgage brokers have the resources of many lenders, including banks and mortgage companies, and can offer a variety of products and programs.
- ◆ Licensed mortgage companies and loan officers are governed and regulated to ensure compliance with all state and federal laws.
- ◆ Most licensed loan officers are trained and tested to measure their competency prior to receiving their license.

Here's the bad news: the mortgage loan officer you contact could be unlicensed and unregulated. Many "mortgage brokers" work part-time under the supervision of a licensed broker who in effect pays a finder's fee for new clients. At the present time, every state regulates mortgage lenders, but most states do not regulate individual mortgage loan officers.

The National Association of Mortgage Brokers (NAMB) and the Mortgage Brokers Association (MBA) offer membership to licensed mortgage lenders and brokers. Both organizations are committed to promoting the highest degree of professionalism and ethical standards for its members. Brokers who are members of the NAMB and/or MBA are committed to enhancing professionalism in the real estate community through industry-wide certification programs and an ongoing pledge to the accuracy and quality of products and services. Check licensing and membership through the resources listed in the Appendix, or visit our online resource page at www.TheMortgageMyths.com.

"There's no real barrier to entry to the loan officer business," said Amy Tierce of Fairway New England Mortgage. "I'm all for loan officer regulation and certification. And, every borrower should try to get a referral from someone who has some personal experience with the loan officer you're considering; a personal referral speaks volumes."

Barry Habib is the CEO of Mortgage Market Guide, and agrees. "Borrowers need to understand how the system works, and deal with professionals who know what they're doing. Check to see if they have any additional credentials and training, such as a CMPS (Certified Mortgage Planning Specialist) or CMC (Certified Mortgage Consultant) designation, which indicates a greater level of commitment to the consumer."

Get referrals and recommendations and interview potential mortgage brokers before you start signing documents. Real estate agents and other real estate professionals will be happy to give you recommendations—and their input can be valuable. If your agent recommends a lender or loan officer, ask for reasons for the recommendation: in some cases the agent will reply that the loan officer is easy to work with and always closes loans on time. That may be important to the real estate agent, but what is important to you is that you get the best mortgage for your financial situation, and that you feel comfortable with the business relationship you establish. Once you have a short list of lenders to contact, interview them: ask about their licensing and whether they belong to any professional organizations such as NAMB. Ask for references if you're the least bit uncomfortable. If your loan officer works at the local bank, you can feel comfortable that you are working with a licensed professional; if you've responded to an ad in the classified section of your newspaper, check credentials and qualifications thoroughly.

"In Florida, consumers can check the Department of Financial Service's website to get information about mortgage companies and individual loan originators," says Patrice Yamato, owner of Plaza Mortgage in Jacksonville, Florida. "Most states have a corresponding office or department. While it may be helpful to check with the Better Business Bureau, the state should be your first choice for ensuring the originator you're considering is licensed and registered."

Tim Wooding is the president of the Kansas Association of Mortgage Brokers, and the owner of Executive Mortgage Group. An experienced top-producing veteran, he's closed over a billion dollars in mortgage loans in his career. According to Tim, the NAMB is working to establish a national database that states can access to share reciprocal information on broker licensing and qualifications. NASD, which tracks securities dealers, is also working on a similar system for loan originators. In the meantime, his advice is to seek out NAMB-certified brokers because of their training on loan origination procedures, best practices, and professional ethics.

"Unfortunately," says Tim, "many borrowers may simply go to their local lender because of the bad press generated by a few bad apples in the lending business. That's a shame, because a good mortgage broker may be able to find the borrower a great program that will save thousands of dollars." What is his advice for borrowers? Ask for referrals from friends and real estate professionals, check for NAMB certification, ask for qualifications, and call the Better Business Bureau to see if any complaints have been registered. "A good lender seeks to find the best possible program available for his or her clients," says Tim, "and if you do your homework, you'll find a lender that's right for you."

"Ask a lot of questions, and if you aren't comfortable with the answers, then go elsewhere," advises Joe Falk, long-time industry veteran and past president of the National Association of Mortgage Brokers. "Asking questions will help you learn about the business, and quickly determine the experience level of the originator."

Your goal is to find an originator who is fully qualified, offers the products and services you need, and is somebody you can partner with. "A great originator will counsel you and collaborate to help you make sound decisions on what you need," continues Patrice. "He or she will ask about your career, your goals for the next five years, whether your family will grow . . . the purpose of that conversation is to help you decide what loan package is best for you. We don't make decisions for you—we help *you* determine the best decision for *your* situation and *your* goals. If your originator is just an 'order taker,' move on. Find someone who wants to help you make sound financial decisions that fit your financial plan."

Joe, who has worked with thousands of first-time homeowners and spends an enormous amount of time working to protect the rights of borrowers and brokers around the country, also offers this advice. "Seek help from a trusted friend or advisor, or a family attorney who can help give you a sense of your 'life circumstances.' The perspective of a 23-year-old newlywed is different from that of a 45-year-old executive, so get their opinion and advice. They can help provide information, guidance, and resources to check and evaluate your final selection of a broker, loan officer, and loan program, which will drive other important decisions in your life."

 Real estate investors can team up with loan officers and mortgage brokers for more than just financing their investment purchases. If you invest in foreclosures, an experienced loan officer can often help your clients (distressed homeowners) with their financing needs. In addition, if you're a buy, fix, and sell investor, the prospective buyers may need financing to close a deal. By having a loan officer on your team, you cover all your bases.

 When doing your research, make sure to search the Internet search engines for both the name of the company, *and* the loan officer! You never know what might show up!

MYTH # **8**

Big Lenders and Major Banks Are Always Better.

Fact: Size Doesn't Equal Security—or Savings

Kathy walked in to Chip's office on a sunny August afternoon. He instantly recognized the lapel pin on her jacket—it was from the investment bank down the street. Chip quickly learned that she was the Branch Director of the Securities Division, where she bought and sold mortgage securities— and she was shopping for a loan! She explained that she knew that all the mortgage funding came from essentially the same source—Wall Street. As a mortgage broker, Chip had access to hundreds of banks and programs, and she knew the value of his expertise. He took out the application and started writing.

At face value you might think that major national banks and lenders are the most secure source of funding and information protection—they have the resources and funds, and can provide the highest level of security for their customers' personal information. While they may have greater resources, major banks and major lenders don't necessarily enjoy bullet-proof information security. In 2005, ABN AMRO Mortgage Group (which owns LaSalle Bank and also InterFirst Mortgage at the time) lost the data for 2 million residential mortgage customers, including customer names, account information, payment histories, and Social Security numbers. Earlier in 2005, 1.2 million customer records were accessed by hackers from Bank of America. (Imagine how happy they—and their customers—were.) Wells Fargo has been hit by hackers three times in the past few years, and Citibank has been hit too. The reality is that *any* organization is potentially vulnerable.

Does that mean major banks and lenders are less safe? Of course not—what it does mean is that information piracy can and does occur, both at small banks and at major, multinational banking corporations.

There's also no guarantee a big bank will give you the best deal on your mortgage, even if you're currently a customer. (In fact, very few lenders offer better terms to current customers than they will offer to noncustomers.) They may offer the best deal—or they may not. The only way to know is to shop around for the best mortgage.

A bank is not necessarily safer or better than a mortgage broker, either: Once your loan is approved and underwritten there's no real difference in safety or security between a major bank and the loan provided by a mortgage broker. (In fact, the major bank will probably sell your mortgage on the secondary market just like the small broker down the street, and it could be serviced by someone else within months of closing.)

"The little guy can often be a better place for the consumer to go," indicates David Acquisti, president of MSource Financial Group, and the past president of the Michigan Mortgage Brokers Association. "For example, some big institutions offer all-inclusive loan programs, but they charge higher rates for the privilege. The consumer can often wind up paying higher fees by going to a larger institution. Brokers have a variety of different programs they can offer, whereas a large bank is limited in their products and don't have the ability to shop around for the consumer."

Because loan officers deal with fewer programs, they can also be less likely to understand the dizzying variety of programs currently available. "An attorney asked me to take a look at a loan on behalf of his client," said

Dave. "The borrower thought they were getting a 1.25% interest rate for 3 to 5 years, and after I took a look at the loan (it was called an option-ARM) and explained it, they could not believe what was going to happen to them. I've taken three-day classes on the program to ensure I understand it, and while it does offer a number of options it also can create potential pitfalls that can have major repercussions for a borrower. In fact, I recommend that my clients consult with a financial planner to make sure they can take advantage of all the options. That's the number one complaint today: the loan officers don't understand all the products available, so the average consumer has no way to understand all the products available."

Here's the bottom line: shop aggressively and find the best deal for you. Shop with major banks, smaller banks, major lenders, smaller lenders, mortgage brokers, online lenders . . . shop aggressively—find someone you are comfortable dealing with, and have them find you the best deal.

 Getting a second opinion is always a good idea. We don't think twice about asking a doctor for a second opinion, but when it comes to our financial health and well-being, we're often reluctant to seek advice from another expert. If you suspect your loan officer doesn't quite understand what he's explaining, ask another loan officer for clarification.

 Be careful of out-of-state banks and brokers. They may not understand local market conditions, and may only have an "impressive sounding" name and not much else!

 MYTH # **9**

My Best Bet Is to Use a Friend (or Someone Local).

Fact: Using a Friend May Cost You a Friendship—and More

All the potential sources of mortgage financing available—banks, lenders, mortgage brokers, online lenders, and so forth—can seem overwhelming.

It's tempting to turn to someone you trust or at least feel safe with, especially if a friend or relative is in the mortgage lending business. If you don't have a friend in the business, it's tempting to turn to a local banker or lender—after all, that's safer, right? Plus, you figure, they know the local market, and they'll take care of me, right?

Not necessarily. Unscrupulous people can be found anywhere, whether on the Internet, at a large bank in another locality, or right around the corner. Integrity isn't geography-related. And while a local lender may know the local market, that's no guarantee he or she will offer you the best deal, or put together the right mortgage package for your individual needs. They may—or they may not. You should always shop locally, but make sure you shop other sources, too: it's your money, so make sure you put it to its best use.

If you do have a friend in the lending business, consider carefully whether it's in the best interest of your friendship to use your friend to handle your mortgage. At the very least you'll have to share your financial information: your credit history, your income, your debts . . . your friend will know all about your finances. Are you comfortable sharing that information with your friends? Does the thought of discussing your salary or discussing the time a couple years ago when you got three months behind on your car payments sound like a fun thing to do at a dinner party? It won't be any more fun to discuss when you're sitting in your friend's office.

In our experience there are very few times when sharing financial information has been positive for the relationship, especially one-way sharing, since your friend won't have to share any of his own financial details with you. Even worse, what if later on the "great deal" you thought you were getting doesn't turn out to have been so great? How will you feel? More importantly, what will that do to your friendship?

A few years ago a real estate agent called Chip and said, "I need your help: my client was prequalified by a good friend of hers, but there looks like there's a major problem. Can you take a look at it?"

After a little investigation Chip learned that the borrower had decided to sell her home in order to purchase a new one, and had been prequalified by a friend who, unfortunately, was an inexperienced loan officer.

Sadly, the loan officer hadn't noticed there was a second mortgage on the property. In order to sell her home to buy the new home, the borrower needed to come up with $10,000 at closing to satisfy the lien. Because she was under contract she had to sell her home, but after paying off the second mortgage she didn't have the cash to purchase the new home. Instead of moving into a new dream home, she ended up having to rent. Had her loan officer friend done her homework, they would have known about the lien, and she could have stayed in her home.

With so many lending options available, it's very likely that mixing friendship with business isn't such a great idea. The final decision is one only you can make, but please think very carefully about the possible impact on your relationship before you use a close personal friend for your next mortgage.

Sometimes, of course, it can work out great! Chip never would have dreamed that he would be financing the home of his ex-wife and her husband, but it turns out that she still trusted him more than anyone else to protect her interests. He's even had the privilege of financing a few homes for his wife's ex-husband!

"Good thing I didn't screw those up!" adds Chip.

And as for using a local lender—that may turn out to be a great option, but only if the rate, terms, costs, and so forth are the best ones for you. It may seem comforting that you will, for instance, be mailing your monthly payment to a local address, but does it matter where the check is sent? Not in the least.

A couple years ago the manager at a local branch of a national bank came to Chip for a loan. He was happy to help, but he was also curious.

"You work at a bank—I love doing business with you, but why do you want to use me for a mortgage?" Chip asked. "Isn't it more convenient to get a mortgage from your bank?"

"If I get a mortgage through my own bank," she replied, "all of my associates have access to my personal and financial information. If I work with you I know you'll maintain confidentiality. My privacy is important to me, and I know you'll protect it."

Most mortgage brokers can access the same products. A key difference is the professionalism and service they offer. "Don't just shop for the best deal—also shop for the right mortgage officer for you," says Ruth Faynor, National Education Consultant for the National Association of Mortgage Brokers (NAMB). (Ruth's responsibilities include coordinating training classes and procedures for 48 U.S. states.) "Look for someone you feel comfortable with and can trust. Are they the type of person who will help you and take time to explain things to you? Good brokers are willing to sit and talk to their customers, and will talk in language you can understand. Good brokers are interested in *you*."

Remember, what's important is finding a great loan officer and finding the best deal possible on your mortgage—not *where* you find them!

Beware of overly friendly loan officers who promise to "take care of everything" for you. Some unscrupulous loan officers and other real estate professionals simply use loan applicants for fraudulent schemes. If a loan officer tries to encourage you to borrow more money than the property is worth so you can obtain cash back at closing, or offers some other deal that sounds too good to be true, consult another loan officer or a real estate attorney for a second opinion.

MYTH # **10**

I'll Find a Better Deal on the Internet.

Fact: It's a Good Way to Shop Around, But Who Will Help if You Have a Problem?

Frantic and hopeless. That's the only way to describe what Chris and his new wife Lisa felt when they walked in. They had found the home of their dreams, and were three days away from closing on the deal. Or so they thought.

"Everything had been going smoothly," Lisa started, "then it came undone ..." They had decided to go with an Internet lending company that seemed to have a great rate and terms. Although they had never heard of the company before, the sales rep assured them they could complete everything in a "virtual environment." Then came the call from the FTC. The Federal Trade Commission told them that they had been the victims of fraud, and there was no "real" lender—just a front for a well-organized crime ring. They had no loan, no deposit, no paperwork, no closing, and no new home. And no one to go and yell at! Fortunately, the story had a happy ending, as a local mortgage broker stepped in and put the pieces back together. Chris couldn't believe it. "The closing was delayed by a couple of days, but we got in the home!"

Don't get us wrong, there are plenty of good Internet lending companies out there. But there are several factors you need to consider when selecting the right lender. It shouldn't surprise you to learn that experts estimate that nearly 82% of potential homebuyers start their mortgage shopping online. It's a quick and easy way to gather basic information about programs, rates, terms, and lenders—and you can do so anonymously (at least up to a point). You can quickly access payment calculators, qualification tools that will help you determine—in a general sense—how much house you can afford, and other tools that help you calculate your down payment requirements or rent-vs.-own comparisons (we already know which one wins there!). Check out our resource page for several easy-to-use calculators at www.TheMortgageMyths.com. In short, the Internet is a great place to gather basic information.

So, is the Internet the best place to get a mortgage? Like most things in life, the answer is: it depends. A great mortgage is one that has the right combination of professional guidance and service, interest rate, fees, points, down payment, closing costs, and so forth for your individual situation. You may be able to find that loan from an online mortgage source, or you may find that a local lender can provide you with the best mortgage. Online lenders claim you'll get a better deal because the application process is streamlined and automated, and because many online lenders don't have to bear the expense of maintaining branch offices for customers to visit, so as a result the savings are passed on to you. That may or may not be true: what is true is that the mortgage you choose must meet your financial needs and must be the most cost-effective for you, regardless of where you find it. And you also need to be able to rely on the mortgage lender. The Internet should be a tool to help you accomplish the process—not replace real people.

"A buyer asked me for a quote, and then found a 'better rate' on the Internet," said Amy Tierce of Fairway New England Mortgage. "About 10 days prior to closing she still didn't have a commitment, and the 'better rate' had never been guaranteed in writing. I found her a great program and she ended up locking in the loan at a better rate . . . and in less than

10 days, even though the Internet lender had waffled on rates and terms for almost four weeks."

There are two basic types of Internet lenders. Some mortgage brokers and lenders offer web-based application tools as a convenience to their customers. "We offer Internet application tools to make our customers' lives a little easier," says Tim Wooding. "We're not necessarily trying to generate new business from our web tools, but we are trying to make the process easier for our clients." Other Internet lenders are just that—they only offer loans over the Internet.

So what do you do? Shop around. Begin your mortgage search on the Internet—check online providers and gather information on rates, terms, and the various programs available. If you like, fill out the online forms and receive quotes. Then, armed with the information you gathered online, shop your local lenders. (Feel free to let local lenders know you've contacted online lenders; creating a little competition may help you negotiate better terms.) Then compare *all* the offers you receive and pick the mortgage that meets your particular needs. If an online lender's offer is similar to a local lender's offer, you may want to choose the local offer to gain the peace of mind that help is around the corner if you have problems.

"Most consumers understand what rates and points are, so some lenders hide additional fees in other areas," says Tim. "Look at all the costs, including the Annual Percentage Rate, in order to decide which program offers the best terms and costs."

Here are some tips from Tim for using online lenders and online lending auction sites:

- Before using any site, decide whether you want a fixed- or adjustable-rate mortgage, as well as your preferred loan term, down payment, and points. Auctions don't work if the item being sold is not precisely defined. If necessary, do some homework. If you would rather not bother, see a mortgage broker or traditional lender.
- Fill out the questionnaire as accurately and completely as you can. The information you provide is used to match you with the right lenders.
- Mortgage rates and price information comes not from the site but from the lenders who contact you. The quality of information

they give you may depend on what you ask for. On fixed-rate mortgages, you need the interest rate, points, and dollar fees. While some lenders are not in the habit of providing their dollar fees in initial price quotes, you should insist upon it. Ask for a *"Good Faith Estimate" (or GFE)*. On adjustable-rate mortgages (ARMs), you need to know more than the rate, points, and loan fees; also ask the lenders for the interest rate index, margin, when the rate can adjust, all rate adjustment caps, and the maximum possible rate.

◆ Ask lenders to e-mail or fax their quotes and GFE to you. (Receiving price quotes over the phone is a problem because you'll have nothing in writing as a backup.)

◆ The interest rate and points quoted to you by a lender apply only on the day you receive them. The lender is not bound to them on the following day since the market may have changed. For the same reason, it's not safe to compare a price received on Monday from one lender with a price received on Thursday from someone else.

NAMB past president Joe Falk agrees that shopping and comparing is the key. "A borrower cannot do enough shopping. Talk to several brokers and get lots of estimates, and keep asking questions about the program and rates."

The best way to get the best deal is to shop aggressively, and understand the process. Get as many quotes as you can—you'll learn more as you go, you'll be a better consumer, and your chances of saving the most money on your mortgage go way up. Don't be lazy—you can save thousands of dollars by hunting down the best mortgage for you.

If you do choose an online mortgage, remember that the level of service you'll receive is likely to be less than what you'll find with a local lender. As Tim says, "You can't yell at or ask advice of a computer when you have a problem." While service may not be an issue for you, if there are problems a local lender is usually in a better position to help you. For example, forms and disclosures must be specific to your state, not to the state the loan originated in, so if you chose an online lender located in another state, you'll need to make sure the forms meet your state's requirements. For your own protection, close the transaction with a knowledgeable closing officer—such as someone from a title company—or with an attorney. You'll protect yourself from signing incorrect mortgage documents that could create a title error.

"There are a number of reputable Internet lenders," says Tim. "There are also some cases where individuals have been taken advantage of. An individual came to me who had gotten a loan over the Internet. She was a high credit score borrower (her score was 820), she had held the same job for over twenty years, and she owned her home free and clear. She wanted to do a cash-out mortgage to finance an addition to her home. She found a loan on the Internet and it sounded like a good deal, but at closing she learned she was paying over $8,000 in fees, which equated to almost 7 points. She did get the low interest rate she was promised, but not on a fixed-rate loan; she instead received an adjustable-rate mortgage and the rate could change after six months. At that point there was little I could do to help her, and in her words, the person she spoke to was a 'slick-talking salesman.' Again, there are a number of reputable Internet lenders—just make sure you know who you're dealing with and that you compare apples to apples when you're shopping various lenders for the best program available to you."

When searching the Internet for great deals, beware of really great deals, like ads for CASH BACK AT CLOSING. Many Internet sites that promise to obtain loans for people who can't otherwise qualify are simply looking for victims and accomplices. Deal only with reputable, licensed mortgage brokers or lenders.

MYTH # **11**

I Can Get a Higher Return by Investing in Stocks.

Fact: You Can't Live in Your Portfolio While You Create Wealth

If you bought shares in Google stock a couple years ago at $100 per share, and you've held onto them (even though selling and cashing in has to have been awfully tempting), today you're a pretty happy camper: Google stock

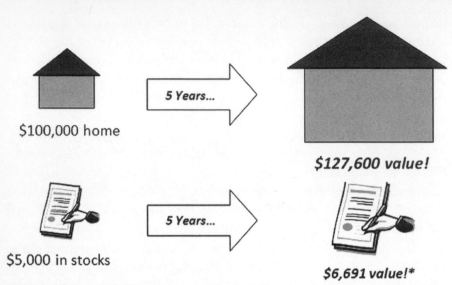

$100,000 home

5 Years...

$127,600 value!

$5,000 in stocks

5 Years...

$6,691 value!*

*Calculated at 6% annual return.

Figure 1.5 Appreciation versus Stocks. Real estate values increase faster than stocks, and you get to live in your investment!

currently trades at more than $520 per share. If you bought $100,000 worth of shares in 2004 those shares are worth over $520,000 today. (Sounds like a percentage gain similar to people who invested in Southern California real estate!) You might be thinking, "If I can find the next Google, why should I put my money in a house?"

If you can find the next stock that will perform like Google, maybe you should. (But first let us know which stock it is!) Returns like that are rare, though—most investors are very happy if they can earn between 8% and 10% over the long term; many mutual fund managers struggle to achieve those kinds of returns on a long-term basis.

Investing in stocks should be one component of your investment portfolio, but let us ask you: Can you live in your shares of stock? Of course you can't. We all have to live *somewhere*—it makes sense to build wealth through real estate first, then expand through other investments. Paying rent really is like paying someone else's mortgage. The one thing almost all financial experts agree on is that investing in real estate, especially in your personal residence, is a key component of almost everyone's investment portfolio. As the "house vs. stock" chart below illustrates, if you have $100,000 to invest and you don't own your residence, put at least some of that money towards a house—you'll build wealth and security while you take care of a basic need. And you can always buy the house with $10,000 down and invest the rest in other ways! (See Figure 1.5.)

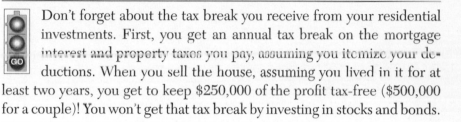

Don't forget about the tax break you receive from your residential investments. First, you get an annual tax break on the mortgage interest and property taxes you pay, assuming you itemize your deductions. When you sell the house, assuming you lived in it for at least two years, you get to keep $250,000 of the profit tax-free ($500,000 for a couple)! You won't get that tax break by investing in stocks and bonds.

SECTION 2

Playing the Mortgage Game

As kids, one of our favorite games was Monopoly. Growing up to play in real life is even more rewarding, but it has had its share of "Do Not Pass Go" moments! It didn't take long to figure out that the one who knows how to play the "game" within the game . . . is the one who wins.

We can't afford to look at your financial life as a game, but since you only get to play a few times—it's better to know some of the rules! In this section, we'll get you prepared for the mortgage process. Products and information details you need to be familiar with, as well as avoiding pitfalls that can cost you dearly. In all our years of writing mortgage loans, working in real estate, and talking to consumers and industry people from every corner of the world—the #1 "myth," and the costliest mistake borrowers make—is shopping by interest rate. So let's jump into the game, and start with that.

MYTH # **12**

My Main Goal Is to Snag the Lowest Interest Rate

Fact: Low Interest Rates Can End Up Costing You a Lot More

Would you shop for a car by only looking for the lowest price? Of course you wouldn't—first you'd decide on the type of car that's right for your lifestyle, your family, and your financial situation, and then you'd look for the best deal on that car. The same approach makes sense when you're shopping for a mortgage.

Just like cars, there are different components that go into justifying the "value" of the price. One of the complications of selecting the value of a mortgage is that the "price" has at least five components. Understanding the dynamics of mortgage pricing is definitely a key to saving you money.

The first component of pricing is the interest rate, which is the number that is multiplied by the loan balance to get the interest payment that is due to the lender. The rate quoted on a mortgage is an annual rate, but it is applied monthly. On a 6% mortgage with a $100,000 balance, for example, the monthly interest due is .005 (.06 divided by 12) times $100,000, or $500. This amount changes monthly, through a miracle known as "amortization" which we will discuss at length later!

On a fixed-rate mortgage (FRM), the interest rate is set for the life of the loan. On an adjustable-rate mortgage (ARM), the rate is preset for an initial period, ranging from 1 month to 10 years, and then is adjusted periodically.

The second component of pricing is "points." Points are upfront charges expressed as a percent of the loan amount. Two points amounts to 2% of the value of the loan. If the loan is for $100,000, then two points would cost you $2,000. You'll get to pay that up front as a cost of the loan.

Points are related to the interest rate. For example, if a lender offers a 30-year FRM at 8% and zero points (this is referred to as the "par" rate), you may be able to purchase a 7.5% loan for 1.75 discount points. In effect, the points "buy" you a lower interest rate.

The third component of pricing is rebates. Rebates can be offered in the form of points paid by the lender to the borrower for accepting above-par rates. The lender who charges 1.75 points for a 7.5% interest rate, for example, might rebate 2 points for a 9% rate. The 2 points would be available to defray a borrower's settlement costs. (Just in case you'd like to know insider's language, on the banking side of the mortgage industry, a rebate is referred to as an "overage." whereas on the brokerage side it's known as a "yield spread premium" or "YSP.") YSPs are not a "bad" thing, and will be listed on your GFE and HUD-1 closing statement. They are just another element of the cost of the loan.

The fourth component of pricing is the origination fee. Origination fees are really points—they're just disguising themselves. The typical origination fee is 1 point and is tied to the par rate. What does this mean? It means that when you call a lender for a rate quote what you could receive is the lender's par rate with a 1% origination fee.

An advantage lenders sometimes have is that reporting services and newspapers show rates and points but not origination fees. Thus, if you were to check the newspaper for today's rates, the lender who charges 1 point and a 1% origination fee for a 6% interest rate seems to be offering a better deal than the lender charging 2 points and no origination fee. To the borrower, points and origination fees are the same—it's money out of your pocket in either case.

The fifth component of pricing is "third-party fees" and "junk fees." Both are usually expressed in dollars rather than as a percentage of the loan. Third-party fees are a necessary part of the mortgage transaction because you need the third-parties services to get the loan closed. These would include things like the credit report, appraisal, attorney fees, recording fees, and flood certification, just to name a few. Usually, third parties invoice the lender who in turn collects from the borrower on their behalf.

"Junk fees," on the other hand, is a term sometimes used to describe all other upfront charges by the lender or mortgage broker. The two most common junk fees are the "processing fee" and "underwriting fee," although both can be waived if you negotiate hard enough. Yes, the lender does have to cover costs, but we've seen cases where the lender is charging an underwriting fee, a processing fee, a loan service fee, a broker fee, an application fee, an overnight fee, a verification fee, a research fee, and a document fee. We've even seen a charge for an e-mail fee! There's a long list of other items that lenders may charge for, but for you—the only total that really matters is the amount charged! It's easy for a lender to say that they're not charging any points or origination, but on closer examination—they have $2500 in miscellaneous fees built in! Don't fall for it. (See Figure 2.1.)

As you can tell from the above chart, the interest rate itself can be misleading when it comes to the overall cost of the loan!

So, the price of a fixed-rate mortgage has five components: interest rate, points, rebates, origination fee (all expressed as a percent of the loan), and

Interest Rate	Extra Cost	Payment	Savings	Break Even Point
7.00%	$0	$665.30	$0	N/A
6.75%	$1000	$648.60	$16.70	59 months
6.50%	$1500	$632.07	$33.23	45 months
6.00%	$2000	$599.55	$65.75	31 months
5.50%	$3700	$567.79	$97.51	38 months

Figure 2.1 Interest Rate versus Cost Comparison. Rates are not always what they seem. A low rate may mean extra costs (in points), which could take years to recoup. (Example based upon $100,000 loan for 30 years.)

third-party/junk fees (expressed in dollars). So why is it so important to understand these five components? Because they are the profit centers for both the lender and the loan originator—it's how they get paid, and it's coming out of your pocket one way or another.

Get three to five quotes from different lenders. Don't just get interest rate quotes—get quotes for points, fees, and all the other costs involved. When you have information about all five components, you can make fair comparisons between the loans. The annual percentage rate, or APR, should also be disclosed, which includes those costs, points, and fees, and allows you to make an apples-to-apples comparison.

Pam Bennett of Benchmark Mortgage has underwritten over $1 billion in loans in her lending career. "The APR lets you know the true interest rate of the loan after any fees and loan closing costs are factored in," she said. "If you're quoted a 5% interest rate, once other fees are added in the APR could be much higher. Make sure you compare APRs—that way you know the true cost of the loan. While .25% may not sound like much, on a $200,000 15-year loan, the extra amount on your payments will add up to over $700 more per year."

Again, make sure you get all the rates quoted on the same day because rates are subject to change on a daily basis. Then use the lowest quote as leverage with the other lenders. Let everyone know what the lowest rate was, and give them a chance to compete for your business. By shopping for more than just the lowest interest rate, you'll make sure they're competing—and you're evaluating—on a level playing field.

"The lowest interest rate isn't the only factor," continues Audrey Acquisti, a certified national mortgage trainer, and president of MSource Training and Consulting. "If a consumer calls Company A and gets an interest rate quote of 6%, and gets a quote of 6.25% from Company B, the consumer will naturally choose the lower rate offered by Company A ... not realizing that Company A is charging $7,000 up front for that interest rate, and Company B is charging $2,000 for their interest rate. So, in reality, Company B is offering the best deal—but if you only look at the interest rate, you won't realize it. You have to compare everything, and compare all costs, to know what the best deal is."

"Shopping strictly by interest rate is a mistake," said Amy Tierce. "The interest rate you get is definitely important, but your lender should also be someone who will treat you as their client for life."

Borrowers who pay points to get a lower interest rate generally end up paying far more in borrowing costs than if they had selected the higher rate with "zero points." So says a 2006 study released by Freddie Mac and Pennsylvania State University, which examined 3,785 mortgage transactions between 1996 and 2003. It was found that only 1.4% of borrowers actually kept their loans long enough to benefit from the points that were paid. In addition, only 1.5% of homeowners who did *not* purchase points should have! On average, these borrowers paid off their loan 37.5 months too early to reap the rewards of the lower rate. Don't fall for that trap. Things change. With job changes, relocations, children, financial changes—you will rarely keep a mortgage for as long as you think.

Yes, it may be possible to get a 1.50% interest rate (*and it sounds good!*), but the terms may be so painful and expensive—you could even end up "upside-down," owing *more* money than you borrowed or even what the home is worth!

The best way to compare loans is to determine the total cost of the loan over the life of the loan:

1. Jot down the upfront loan expenses, including the loan origination fee and other closing costs.
2. Multiply the monthly payment times the number of months you plan on paying on the loan.

3. Add the two amounts from steps 1 and 2 to determine the total cost of the loan.
4. Subtract the total amount of money you're borrowing (the principal).

The result is the total cost of the loan to you. Now, simply choose the loan that costs the least.

MYTH # **13**

The Federal Reserve Controls Interest Rates.

Fact: Mortgage Rates Have Very Little to Do with the Fed Rates

With the closing two days away, Ed called Chip in a panic. "I just heard the rates went down a quarter percent—can I get my rate lowered by Friday?" Chip had told him not to watch so much TV, but had to break the news to him anyway—it didn't matter.

The Federal Reserve (which is led by chairman Ben Bernanke) controls the rate at which banks lend money to each other overnight, and the rate at which the Federal Reserve Banks lend money to commercial banks for very short periods of time. It was news to Ed, and thousands of others, that the Federal Reserve does not control or mandate mortgage rates. While short-term loan rates and long-term rates are sometimes related by trends, typically short-term rates are much more volatile than long-term rates. A .25% increase in short-term rates may have no effect on mortgage rates, at least not in the short term.

Mortgage rates are much more affected by 30-year bond rates, because a 30-year bond is a more comparable investment to a 30-year mortgage. (In other words, an investor will not lend money for a mortgage if a greater return can be found in the bond market—so, they two tend to track fairly closely.)

The Federal Reserve does control the flow of money, and the fiscal policy they set does have long-term repercussions in all the financial markets, including the stock market, the bond market, futures markets, and the market for mortgages, but it's not a direct link, as Ed thinks it is.

Whenever the Fed lowers the interest rates, we expect a number of customer calls the same day looking for a lower interest rate. Just because the Fed raises it a quarter of a point doesn't mean interest rates will change, so don't be fooled into thinking that if the Fed lowers their rate by .5% that mortgage rates will instantly follow. Most of the time they won't. On the flip side, however, sometimes mortgage rates come down—and the Fed didn't have a thing to do with it!

 The rate you're offered depends much more on how attractive you are as a borrower than on the Federal Reserve. If you have a credit score of 700 or higher, a long history of borrowing money and paying your bills on time, and a credit report that has no blemishes, you're more likely to qualify for lower interest rates. Obtain your credit report, inspect it carefully, and work towards improving it.

MYTH # **14**

Stay with Fixed Rates—ARMs Are Just Too Risky.

Fact: Specialized Adjustable Programs Have Been Designed to Save You Money

While an adjustable rate mortgage (ARM) can expose a homeowner to risk, in many cases an ARM is a great—and relatively safe—mortgage choice. Before we look at why, first let's make sure you understand what an ARM is.

Adjustable rate mortgages incorporate terms that change over the life of the loan. There are two phases in the life of an ARM. During the first phase, the interest rate is fixed, just as it is on a fixed-rate mortgage (FRM). The difference is that on an FRM the rate is fixed for the term of the loan, whereas on an ARM it is fixed for a shorter period. That period can range anywhere from one month to 10 years!

At the end of the initial rate period, the ARM rate adjusts periodically for the remaining life of the loan. The adjustment rule is that the new rate will equal the most recent value of a specified rate *index*, plus a *margin*, and then rounded (usually up) to the nearest 1/8%. (The margin is specified in the original note and remains unchanged throughout the life of the loan.) The index on the other hand, changes based upon market conditions, and can be based upon a variety of financial instruments. Indexes commonly used include Treasury, LIBOR (London Interbank Offered Rate), COFI (Cost of Funds Index), Prime Rate, and a few others. Regardless of the index, the calculation method remains the same. For example, if the index is 3.54% when the initial rate period ends and the margin is 2.75%, the new rate will be 6.375% (or 6 3/8%) (this is 3.54 + 2.75 = 6.29 rounded to 6.375).

This rule is subject to two conditions. The first condition is that the increase from the previous rate cannot exceed any rate adjustment cap specified in the ARM contract. An adjustment cap, usually 1% or 2% but ranging in some cases up to 5%, limits the size of any interest rate change.

The second condition is that the new rate can't exceed the contractual maximum rate. Maximum interest rates are usually 5 or 6 percentage points above the initial rate.

During the second phase of an ARM's life, the interest rate is adjusted periodically. This period may or may not be the same as the initial rate period. For example, an ARM with an initial rate period of 5 years might adjust annually after the 5-year period ends. This is referred to as a "5/1 ARM." There can also be 3/1, 7/1 and 10/1 ARMs. In some cases, the second adjustment period could be on a monthly basis—that means your payment could actually change every month.

The initial fixed rate and adjustment phases, and the subsequent rate caps, are all defined by the lender's "ARM Disclosure"—make sure you ask for it. In addition, you are entitled to a "CHARM Booklet," which illustrates how ARMs work, and is included in the Appendix section of this book, or visit www.TheMortgageMyths.com for a printable copy.

At the top of the program disclosure you'll see a description, for example, 5/1 (5/2/5). The 5/1 indicates that the initial rate is fixed for 5 years and then becomes adjustable once each subsequent year. Also know as *caps*, the 5/2/5 means the initial rate cannot exceed (or is capped at) 5 points over the start rate at the first adjustment, cannot move more than 2 points up or down every year after, and cannot exceed 5 points over the start rate over the life of the loan.

The rate that is quoted for an ARM on the news and by loan providers is the initial rate—regardless of how long that rate lasts. When the initial rate period is short, the quoted rate is a pretty poor indication of the real interest cost to the borrower. The only significance of the initial rate on a monthly ARM, for example, is that it's the rate that may be used to calculate the initial payment.

The index plus your margin is called the "fully-indexed rate" (FIR). The FIR based on the most recent value of the index at any given time indicates how the ARM rate may adjust when the initial rate period ends, tempered only by your caps.

For example, assume the initial rate is 4% for 1 year, the margin is 3%, and the rate adjusts every year subject to a 1% rate cap. If the index value is 2.5% at the end of the first year, the FIR is 5.5% but your rate will only adjust to 5% because of the 1% cap. As a result, it's important to know what index your ARM is tied to. (Ask your lender for the index and for details on how you can monitor it yourself.)

"Make sure you know how your ARM works," says Patrice Yamato. "Look ahead and make sure you know what your payment might be in a year or two. Don't just look at today: look at what might happen and make sure you're prepared for that eventuality . . . and if you're not, that particular ARM might not be right for you. Your originator should help you walk through different scenarios to make sure you understand exactly how your ARM works and whether it's right for you."

So, which type of loan is right for you, a fixed-term or an ARM? It depends, like most things, on your situation.

If you're happy with the current interest rate being offered on a fixed-term mortgage, and you're planning to live in the home for more than a few years, and you are conservative by nature—go with a fixed-term mortgage. While interest rates may fall later, as long as you're comfortable with the loan you've gotten, you won't have to worry that in years to come your payments will go up because of interest rate spikes. And if interest rates fall steeply you can always refinance to take advantage of lower rates.

If you're not planning to live in the home long, or anticipate changes in your income or financial plan, then an ARM is the better way to go. Your monthly payments will be lower, and it doesn't matter that you're not paying down the principal much—in the first few years you pay down very little of the principal on a fixed-term loan anyway.

Some years ago a colleague and his wife moved from one state to another and bought a new home. They only planned to live in the home for about a year, because they planned to then move to another state and start their own business. Interest rates were low at the time, and they took out a fixed-term mortgage. It was an expensive house, and their monthly payments were almost $2,000 per month. A year later they in fact did sell their home and move, just as they planned.

If they had taken the interest-only ARM mortgage available at the time their monthly payments would have been $400 less per month. They would have saved almost $5,000 in mortgage payments—in one year.

What's the moral of the story? John and his wife were foolish not to get an ARM instead of a fixed-term mortgage. Why did they make that decision? They decided on a fixed-term mortgage "just in case." "Just in case" they didn't move. They were trying to be safe—but they ended up spending a lot of money needlessly. With planning and discipline, here's how an ARM mortgage can work for you—*even* if rates go up (see Figure 2.2).

The key is to stick with the plan and use the ARM as a financial tool! Even though the interest rate gets higher in later years, you owe less money, have greater equity—all with the same payment!

ARMs have received a lot of bad press lately. Why? As rates have risen, some homeowners haven't been able to make the new payments—and they've lost their homes. An ARM is a great choice for certain borrowers, especially those who know they are going to move within a few years (relocation, etc.) or people who are leveraging principal reduction—but you should always know the risks. The simplest way to stay safe is to calculate the maximum rate of increase and ensure you can meet that payment—if you can't, and rates rise, you'll find yourself in trouble. Take a look at the worst-case scenario and make sure, if it happens, you won't be stretched too far.

Interest Rate	Year 1	Year 2	Year 3	Year 4
7.00% Fixed	$98.984.21	$97,895.00	$96,727.06	$95,474.67
6.00% ARM	$98,772.00			
6.75% Yr. 2		$96,602.50		
7.50% Yr. 3			$93,307.35	
8.25% Yr. 4				$88,685.69

After 4 years, you owe $6788.98 less on the ARM program, even though the interest rate is 8.25%! You also saved on the monthly payments of almost $800 in the first year!

Figure 2.2 ARM versus Fixed-Rate Comparison. Adjustable mortgages will perform better in the early stages of the loan—even if rates go higher. (Example based upon $100,000 loan for 30 years.)

 ARMs may be risky for homeowners who already find the monthly mortgage payments a little tight and plan to live in the property for several years. An increase of as little as 1 or 2% could make it impossible for them to make the payments.

 We recommend fixed-rate mortgages for most homeowners who plan on living in the home for several years. Investors who quickly buy and sell properties may benefit from low-interest ARMs because they will be paying off their mortgages before rates have a chance to increase considerably.

MYTH # **15**

A Shorter Term Always Beats a 30- or 40-Year Term.

Fact: Used Wisely, Longer Terms Can Be a Better Deal

If you decide to get a fixed-term loan, your first decision is whether you want a 15-year loan or a 30-year loan. (There are also 10-year and 20 year, 25 year, and even 40 or 50-year loans, but the decision-making process you'll use is the same, so we'll make it simple by comparing 15- and 30-year loans.)

Qualifying is a main consideration, and you will want to maximize your finance-ability. If you can't afford the monthly payment on a 15-year loan, the choice is made for you. Monthly payments are naturally higher on 15-year loans.

If you can afford the 15-year loan, you'll need to decide whether you're more concerned with minimizing your monthly payment or maximizing your ability to build wealth. Monthly payment "minimizers" are mainly concerned with the present; wealth builders are mainly concerned with the future.

For example, the mortgage payment (not counting PMI or escrows) on a $100,000, 30-year loan, at 7%, is $665. On a 15-year loan at 6.75%, it's $885. If your main goal is to minimize your monthly payment, the 30-year loan is your best option because you pay $220 less per month in principal and interest.

On the other hand, after 5 years the borrower who took out the 15-year loan has repaid $22,933, while the borrower who took out the 30-year loan has repaid only $5,868. That amounts to a difference in wealth accumulation of $17,065; to the person whose main goal is to build wealth, that makes a huge difference in a short period of time.

Some borrowers who can afford a 15-year loan choose a 30-year loan because of the flexibility it provides. "I can make the larger payment of the 15-year," they argue, "but I don't have to; if I get into a pinch, I can make the lower payment of the 30-year." Homeowners who take a 30-year but make the larger payment of the 15-year, however, don't pay down the balance as rapidly as they would have if they had taken a 15-year because they are paying the higher rate of the 30-year loan.

But there are other forces at work as well! Look at the chart below (Figure 2.3), and we'll assume that you can afford a $1,000 per month payment (P&I only used), and there is a difference of .25% between the 30-year and 15-year loans. Here's how it stacks up.

Another consideration is flexing your leveraging muscle! Assume that we can again afford a $1,000 per month payment as above, but leveraged that payment into a larger home. Now look what happens after 5 years (see Figure 2.4).

$1,000 per month payment:

Program	Mortgage	Rate	Balance (3 yrs)	Tax Deduction (25% rate)
15-Yr. Fxd	$111,300	7.00%	$97,278.56	**$5,498.24**
30-Yr. Fxd	$111,300	7.25%	$98,155.16	**$5,717.39**

After 3 years, the 30-yr fixed loan is within $876, but is off set by $220 in additional tax savings—even at the higher rate! The net outcome is virtually even, but you have the safety net of opting for a lower payment if unforeseen circumstances arise.

Figure 2.3 Equity Build-Up: 30-year versus 15-year.

If you're interested in making additional real estate investments, or other types of investments, the cash you'll free up on a 30-year loan can go towards those investments. Or if you want to make improvements to your house, you'll have more cash to use. The choice between a 15-year loan and a 30-year loan is based on your situation and your investment goals—there's no one right answer.

Oh—but keep in mind, if inflation is high or interest rates are extremely low, a 30-year loan may be an incredibly cheap loan somewhere down the road—if today you take out a 6% loan and in 10 years interest rates are over 10%, you may end up glad you have a long-term loan with a low payment.

$1,000 per month payment:

Program	Mortgage	Rate	Purchase	Balance (5 yrs)	Equity
15-Yr. Fxd	$111,300	7.00%	$123,700	$86,183.39	**$79,354.61**
30-Yr. Fxd	$146,600	7.25%	$162,900	$138,368.64	**$79,628.26**

The resulting equity is almost identical! However, the 30-yr. program results in an **extra $5781.70** in tax benefits (25% tax rate)!

Figure 2.4 Equity Build-Up with Appreciation. Example uses a $1,000 per month payment; 6% appreciation; 10% down payment.

Think of a mortgage as a financial planning tool, not as a debt. The average life (at the time of this writing) of a loan is 2.8 years. Not everyone is selling their home every 2.8 years—but many of the underlying mortgages are being refinanced. One of the first questions Chip asks new customers is, "How long do you plan to keep this mortgage?" His intent isn't to find out how long they plan to own the home; he wants to determine how the mortgage fits in their overall financial plan.

Chip generally advises customers to go with a 30-year mortgage rather than a 15-year mortgage, and an ARM over a fixed-rate loan. Why? Because you can still make additional principal payments on your own, in effect turning your 30-year mortgage into a 15-year mortgage, take tax advantages, and still have flexibility. Then, if you run into financial problems, you can cut back on your payments for 2 or 3 months (or however long it takes), get your finances back in order, and bump back up to the 15-year payment amount. If you already have a 15-year mortgage, you don't have the luxury of scaling back the payment if emergencies occur. Follow the plan, and let the numbers work for you!

 If you plan to take a 30-year mortgage and pay it off in 15 years, make sure the mortgage does not have an early-payment penalty.

MYTH # **16**

My Credit History Needs to be Perfect.

Fact: Almost Everyone Has a Credit Blip in the Past

It's true: Almost everyone has had a credit blip somewhere along the way. (We have a friend who says, "If you don't have at least one 'ding' on your record, you haven't been trying hard enough.") Very few people have "perfect" credit—and as a result mortgage lenders don't expect your credit to be perfect.

Even though lenders don't expect perfect credit—and in some cases, far from perfect credit—a high credit score can help you qualify for a better loan. How do you get one? Through discipline, and understanding the rules of the game!

To help lenders evaluate the risk of a borrower on a loan, a credit report is obtained. As part of that credit evaluation, a *credit-scoring* system is used to establish the level of risk to a lender. The higher the score, the less the risk.

Most people understand that if you don't pay your bills on time, your credit score suffers. There's a common misconception, however, that if you pay off these delinquent accounts, all will be forgiven—people assume that since the lender has been paid, their credit score will return to what it was before the delinquency occurred. But it doesn't work that way. There are dozens of factors that go into determining your credit score, and doing something like paying off an old debt—might just work against you.

Current and recent delinquencies reduce your credit score because all credit-scoring models view delinquent accounts as evidence of a weak commitment toward meeting your obligations. The evidence is not wiped away when you repay the accounts or catch up on late payments. The delinquencies are still there, and they impact your score. The only thing that will wipe them away is the passage of time and a better payment record.

A similar misconception is that consolidating credit card accounts into a smaller number of cards will improve your credit score. It won't help—it'll hurt—if the consolidation of balances significantly raises the ratio of balances to available credit lines on any one card, which is commonly known as "maxing out" a card. While the credit-scoring models don't like you to have a lot of cards, the models look even less favorably on cards that are maxed out because this may be a sign you're having financial difficulties. This is called your "utilization ratio,"

Here's an example. Let's say you have five credit cards. Each card has a $5,000 limit, and you owe $1,500 on each card. Your total debt is $7,500. Each card has a 33% loan balance to available credit ratio. If you get a new credit card with a limit of $8,000, and transfer all the outstanding balances to that card, you still owe a total of $7,500, but now your balance to available credit ratio is 93%. To a credit bureau it appears you've almost maxed out your credit power, so your credit rating—and score—will suffer.

If you've already consolidated debt and your credit score has already been reduced, don't try to undo the damage by opening more accounts. The credit rating models look unfavorably on multiple new accounts in a short period of time. Why? That can be another indicator of financial distress.

Another way your credit score can be impacted is from credit inquiries. A credit inquiry is what happens when you apply for credit—the lender checks with the credit bureau to obtain your history, creating an inquiry. Credit inquiries negatively impact credit scores because studies show multiple inquiries are associated with high risk of default. Distressed borrowers often contact many lenders in hopes of finding one who will approve them. Fortunately, multiple inquiries *of the same type* (e.g., mortgage lenders), only count as one inquiry within a certain period of time. So don't be afraid to shop around and think that it'll hurt your credit score. On the other hand, don't open up your credit profile to dozens of companies either!

Couples who purchase a home together often find that one of them has good credit and the other one has the income required to qualify. Lenders, however, are concerned with the credit of the borrower (or borrowers) whose income is being used to qualify. Good credit on the part of a borrower without the means to pay is of no use. Income and credit can't be separated.

Many people have no idea how good their credit is. "A client thought his credit was terrible—he had a couple of late payments on a department store credit card, and he assumed it had killed his credit," said Pam Bennett of Benchmark Mortgage. "He was an attorney and he thought he knew how credit scoring worked. It actually had little to no effect based upon his other strong credit. He actually qualified for conventional financing, and on great terms."

Others don't realize their credit may not be as strong as they thought. "Some customers think their credit is good because they pay in cash," continued Pam. "While they don't have negative entries on their report, they also haven't built a positive history of repayment. It's hard for me to loan someone $200,000 when they haven't got a proven track record that they can make some other payments."

The first step is to get a copy of your credit report. There are three primary credit repositories, Equifax, Experian, and TransUnion. Each of these agencies contains slightly different information about your credit over the past several years, and lenders use a combined report, sometimes referred to as a "tri-merge report." To get a copy of your credit report, contact the following agencies:

Equifax
P.O. Box 740241
Atlanta, GA 30374
(800) 685-1111 (8 A.M.–5 P.M. ET)
www.Equifax.com

Experian Credit Services
P.O. Box 949
Allen, TX 75013
(888) 397-3742 (24 hours)
www.Experian.com

TransUnion
P.O. Box 2000
Chester, PA 19022
(800) 888-4213 (24 hours)
www.TransUnion.com

For a *free* copy of your credit report (a website sponsored by the three agencies), you can also go to:

www.AnnualCreditReport.com

If you have questionable credit, you can still get a mortgage—it just may be one that costs you more than if you had great credit. Even if you've had major credit glitches like bankruptcy or foreclosure, you can qualify for some type of mortgage, even if it's one with higher interest and/or more points and fees. Instead of the top "A" category loans purchased by the secondary market (usually referred to as conventional mortgages), a borrower may only be able to qualify for a lower-rated loan category: A-minus, B, C, or D.

Subprime means a category of loans available to borrowers who have had damaged credit on a regular or extensive basis. Problems can fall into three primary areas of credit blemishes: mortgage credit, consumer credit, and public record postings. (For example, public record postings include someone who has had a foreclosure or a judgment against them.)

After scoring and grading the borrower's credit, the lender places the borrower in the appropriate category. An A-minus subprime borrower, for instance, might be someone with a 30-day late mortgage payment in the past 12 months, while a C subprime buyer might have had a bankruptcy discharged 18 months ago.

If you're in the subprime category, the amount of the down payment you can make plays a role in the type of loan you can get. A rule of thumb is that the greater the amount of equity (in other words, the larger your down payment), the weaker your credit can be. Why? Because the more you put down, the less risky you are. So, if you factor in the amount of the down payment, it could be possible for a borrower who previously has gone through bankruptcy to be placed in a higher-category subprime mortgage than someone who has been late twice on mortgage payments. That may sound strange, but it's true. Bottom line: regardless of your credit, there's probably a program for you—all you have to do is look for it.

"If you want to know what your credit score is, go to Fair Isaac's website (at www.myfico.com) and order a credit report from each of the three bureaus," says Ginny Ferguson, one of top experts on credit reporting in the country. "You'll be able to see what's in your credit file without creating an inquiry that will be calculated in your credit score later. Since the consumer is requesting the information, the inquiry doesn't count in the calculation for your credit score. If you order from Fair Isaac's website you know you'll get the credit score that mortgage lenders will use to determine your credit score. If you find problems on your score, take your report to your mortgage broker to get advice on how to clear up any problems."

Sometimes improving your credit report is as simple as making a phone call. "A customer of mine had late payment notations on their credit report for a gasoline credit card account," said Paco Torch of Torch Mortgage Corporation. "I advised my customer to give the company a call and explain the situation. She told them they were trying to refinance their home but couldn't qualify because of the late payment entries. She asked them if they'd be willing to remove the entries, especially since her account had been current for some time. To my customer's surprise, the company agreed."

Is it always that easy? Of course not. But, "If you don't ask, you don't get," continued Paco. "Ask to speak with a supervisor, and be extremely nice."

Here's another important note: the three major credit reporting bureaus have developed a new credit scoring model called a "Vantage Score." While the Vantage Score may clear up confusion between the different scoring systems, mortgage lenders won't tend to use the Vantage Score until the secondary mortgage market adopts the system. Until Vantage Scores are signed off on by the secondary market, we won't see their use in the mortgage market," said Ginny Ferguson. "Vantage Scores may be used in consumer credit situations like credit cards or department score credit assessment, but for now, the Vantage Score has little impact on the mortgage lending business, and tends to cause confusion."

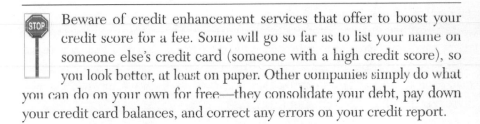

Beware of credit enhancement services that offer to boost your credit score for a fee. Some will go so far as to list your name on someone else's credit card (someone with a high credit score), so you look better, at least on paper. Other companies simply do what you can do on your own for free—they consolidate your debt, pay down your credit card balances, and correct any errors on your credit report.

MYTH # **17**

My Credit Score Determines My Loan's Approval.

Fact: Your Credit Score Is Only One of the Many Factors that Go into the Decision Process

A few years ago a borrower was referred to Chip who had been turned down by several other lenders. After talking with him, Chip learned he had a 502 credit score and he was 90 days delinquent on his current mortgage.

No one was interested in helping him, but Chip asked the magic question: "What happened?" He soon learned that the borrower's wife had been diagnosed with a rare form of cancer and needed medical treatments that were not covered by insurance. He had depleted his entire savings for the experimental treatments, and needed more cash. He wanted to sell his home to buy a smaller property he could more easily afford, but because things had spiraled downward so fast, he had been unable to obtain financing. With a little extra effort, Chip found a solution and a loan for him. He had equity in his home allowing him to make a large down payment, and he had an insurance policy sufficient to pay off the mortgage on a new house if his wife passed away. Positioned correctly, the underwriters agreed this was a good loan.

From a lender's point of view, a "good loan" is a loan made to a borrower who demonstrates both the ability and the willingness to repay it. Qualification has to do with determining the borrower's ability to repay. Your willingness to repay is determined largely by your past credit history and thus your credit score.

Credit scores (sometimes referred to as a "FICO score") range from 300—850, and the higher the better! Most people have scores in the 600s, and your score varies among the three repositories and can change daily.

There are *five* components that go into making up your credit score, and they all have different importance (see Figure 2.5).

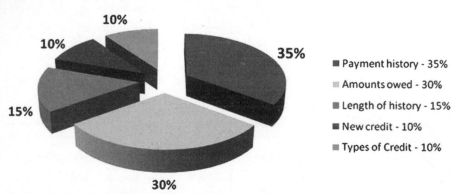

Figure 2.5 Credit Scoring Factors. Breakdown of the various factors used for calculating a credit score.
Provided by Fair Isaac Co. www.My FICO.com.

1. *Payment History*—35% Do you make your payments when they're due? Even a 30-day late payment can kill your credit score.
2. *Balances*—30% How much do you owe, and how much is that relative to your total credit limits?
3. *Length of History*—15% How long have you been a credit consumer? Longer histories will increase your score.
4. *New Credit*—10% Any new accounts or inquiries? A lot of accounts may signal a problem.
5. *Other Factors*—10% A different mix of credit uses and payment patterns can also influence your score.

There are also certain factors that *do not* influence your credit score, including your race, color, national origin, sex, or marital status. Remember, as long as you can pay me—I want to give you a loan!

There are also certain benchmarks for lenders in determining interest rates. As a general rule, your rates and terms get better when your credit score is over 620, better yet at 680, and again at 720. With a score over 800—you get to make the rules! (See Figure 2.6.)

For a loan to be approved, the lender must be satisfied as to your ability to repay and your willingness to repay. This is the difference between "qualification" and "approval." You may "qualify" if you have the ability to repay; you'll be approved if you're also judged to be willing to repay.

Despite credit scores, lenders will still ask two basic questions about a borrower's ability to pay. First, is the borrower's income large enough to service the new expenses associated with the loan, plus any existing debt obligations that will continue in the future? Second, does the borrower have enough cash to meet the upfront cash requirements of the loan? (In other words, can you cover the down payment, closing costs, and monthly payments?)

The lender must be satisfied on both counts for you to get approved for the loan.

In general, the lender assesses the adequacy of the borrower's income in terms of two ratios that have become standard in the industry. The first one is called the "housing expense ratio." It's the sum of your monthly mortgage payment including mortgage insurance, property taxes, and hazard insurance, divided by your monthly income. The second ratio is

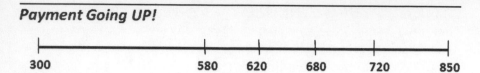

Payment Going UP!

300	580	620	680	720	850

Borrowers with higher credit scores are able to get better interest rates! FICO scores (www.myFICO.com) are used to evaluate the risk to the Lender, and can affect your rate and ultimate cost of the loan — check your score before application!

Credit Score	Rate	Payment*	Pmt. Increase	3-yr Cost!
720+	6.500%	$632.07	N/A	N/A
680-719	6.750%	$648.60	$16.53	**$595.08**
620-679	7.125%	$673.72	$41.65	**$1499.40**
580-619	8.250%	$751.27	$119.20	**$4291.20**
500-579	8.750%	$786.70	$154.63	**$5566.68**

*$100,000 loan amount, 30-year.

Figure 2.6 How Credit Scores Affect Interest Rates. Examples are for illustration only—actual variances will be different based upon lender and market factors.

called the "total expense ratio." It's the same calculation, except that you include your housing expense (above) *plus* all your existing monthly debt service obligations. For each of their loan programs, lenders set guidelines for these ratios, usually between 28% and 36% for the front number, and 36% to 50% for the back ratio.

So for example, if you had $5,000 in monthly income, your housing payment was $1,250, and your monthly credit debt was another $450, your ratios would be 25/34. You can qualify yourself using the "Pre-Qualification Worksheet" included in the Appendix in the back of this book, or try our easy calculator at www.TheMortgageMyths.com.

Maximum expense ratios actually vary somewhat from one loan program to another. So, if you are only slightly over the limit, nothing more may be necessary than to find another loan program with higher maximum ratios. Usually that means you'll pay a little more for the loan, too, because the greater the risk to the lender the greater the cost of the loan. This is a situation where it is handy to be dealing with a mortgage broker who has access to loan programs from many different lenders—chances are at least one will have a program that's right for you.

But even within one program, maximum expense ratios may vary with other characteristics of the transaction, and this can work against you. For example, the maximum ratios are often lower (meaning more restrictive) for any of a long list of program "modifications," such as if the property contains two to four separate dwelling units; if the property is a co-op, a condominium, or a second home; if it's designed for investment rather than owner occupancy; if the borrower is self-employed; if the loan is a cash-out refinance . . . or combinations of any of these.

The maximum ratios are guidelines, and are not carved in stone if the borrower can make a persuasive case for raising them. Here are a few examples where the limits may be increased (within reason, of course):

- The borrower is just slightly over the housing expense ratio but well below the total expense ratio—36/38 for example.
- The borrower has an impeccable credit record.
- The borrower is a first-time homebuyer who has been paying rent equal to 40% of his or her income for three years and has a perfect payment record.
- The borrower is making a large down payment.

If expense ratios exceed the maximums, one possible option is to reduce the mortgage payment by extending the term. (If the term is already 30 years, however, there is very little you can do. Few lenders offer the 40 or 50-year loans.) Still, with a higher credit score—the more options you'll have.

Here's what Ginny Ferguson, co-owner of Heritage Valley Mortgage, had to say about credit scoring.

"Credit scoring models look at all data in a credit file—both positive and negative—and the older a negative mark is, the less impact it has. Good recent credit and good debt utilization, especially in the recent past, works to negate the effect of old delinquent events. After 7 years old marks are eliminated, and typically after 4 years those events have relatively minor impact . . . as long as you've built good credit since that time. If you learn from your errors and move forward in a positive way, you'll be fine. Time, where credit scoring is concerned, really is your friend, because the more positive credit events you have, especially recent ones, the faster old negative marks will lose their impact.

"Think of it this way: a credit score is a numerical snapshot of a person's creditworthiness. For a credit file to receive a score, it must contain at least one account that has been open for at least six months, has had activity, and has had no disputes. (Disputing an item freezes that particular item, and that item will not be scored, but all the other credit is scored. The Fair Credit Reporting Act requires that disputed items be resolved before the account is used to score credit.)

"Credit scores are not the only item that we in the mortgage lending industry review to make a credit decision—far from it. Large down payments, huge amounts of equity, large cash reserves . . . all these factors are considered in conjunction with the credit score.

"Remember, no one can tell you the relative impact of any particular item in your credit history and how that item affects your overall score. So, your best bet is to use your credit wisely in a limited capacity, keep balances low (at 30% or less than the available credit), and make your payments on time."

Your credit score is just one factor your lender will consider. The amount of your down payment, your level of income, the total of your other debts . . . all these factors and more play a part in determining whether your loan will be approved.

Your credit score is not necessarily the deciding factor in whether you're approved for a loan—it's an indication of creditworthiness, but if your credit history is poor and you can document good reasons for those financial problems, lenders may look favorably upon you *even* if you do have a lower credit score.

"If you're told you need a minimum credit score to qualify, keep shopping," says Lorenzo Wooten. "Fannie Mae doesn't require a minimum credit score, although the individual lender you're visiting might. There are hundreds of mortgage brokers who work with Fannie Mae—if your lender requires a minimum credit score, there are plenty of other options available to you."

Take these four steps to raise your credit score over time:

1. Dispute any erroneous items on your credit report.
2. Apply for fewer loans and credit cards. Every inquiry on your credit report can bump down your score, and every time you apply for a loan or a credit card, an inquiry is posted to your report.
3. Pay down the balance on your credit cards to 50% or less than your available credit limit.
4. Make credit card payments by the due date on the statement. Late payments will lower your score instantly.

MYTH # **18**

Be Conservative—Don't Stretch Yourself.

Fact: Think *Big*—Your Wealth Will Grow Faster

Everyone has a different risk tolerance: some people are uncomfortable with anything they perceive to be a risk, while others live at the opposite end of the spectrum and seem to enjoy risk almost for risk's sake. You've probably heard the cliché, "With risk comes reward; with great risk comes great reward," and it's often true. The level of risk you take on has to be appropriate for your situation and for your emotional temperament, though—taking on so much risk you can't sleep at night defeats the purpose of buying a home you'll enjoy.

"A house acts as an investment, but just as importantly it's a place to live," says Terri Murphy, best-selling author, accomplished columnist, national speaker, and active member of several state real estate and commerce organizations. "Buy more 'house' if you can ... but only if it serves your overall financial strategy. Remember, it's not about simply buying the biggest house; it's about developing the best financial strategy. Buy what's right for you—you have to live in it, it's your life, and it's a component of your financial plan."

Here's an example of thinking big. A few years ago a friend moved from Virginia to New Jersey to take a job in Manhattan. (The difference in housing prices from Virginia to New Jersey was quite a shock.) She stretched her budget and bought a home in a commuter town across the river from Manhattan for $219,000—and sold it two years later for $344,000. She then was transferred to Lancaster, Pennsylvania, where she again stretched her finances and bought a home for $319,000—and sold it twelve months later for $358,000. While it's true that in some areas of the country home prices have stayed relatively flat, most areas of the country have seen double-digit increases over the past three to five years. Had she played it conservatively, her gains would have been much lower. Even if the prices had declined slightly, as they have in some markets (short term), she still would have been ahead! See Figure 2.7 for an example of why you should stretch your financial muscles.

As you can see, it makes sense to buy the maximum house you can afford now rather than to continually upgrade a smaller house over time (unless you'll perform the upgrades yourself and can save money in the process). Buying a small house today only to sell three years from now because you need a bigger house means you'll pay closing costs, legal fees, and points all over again. Those costs really add up over time, and if you can avoid them, why shouldn't you?

Stretch!

Here's a look at how far a $10,000 down-payment can be stretched:

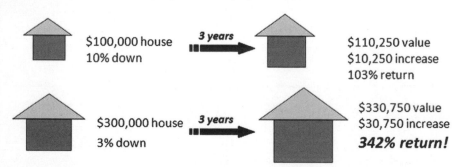

Figure 2.7 Leverage Your Equity. Examples assume 5% annual appreciation. Does not take into account closing costs, liquidation costs, or mortgage insurance.

Here's our best advice: your home is a place you should enjoy and that should meet your family's needs first and foremost. It's also the biggest investment most people make—so think big and put your money to work for you. If you think small, you'll "get" small. Think big—within reason— and your wealth will grow at a rate faster than you may think possible. Just make sure the total of your monthly payments—mortgage, auto loans, credit cards, etc—is less than 50% of your gross monthly income, and in general you should be fine.

"Within reason" is the key phrase. Most buyers want it all: three bedrooms, three baths, huge lot, fireplace, great room, modern kitchen. They stretch themselves too far and end up in bankruptcy. Stretch yourself, but make sure you have enough to pay the mortgage, insurance, and taxes.

MYTH # **19**

I'm Divorced or Declared Bankruptcy, So I'll Never Qualify.

Fact: Many Times, You're a Better Credit Risk after a Life-Changing Event

If you're married and you apply for a loan in both of your names, each person's credit will also be evaluated. (If you or your spouse has great credit, and the other of you has poor credit, you can apply as an individual rather than a couple—but your individual income will be used to determine your buying power. You won't be allowed to claim both parties' income but only one party's credit history. And there's nothing illegal or unethical about applying individually; federal law prohibits lenders from discriminating against you based on marital status, so one spouse's poor credit cannot be used to deny credit to the other spouse.)

If you're divorced, any credit problems created by joint liabilities will show up on your credit report—even ones that occurred after your divorce was final. For example, if you held a joint auto loan, and your name is still on the loan, it will still show as a joint obligation . . . and any late payments that have recently occurred will be "charged" to your credit history even if you aren't responsible for making those payments. Most experts recommend making sure your obligations are sorted out, creditors are notified, and that your credit history is up to date before your divorce is finalized. Ideally you'll want your ex-spouse to requalify for credit and remove you from any debts, but that may not be possible.

As a result, mortgage lenders may require a copy of your divorce decree so they can determine for which debts you are, and are not, responsible, and also which assets you still retain possession of.

But here's the good news: once you are divorced, you can quickly build positive entries on your credit report by satisfying all your debts on time. And you may find that within a short period of time you're considered a better credit risk after you're divorced, especially if your spouse's credit history is disastrous.

Don't let your former spouse control all the finances; keep in mind a divorce decree does not negate the responsibilities of making payments. If the other spouse doesn't pay, you're still liable. And, even in a divorce, if you're liable for another mortgage you don't have to count that debt in order to qualify for a new loan. Sometimes it's even easier to get a new loan if you're inside a Chapter 13 bankruptcy . . . but you can almost always get into a home if you've experienced circumstances beyond your control.

The best thing you can do is talk to the lender about your situation. Bring any documentation you can, to help you explain why you may have had poor credit in the past, and why your change in marital status makes you a better risk in the future. A friend applied for a mortgage and was initially turned down because of several negative entries: two years before he'd missed mortgage and car payments due to a nasty separation. He explained what happened at the time, could show that he quickly brought his payments current and had remained on track since . . . and was approved for the loan.

If you've had a bankruptcy and are seeking a loan, the bankruptcy must be fully discharged and you'll need to have re-established a good credit history. Most lenders require a two-year period between a Chapter 13 bankruptcy and the mortgage application, and a four-year period between a Chapter 7 bankruptcy and the time of application. Fannie Mae's My Community mortgage only requires a two-year period after discharge for both a Chapter 7 and a Chapter 13 bankruptcy. Some programs, such as FHA, will allow you to refinance while you're still in bankruptcy! If you've had a foreclosure within the past four years, you'll probably struggle to find a mortgage since the secondary market usually requires a four-year period between the foreclosure and an application. (But you may be able to find a mortgage from a lender who doesn't intend to sell the loan on the secondary market.)

There are exceptions to the guideline that your bankruptcy must be fully discharged, however. A few years ago Chip worked with a farmer who had struggled to obtain financing through other lenders. The state had determined his cattle were contaminated, and his entire herd was destroyed, creating a major financial setback. Nine months later, the state came back and said his soil was still contaminated, and his new herd was destroyed. Chip was able to show the state's actions forced him into bankruptcy, so from an underwriting perspective he was easier to qualify because his bankruptcy was due to extraordinary events outside his control. If you can document logical exceptions, you can potentially qualify for a mortgage even if you've recently declared bankruptcy.

Remember, loan officers don't expect you to have perfect credit—but when your credit is particularly poor, they may require you to explain what happened and to show reasons why you're now a good risk. Sounds fair to us—after all, they're considering lending you money and taking on a risk; they're entitled to know the risk is a good one.

 If you're embroiled in divorce proceedings, don't forget to separate the finances as well as your marriage. Some divorce lawyers drag out the proceedings, and your ex's attorney may try to charge you his attorney fees. The faster you can get this behind you with a clean break, the better chance you have of obtaining loan approval.

MYTH # **20**

Special Financing Programs Aren't Available to Me.

Fact: There Are Always Multiple Choices Available to Almost Any Homebuyer

The variety of loan programs that are offered has exploded; the potential choices are limited only by the creativity of lending professionals. Some lenders specialize in offering or developing "special" financing programs for clients who have recently faced financial difficulties like bankruptcy; for home buyers with high incomes but very few assets; for home buyers who are self-employed and have incomes that vary greatly from month to month . . . the possibilities are endless. Many banks do not offer special financing programs, but mortgage brokers in particular have access to programs from dozens of different lenders, and frequently can offer several choices to almost any homebuyer. The best way to find out what programs are available to you is to sit down with a lender, thoroughly describe your financial situation, and allow him or her to determine which choices could make the most sense for you.

Here's an example of a special program. You've probably heard of FHA loans—FHA loans are insured by the Federal Housing Administration. (Chip wrote the book *The ABCs of FHA Lending*, and he trains loan officers and companies around the country how to do FHA loans.) FHA loans are intended for borrowers who seek loans no larger than the loan size limits set by the FHA program, can meet a 3% investment requirement, have poor credit or no credit history, or other difficult circumstances.

Most FHA borrowers make total cash investments (including down payment) of 3% or less. FHA loans even allow you to buy a home with none of your own money! Private mortgage insurers require 5% down on most loans, and only allow 3% down on special programs. FHA is also liberal in allowing gifts to be used to pay the settlement costs—up to 100%!

FHA lenders also usually have weaker credit requirements than private insurers or conventional lenders will typically accept. FHA allows higher ratios of expense to income, is more tolerant of existing debt, and will allow the income of co-borrowers who don't live in the house to count fully in measuring income adequacy. FHA loans are also very forgiving of buyers with poor credit. For example, a borrower only has to be out of a Chapter 7 bankruptcy for 2 years and can even get you out of a Chapter 13 bankruptcy!

While FHA loans are intended to help home buyers with poor credit, insufficient down payment funds, and so forth, borrowers who meet the requirements of a conventional loan can also qualify for an FHA loan. Many conventional borrowers like FHA's ability to provide a 95% LTV cash-out loan! You can't do that anywhere else.

FHA loans are generally available in the market at about the same interest rate and points as conventional loans with the same term. There may be a difference in mortgage insurance premiums, however.

Talk to at least three mortgage brokers or lenders. Make sure you find a variety of options so you can decide which program is best for you. Many people who accept subprime loans do so because they didn't shop around; the first lender they called may have only offered them a subprime—when they could have qualified for a more conventional mortgage or an FHA-insured loan.

So don't despair—no matter what your situation is, there's likely to be a special loan program available for you. Ask a lender for assistance and guidance—or better yet, ask several—you'll be glad you did.

 Some loan officers specialize in FHA, VA, and other government-secured loans that other loan officers may have little experience securing. If you think you might not qualify for a mortgage loan, that's a pretty good sign that you may have the right qualifications for a government loan.

MYTH # **21**

I Should Avoid Mortgage Insurance.

Fact: Creatively Used, Private Mortgage Insurance (PMI) Can Save You Thousands.

Most homeowners prefer to avoid private mortgage insurance (PMI) if possible, but there are situations where PMI can be helpful and can even save you money. First, let's take a look at what PMI is.

Mortgage insurance isn't like regular insurance—you can't get it on your own, and you can't get it from State Farm or the insurance company where you get your homeowners or auto insurance.

PMI isn't particularly popular with consumers, and at face value that opinion makes sense. After all, why pay insurance that covers your lender? "Keep in mind that once upon a time if you didn't have 20% to put down you couldn't buy real estate," said Amy Tierce. "Private mortgage insurance has made home ownership possible for millions of people."

PMI typically insures the top 20% of the new loan against the borrower's default. What does that mean? That means if you default on your loan, the lender is covered for up to 20% of the loss they might incur disposing of your home after foreclosure. If you owe the bank $100,000 on your home, and the bank sells if for $95,000, PMI reimburses the lender the $5,000 difference. In effect, it means the bank has very little risk in making the loan—and even better, you pay the insurance premiums, not the bank. It's a win/win situation . . . for the lender, at least.

So, lenders require PMI on any loan that exceeds 80% of property value. The larger the loan is relative to the value of the home, the higher the insurance premium will be. While the insurance premium is assessed against the entire loan, the cost should be allocated entirely to the portion of the loan that exceeds 80% of value.

Assume you can get a 30-year fixed rate mortgage at 7.5% and zero points to purchase a $100,000 house. Without mortgage insurance, you could borrow up to $80,000 (80% of property value), whereas with mortgage insurance you could borrow up to $95,000 (95% of property value). Let's say the insurance premium on the $95,000 loan is .79% of the balance per year for the first 10 years, after which it drops to .20%. Without PMI, if you didn't have the down payment funds available to put down the 20%, you may not have qualified for the loan at all.

In addition to putting 20% down, there are two common ways to avoid purchasing PMI.

One way is to pay a higher interest rate instead of PMI. When a borrower accepts this option, the lender buys PMI for less than the borrower would have to pay. The higher interest rate covers the insurance cost to the lender plus a profit margin. Some, but not all, lenders offer this option.

Why would you consider this? The sales pitch for the higher rate as a replacement for PMI is that interest is tax deductible whereas PMI premiums are not.

The other side of the coin, however, is that you must pay the higher interest for the life of your mortgage, while mortgage insurance will be terminated when the loan value is less than 80% of the home's value.

The second way to avoid paying for PMI is to take a first mortgage for 80% of value and a second mortgage for 10% or 15%. These are known as 80/10/10s and 80/15/5s, where the last number is the down payment percentage. So, an 80/10/10 means you're getting an 80% first mortgage, a 10% second mortgage, and you're putting 10% down.

In general, combination loans are more attractive the higher your tax bracket, the smaller the difference in rate between the two mortgages, and the shorter the term of the higher-rate second loan. Expected rapid price appreciation reduces the attractiveness of combination loans because it means that mortgage insurance will terminate sooner.

A creative way to avoid PMI is to have the seller pay it for you. Some sellers are willing to make a one-time PMI payment, typically 2 to 3% of the loan value. This option can be a win-win for both parties. The seller may be able to get the price they wanted for the property, and the buyer can purchase the property with a lower down payment (that they don't need to use to avoid PMI) or a lower monthly payment (since each payment won't include an amount for PMI).

Most people focus on avoiding PMI, but smart investors frequently choose to accept PMI in order to free up cash for other investments. If you're buying a $300,000 home and you wish to put down less than

$60,000 (20%), PMI allows you to do so, making it possible to invest that cash elsewhere. Or, if you're considering making improvements to the home, you may wish to save some of the down payment to use to make those improvements. You can always have the PMI eliminated once your home appraises for a higher value.

If you don't have the cash and want to avoid PMI, you'll have to take a second mortgage to cover the additional down payment required to reduce the loan value to less than 80%—and at higher rates than the first mortgage.

Those costs will be carried over the life of the loan, whereas PMI generally extinguishes once the loan value is less than 78% of the home value. You'll typically have to wait two years before you can extinguish PMI, though, and may have to pay for an appraisal to confirm value. FHA loans also have a form of mortgage insurance—it's called Mortgage Insurance Program, or MIP. It's required on every FHA loan, regardless of the LTV, and you'll have to own the home for five years before MIP can be extinguished.

If you've been late on payments, or if the area has declined in value, the lender may elect not to eliminate PMI, though—yet another reason to make sure you stay current on your mortgage payments. If your house appreciates rapidly, you could find yourself able to eliminate PMI within a few short years; whereas, if you've taken a second mortgage, the only way to eliminate that cost is to pay off the second mortgage itself.

Another great advantage of using PMI, is that as of January 1, 2007—it's tax deductible! Although there are some restrictions, the "deductability factor" alone can add up to substantial savings. For example, check out the chart below (Figure 2.8).

You don't necessarily need to carry the PMI for the life of the loan. When you have 20% equity built up in the property, ask to have the PMI removed or consider refinancing your mortgage to have the PMI removed.

If you hear of a lender offering 100% financing with NO PMI, they're typically paying for it and including it in the rate—check the increased costs carefully!

Example for a $166,667 Purchase; 25% Tax Bracket:

	95 LTV Loan		100% LTV Loan	
	Borrower Paid Mortgage Insurance	80% First 15% Second	Borrower Paid Mortgage Insurance	80% First 20% Second
Tax-Deductible Interest	$9,923	$10,549	$10,445	$11,280
Tax-Deductible: MI	$1,236	-	$1,596	-
Total Deductible Payments	$11,159	$10,549	$12,041	$11,280
Estimated Tax Benefit	$2,790	$2,637	$3,010	$2,820

Figures provided courtesy of MGIC.

Figure 2.8 PMI versus "Piggy-Back" Loan. Estimated tax benefits for a 95% LTV loan and a 100% LTV loan with and without using Private Mortgage Insurance.

MYTH # **22**

The Good Faith Estimate Guarantees My Closing Costs.

Fact: The GFE Doesn't Even Have to Be *Close*, and It's Certainly Not a Guarantee of Your Final Costs

The Good Faith Estimate (GFE) is just what it says it is: it's an *estimate* of the costs for a potential loan. The Good Faith Estimate is not legally binding. If the lender originally estimates you'll need $4,000 at closing, and the costs total close to $7,000 on the day you close, you'll have no recourse against the lender. So while the GFE is intended to help you comparison-shop for a mortgage, it usually isn't much help, because the costs shown can and almost always do change. Here's a rule you should live by: Only depend and count on quoted rates and points when you have received written confirmation from the lender that your terms have been locked.

"The Good Faith Estimate and Truth in Lending documents are basically useless," said Amy Tierce. "Lenders don't have to stand behind them, and there's no penalty if they don't turn out to be accurate."

Lenders are required to provide you with a GFE within three days of your loan application. Some costs may or may not be listed on your GFE, including escrow fees, appraisal fees, county title recording fees, and so forth. (They typically are listed, and the amounts listed tend to be accurate because the costs for most of these items are relatively fixed.) While they're important fees, they tend not to change much. What you should pay much closer attention to are the lender fees: loan origination fees, processing fees, underwriting fees, and "miscellaneous" fees. Unscrupulous (or simply sloppy) lenders can and often do increase these costs greatly between the time the GFE is generated and the actual closing.

"The difference between the GFE and actual costs shouldn't be more than about $50," said Paco Torch, president of Torch Mortgage Corporation. "While it's common for the total to be slightly higher, it shouldn't vary by a lot—and if it will, your lender or mortgage broker should explain that to you ahead of time."

Remember, your closing costs aren't "fixed" until they appear on your HUD-1 settlement statement. Always review the settlement statement at least one day before closing; if you wait until closing to check it out, you may be in for an unpleasant surprise.

Here's the bottom line: The GFE is only as good as the lender standing behind it, because there's no penalty for providing a "bad" one, so evaluate who you deal with carefully.

 Contact the title company or attorney in charge of the closing and request a copy of the closing papers at least three days prior to closing. Compare the numbers on your Good Faith Estimate to the numbers on the closing papers to see if anything has changed. If the numbers are different, call the title company or attorney and ask for an explanation.

MYTH # **23**

I Have to Use the REALTOR®/Builder's Loan Officer.

Necessarily Working

...ders are generally to individual ...ompanies. An agent with great ... to refer clients even when the

...nterest as buyers in completing ... providers who can generally be ..., and closing on time, is the real ...ncern of borrowers as well. (It's ...uilder, because that's when they

... in the mortgage price or whether ... mortgage. Although, in fairness, ...o far out of line or the service so ...d blames the agent.

...te agent, in most cases he'll refer ... It's simple: the real estate agent ...ped a business relationship. The ...t their clients courteously, to work ... overcome any problems that pop ... estate agent doesn't get paid until ...lly refer you to a lender he thinks ... necessarily to the lender who will ...l also tend to refer you to someone who makes their jo...

When a friend bought his last home, the agent asked who was handling his financing. (She had seen his preapproval letter early on, but she obviously forgot.) He told her he was using an online lender. She frowned and said, "Oh, I don't think that's a good idea." He asked her why she felt that way, and she said, "I just wouldn't. They're unreliable. You don't know who you're dealing with, and they may try to take advantage of you . . . I'd use someone local . . . someone you can trust."

Now, to be fair to her, she may indeed have been sincere and well-intentioned. And her advice may in some cases be accurate. From her point of view using an online lender was a problem—well, a problem for her, at least. Real estate agents are responsible for helping a sale close: they keep in touch with the loan process, they send appraisal forms and other information to the lender, request information back . . . and it would be a lot easier—again, for her—if he used a local lender she was comfortable with. She could count on the local lender to make her job easy because that lender has an interest in getting referrals from her. An online lender, on the other hand, has no interest whatsoever in keeping a local real estate agent happy. So from the agent's point of view using an online lender was a mistake.

Just to humor her, our friend talked to the lender she recommended. His "best" loan was more expensive by a considerable amount. Our friend's monthly payments would have been almost $120 higher, and he would have paid over $3,500 more in closing costs. His agent's job would have been easier . . . but at his expense.

What's the moral of the story? Accept referrals from real estate agents and builders . . . but make sure you shop around, too.

Sometimes a real estate agent will try to tell you how much you can afford. Chip doesn't tell real estate agents how to sell houses, for example, and they shouldn't tell you what you can afford, because we all have our specialties. The lender will tell you how much you can really afford.

By contract, real estate agents are obligated to protect the seller, not the borrower, unless you have an agency contract with a specific real estate agent. Their agreement specifically binds them to work for the seller. The lender's job is to protect you, through an appraisal, title insurance, inspections, and so forth. If an appraisal comes in low, for example, don't expect to get a new appraisal because what you've learned is the house isn't worth what you think it is. The appraiser is simply trying to protect your collateral.

You may fall in love with a house, but you may not want to invest the money in that house if it isn't worth the money.

Having checks and balances in any real estate transaction is a good idea—it keeps everyone honest. In some fraudulent real estate schemes, the REALTOR®, loan officer, appraiser, and seller conspire to sell a home for more than it's worth to an unwary buyer. If you suspect that a home is worth significantly less than everyone else is telling you it's worth, consider hiring your own appraiser. An unbiased appraiser is often your best protection against fraud.

SECTION 3

Selecting the Right Home

MYTH # **24**

I'll Save Big Money Buying FSBO.

Fact: Buyers Usually *Lose* Money Dealing Directly with Sellers

When real estate markets are hot and demand outweighs supply, some homeowners are tempted to sell their homes themselves, without the assistance of a real estate agent. (Some are tempted to do so regardless of current market conditions.) A For Sale by Owner (FSBO) home is just that: a home for sale by its owners. When the house is sold, the owner will not have to pay a commission to a real estate agent, potentially saving thousands of dollars. In theory some of those savings will be passed on to you, right?

It's not likely. First, you don't save any money on commissions—buyers do not pay real estate commissions, sellers do. If you buy a home listed by a real estate agent, you won't pay the commission on the sales price; the seller will. So, buying a FSBO property won't save you a dime on real estate commissions.

— 77 —

You also won't save any money on loan costs (unless the owner offers seller financing). Your lending institution won't care whether a real estate agent is involved or not—you'll qualify for the same terms either way.

You're also not likely to buy the home for a lower price. (In fact, you're less likely to, because the seller will not have the benefit of receiving informed and educated advice from a real estate professional—most FSBO sellers are notorious for overpricing their homes.)

Here's at least one reason why. Let's look at it from the other side and assume you're selling your home. If you sell your house on your own, you save the 5%, 6%, or even 7% commission you would have paid to an agent. (On a house that sells for $300,000, that commission could be as much as $21,000—and that comes out of your pocket.) Sounds like a no-brainer to sell on your own, right?

The problem is that most potential buyers also understand what you're trying to accomplish. With FSBO houses they believe the owner most likely has overpriced the house; what the owner really hopes to get is a price that is inflated by the amount of a potential commission. That way, if the owner can't sell the house and has to turn it over to a broker, she can leave the price the same and still get her bottom-line figure for the house—even after taking into account the agent's commission.

If this logic makes sense to you, you can bet the average FSBO seller has thought of it, too. And as a result the house is overpriced.

Terri Murphy has this to say about FSBO properties: "The average consumer is certainly better informed than they used to be, but they're not *that* informed. The Internet offers great information 24–7 . . . and the consumer can fall prey to thinking the information they can get is *all* the information they need to get.

"Just because four or five houses have sold at a specific price point doesn't mean that others will sell for the same price. Multiple Listing Service prices reflect houses that were sold by brokers, not FSBOs. A REALTOR® understands that even if you have a ready, willing, and able buyer willing to pay top price, the lender may not loan that amount after an appraisal.

"FSBO listings and sales are on the decline, and for good reason. Take apartments in Manhattan—they all look the same from the outside, but they vary wildly on the inside. REALTOR®s understand property values. Few FSBO buyers or sellers perform the in-depth due diligence to understand what the true value is. Then, a few years later, if the buyer has to sell, they may not recover the price they paid.

"Here's the bottom line: a real estate agent knows the questions to ask and the answers you need. FSBO owners aren't in a position to tell you what you really need to know, and unless you're a real estate professional, you probably won't know what to ask, either."

An alternative is to visit a FSBO property with a buyer's agent. Some FSBO sellers include provisions for paying a commission to a buyer's agent who finds a buyer for the home. A buyer's agent can steer you through the process and apply his knowledge and expertise to your home-buying efforts—especially if you're considering a property that's FSBO.

If you do purchase a FSBO house, here's some advice:

- Use a certified home inspector to check for problems. Make sure they do a comprehensive and thorough inspection.
- Pay close attention to the survey and to any covenants or restrictions on the property.
- Double-check all documents for accuracy, and have the contract and any other agreements checked by a lawyer.
- And absolutely, without fail, make sure you purchase title insurance.

Here's an example of a FSBO horror story. A couple was purchasing a FSBO home. The owner didn't know how to write a good sales agreement, and the buyers didn't know what to look for in a good sales agreement, so the agreement contained none of the typical clauses that protect buyers—and contained a number of unusual clauses that weren't in the buyers' best interest. For example, the agreement allowed the sellers to store personal items in the garage for a period of time after the closing. Because no real estate agent was involved, the sellers and buyers negotiated directly, and those negotiations became incredibly frustrating and personal. (In fact, Chip ended up acting as the intermediary between the sellers and buyers.)

After a long struggle the buyers did finally purchase the home, but tempers had frayed to the point that they had to have separate closings, and the borrowers ended up accepting terms and taking actions they were unhappy with . . . if they'd dealt with a good real estate agent they could have saved time, money, and a tremendous amount of hassle.

Ralph bought his first house on his own from a mother and her daughter. He didn't use a REALTOR®, attorney, or title company. Soon after handing over his money, Ralph learned that the daughter who sold him the house wasn't the daughter who owned it. This little mess took Ralph four years to straighten out. If you're looking to buy a FSBO home, we suggest hiring a broker to at least write up the deal for a fee.

MYTH # **25**

I Have to Shop Within a Certain Price Range.

Fact: Buy Based Upon Value—Not Price

Buying a house you can afford is certainly important; if you stretch yourself too thin, you may dig a financial hole you can't escape from. At the same time, automatically limiting yourself to a specific price range can cause you to miss out on a great deal. The buying decision you make should be based on value, not on price.

Why? Price is a subjective thing; the price of a house is what the owner hopes to get. Most owners, especially if they don't listen to the advice of their real estate agent, will overprice their home. It's a natural mistake—after all, it's your house . . . so it must be worth a lot, right?

Restricting yourself to a tightly-defined price range could cause you to miss a great deal. Say you decide you're in the market for a house in the $325,000 to $350,000 range. You refuse to even look at houses above $350,000 because you can't afford them. Sound sensible?

It's not. A house listed for $370,000 may be overpriced. What if it's perfect for your needs, and after a little negotiating you could get the owner to accept $340,000? Wouldn't that be great?

You'll never know, because you've limited yourself to a specific price range.

Our advice is to look at homes priced at least 10% under and over your target price range. Unless the market is extremely hot, a 10% reduction in price, while certainly not the norm, is also not unusual. The owner may have set a (wishful) high price but may also be desperate ... and could turn out to accept any reasonable offer presented. Or you could find a great house containing a small apartment with a separate entrance suitable for renting—but if it's outside your price range, you'll never check it out.

You won't decide a house is a great deal based on its price—you'll decide it's a great deal based on its value. Value is what you get for the price you pay; make sure you shop for value, not for price. If it helps, think of it this way: almost every home is probably overpriced. Before you buy any home, check out at least 10 other homes; you won't have a good sense of what value is until you have a basis to make comparisons. To be personally satisfied with the value you'll receive, look at a lot of homes so you can make educated and informed comparisons. Check out higher-priced homes *and* lower-priced homes; you may find a great value ... and *that's* what you're looking for.

Eric Weinstein, President of Carteret Mortgage, says, "Here's advice I give all first-time homebuyers:

1. "Check out neighborhoods thoroughly. Drive by the schools, and stores. Drive by during the weekends and during rush hour. Get familiar with the general vicinity to be sure you like the area first.
2. "Most people tend to jump, and over-buy on price. Stay within your comfort range, and don't get emotionally attached to the home or the deal—you'll lose money (and sleep) every time. Look for the value within the price.
3. "Deal with people you trust. Check them out, and if you're not comfortable—find someone else."

Don't limit yourself to searching for homes listed in the standard channels. Consider checking foreclosure notices, exploring government-seized properties, buying properties from a bank's REO (Real Estate Owned) department, or purchasing FHA or VA foreclosure properties through a broker who specializes in those properties. You don't have to be a real estate investor to capitalize on these great deals.

Check how long the home has been on the market—including with different agents. A long shelf life may indicate problems, or that it was incorrectly priced from the beginning.

MYTH # **26**

Everything Is Included in the Sales Price.

Fact: If It Ain't in Writing, It Ain't Gonna Be There

Let's look at a couple of definitions. *Real property* is defined as "the interests, benefits, and rights inherent in real estate ownership; land and anything else of a permanent nature that is affixed to the land." *Personal property* is defined as "any items belonging to a person that is not real estate or is property that is movable and not fixed to land."

Does that clear it up? Probably not—and that's a problem when you buy a home. The owner is selling you real property; he or she is taking personal property.

So—is the Tiffany hanging lamp in the hallway part of the purchase? Maybe—and maybe not.

"I was a REALTOR® in a small town," says Terri Murphy, "and I listed a home owned by a local landscaper. I found a buyer fairly quickly, handled the negotiations, and we reached an agreement. Then, on the day of the walk-through, we found he'd taken all the decorative stone from the flower beds. (I had him bring them back, by the way.) A good real estate agent—and a smart buyer—makes sure to specify exactly what will convey and what won't. Remember stating that "a" washer and dryer is included doesn't mean "the" washer and dryer is included—I go so far as to note serial numbers. I've seen sod rolled up and removed, rose bushes and rhododendrons taken out . . . you name it and I've seen it. Just because landscaping is attached to the earth doesn't mean someone won't try to take it when they move.

If an item is permanently attached, it's considered to be real property and will remain. Kitchen cabinets, for example, are considered part of the property. An island on wheels used in the kitchen may not be considered part of the property, especially since it's not attached.

Some sellers may complain (and some real estate agents may complain), but your best bet is to write everything down that you expect to remain with the home; if you and the seller disagree, negotiate until you reach agreement. Once you close on the home, you'll have no recourse, so write down every item when you create a contract and check to be sure they're in place when you do your closing day walk-through. If any items are missing, don't close until they're returned or unless you reach an agreement on a fair price the seller will pay for those items.

Chip found a mortgage for a couple who learned at the preclosing walk-through that the shrubs had been pulled up, the refrigerator, washer, dryer, mirrors, and light fixtures were removed, a chandelier had been replaced with a $15 substitute . . . none of those items had been noted on the FSBO sales agreement they signed, so the seller removed them.

Remember: if it isn't in writing, it probably won't be there when you close. Don't allow room for misunderstandings; write down everything, and make it part of your purchase agreement.

Nothing in real estate is legally binding unless it's in writing. If the homeowner promises you that the oriental rugs are staying, get it in writing. If the rugs are gone when you move in, you won't have a leg (or a rug) to stand on.

MYTH # **27**

The Appraiser Will Specify the Value and Any Required Repairs.

Fact: The Appraiser Doesn't Determine the Final Value; the Appraiser Works for the Lender to Establish the Collateral Value of the Property

What is an individual home truly worth? A home, like any other commodity, is only worth what someone is ready *and* willing to pay for it. The actual sales price reflects its value, at least to the buyer and the seller. Anything else is simply an estimate.

Lenders determine the value of a property through an appraisal. There are three basic types of appraisals: sales comparison, cost, and income capitalization. Remember—each type only provides an estimate of value; none specifies what a house is truly worth.

- **Sales Comparison.** The sales comparison method estimates a property's value by comparing it to similar properties that recently sold in the area. Those properties are called comparables, or "comps." An appraiser will compare "comps" to the subject property to help determine its value. Sales comparison appraisals are typically used to evaluate single-family homes, townhouses, and duplexes.

  Appraisers are generally required to compare the subject property to at least three comps. Since very few houses are identical, the appraiser will adjust the values according to some standard formulas: for instance, if the subject property has a deck and a comp does not, the appraiser will adjust the value of the subject property upwards to compensate for the additional feature.

  Sales comparison appraisals are part art and part science: the appraiser has a fair amount of latitude within which to determine the value of the property. If two different appraisers evaluate a property, they'll rarely agree exactly on the property's value.

- **Cost.** The cost method determines a property's value by calculating how much it would cost to replace the home. The appraiser estimates the value of the property if it was new, then deducts an amount for depreciation (wear and tear) based on the property's current condition. The value of the land is determined by using recent sales of comps. (There is no way to estimate land value by a cost method since the land can't be replaced.)

  Cost appraisals are more accurate when the property is fairly new, since it's easier to estimate the replacement cost. With older properties, it gets harder to reproduce or duplicate the setting and feel of the neighborhood. Cost appraisals are also useful when a property is somewhat unique and suitable comparables can't be found.

- **Income approach.** The income approach, or capitalization appraisal places a value on a property based on its ability to produce income. Income capitalization appraisals are most commonly used to estimate the value of office buildings, commercial real estate, and other rental properties. Appraisers look at the property from the investors' point of view. In effect the investors are determining how much they're willing to pay based upon the return on equity—which becomes what the property is worth (to them.) You'll see why investors perform this calculation in a moment.

   The process is simple: first calculate the gross income (rent) for the property and then subtract an amount for typical operating expenses like taxes, utilities, maintenance, insurance, and other costs. The result is the net income the property is expected to provide. That net operating income (or NOI) relative to the cash investment required provides the basis for total price investors are willing to risk.

Appraisals are important to buyers, sellers, and lenders. Lenders use appraisals to make sure they don't loan more than the property is worth. Buyers use appraisals to make sure they aren't overpaying for a property, and sellers use appraisals to help them properly value their properties for sale.

What you hopefully noticed is that while an appraisal may reference the overall condition of the home, it does not describe problems or issues with specific house features, items, or appliances. The appraiser will spend very little time assessing the condition of individual features; remember his or her job is simply to estimate the value of the home.

In order to determine if any repairs may be necessary, a home inspection performed by a qualified and licensed home inspector is necessary. Six months after he closed on his home, a customer learned that the home was infested with termites. He assumed the appraisal also served as an inspection, and he figured he'd save a few dollars by skipping an "unnecessary inspection." He may have saved a couple hundred dollars initially—but the termite problem ended up costing over $60,000 to fix.

If it's helpful, think about an appraisal in the same way you'd consider the blue book value of a car. The book value is simply an indication and a guide to a car's value; it's no guarantee you can buy or sell the car for that price. An appraisal is the same: it's an indication and an estimate of a home's value. You would not expect to be required to pay book value for a car—don't feel you're required to pay any more or less than the appraisal value of a home.

 The value of a property is determined by what a buyer is willing to pay for it and the seller is willing to accept for it. The appraiser's job is primarily to protect the lender from approving a loan for significantly more than the house is worth. His job is not to tell you how much to pay for the house—or to tell the seller how much to accept for it.

 You are entitled to receive a copy of the appraisal (as long as you paid for it), but must request it in writing within 90 days. Make sure to get one!

MYTH # **28**

The Real Estate Agent Will Protect Us.

Fact: Most Agents Are Under Written Contract to Represent the Seller, Not the Buyer

There are two basic roles a real estate agent can play: as a seller's agent or as a buyer's agent. (And in some states a real estate agent can be a dual agent.) By far the most common role agents will play is that of a seller's agent: in short, they act on behalf of the seller of the home to sell the property. Because they work for the seller, they can't disclose confidential information to buyers of the property. They also aren't negotiating on your behalf—their goal is to get the best price they can for the seller, not for you. In fact, they're contractually, and ethically, required to do so. As a friend likes to say, the real estate agent may be *friendly*, but he or she is not your *friend*.

In the past many buyers were unaware that the agent wasn't working on their behalf. After all, they may have seen a house they liked and called the agent ... so shouldn't the agent be *working* for them? No. Some buyers would tell the agent the maximum they were willing to pay for a particular house, for instance ... unaware that the agent could and would pass that information on to the seller.

As a result of the potential confusion, agents are now required to disclose they are agents for the seller; in most cases the disclosure must be in writing. (Even though disclosure is a requirement, oddly enough many buyers don't pay attention to what the disclosure actually means and continue to assume the agent is working for them.)

While seller's agents are working on behalf of the seller, they are required to disclose "material" facts about the house. They must disclose material facts about property condition, for instance. If, for instance, the roof is leaking, appliances are broken, or the heating system has failed, the agent is required to disclose those facts to potential buyers if he or she is aware of the problem. Disclosure is also required if the property fails to meet zoning requirements or building codes.

Agents are not required to disclose personal information about the sellers, though. The agent does not have to tell a buyer how motivated the sellers are, what their bottom-line price is, why they're selling the home, and so forth. (In fact, they shouldn't—doing so would be unethical.)

Buyer's agents agree to work on the behalf of a buyer. They do not operate on behalf of the seller, so in effect the confidentiality relationship is reversed.

Most buyers' agents will require you to sign an exclusivity contract stating you will work only with them for a specified amount of time. (In fact, some agreements state that you must pay the buyer's agent a commission if you purchase a house using another agent.) Why does a buyer's agent require an agreement? They'll put a lot of work into finding a house for you and representing you—as a result they want (and in truth deserve) some guarantee that work will pay off for them.

Buyer's agents can be very helpful, and best of all they also are required to disclose material facts about properties they show. They can research past sales to help you determine how much to offer for a property; they can help you negotiate with the seller and the seller's agent, and they can help walk you through the closing process.

Why are there fewer buyer's agents than seller's agents? It's simple: if agents list a house for sale, as long as the house sells they're paid a commission. It doesn't matter whether they found the buyer or not (although their earnings are higher if they do). A buyer's agent has to hope that you find the right house and complete the purchase. Their odds of earning a commission are without a doubt—lower.

Using a buyer's agent is a good idea. If you use a buyer's agent, you can negotiate the terms of your agreement. For instance, you can specify:

- *The geographic area.* If you're looking at properties in a fairly broad area, you can limit your agreement with the buyer's agent to a particular city or county, for instance.
- *The time period.* You can agree to a long-term relationship (30, 60, or 90 days), or to a time period as short as 1 day or even the showing of 1 house. Keep in mind that the longer the term you agree to, the longer you're required to work with the agent. On the other hand, in general the longer the term the harder agents will work for you, because they'll know they have a better chance of earning a commission.
- *Basic exceptions.* For example, you could negotiate that if you find a property that's being sold by its owner you have the right to purchase it without paying the buyer's agent a commission.

If you use a buyer's agent, make sure you understand all the terms of the agreement. A friend signed a buyer's agent agreement without realizing that she had agreed to pay a fee at the end of the agreement even if she had not purchased a property. The contract can state any terms you both agree to—so make sure you fully understand what you're agreeing to.

Agents can also be considered dual agents. A buyer's agent automatically becomes a dual agent when showing a property listed by his or her real estate firm. Some states won't allow dual agency because it's a little confusing to consumers, since the agent has responsibilities to both parties. The agent can't disclose personal information to either client about the other, but still must make sure to meet the needs of both. It can be difficult being in the middle, and it's a tight line the agent is required to walk. Dual agency must be disclosed to both sellers and buyers in writing, so you'll know if your agent is acting in a dual agent capacity.

It's easier to work with a dual agent if she isn't the person who actually listed the property. In that case she may not be aware of personal information about the sellers, so confidentiality is easier to maintain. If you have a buyer's agent agreement with a particular agent and she wants to show you a home she's listed, many firms will require the agent to "hand you off" to another agent in the firm for that showing and possible transaction.

Most people also don't realize they have the right to be at the presentation of their offer to a seller. One reason is to ensure your offer is communicated in a timely fashion; agents are supposed to present offers as soon as practicable, but less-than-ethical real estate agents may purposely hold offers until another one comes in to create a small bidding war. You also may want to attend the presentation to explain personally why your offer is a good offer, especially if it's a creative offer. If you think the agent won't thoroughly understand the offer and be able to present it well, you have the right to be there, especially in complex or unconventional situations.

Here's the bottom line: if you haven't signed a buyer's agent agreement with a real estate agent, the agent is a seller's agent and is working on the seller's behalf, not on yours. (No matter how helpful the agent may seem to be.) If you've signed a buyer's agent agreement, the agent works for you, and you'll know he or she is working on your behalf.

 You're driving around town and notice a For Sale sign planted on the front lawn of a house you find appealing. You call the number for the agent listing the house. You're now working with the seller's agent, who is contracted to represent the seller—not the best move. Draw up a contract with a buyer's agent who represents you. The commission you'll pay is the same—the seller's agent simply splits the commission with your agent.

MYTH # **29**

Condos Are Bad Investments and Hard to Finance.

Fact: Condos Represent One of the Fastest-Growing Forms of Home Ownership

Why? First, buying a condo increases your purchasing power. Try this test: compare the price of a two-bedroom condo to a two-bedroom single-family home located in the same neighborhood. You'll find that most condos sell for at least 15 to 30% less than the same-size single-family home. Why? You share the cost of owning the roof, foundation, and plot of land with the other owners. If you're a first-time homebuyer, buying a condo may be the only way you can afford to become a homeowner instead of a renter.

Condo purchases are also not typically difficult to finance. In some ways they can be easier to finance, because the lender can feel confident in the appraisal value since comparable sales are easy to find. Most lenders are no more hesitant to offer condo financing than they are to offer single-family home financing.

On the other hand, some online lenders can create problems for condo buyers. "A REALTOR® called me looking for help," said Amy Tierce of Fairway New England Mortgage, a veteran of the mortgage industry with over 15 years experience. "Her sellers were going to hold the buyer's deposit if the loan didn't close by the next Friday. The buyer had applied with an Internet lender, and the lender required amendments to the condominium agreements. There was no way that was ever going to happen. Even on short notice, I was able to get the loan approved and closed on time—there was no reason for the loan to not be approved. Better yet, I was able to get the borrowers better terms than offered by the online lender.

"It stunned to me to realize that a borrower would put their trust into a nameless, faceless online entity and risk a tremendous amount of money. In Massachusetts buyers are required to put 10% down when they sign a purchase and sale agreement; this buyer was going to lose about $30,000 if the purchase didn't close on time."

Generally speaking condos are no more difficult to finance than single-family dwellings, and they offer other perks. Here are some advantages to condo ownership:

- Condos usually cost less to maintain than detached homes. Replacing, for example, a roof may cost the same in absolute dollars, but the cost per owner will be less.
- Condos may have amenities that you couldn't otherwise afford: swimming pools, tennis courts, playgrounds, and so forth.
- Condos can be perfect homes for empty nesters, especially since you may not be responsible for maintenance, yard work, and so forth.
- Condo prices tend to be stable due to other units, and finding comparable recent sales is easy, allowing you to have a good sense of the condo's value before you make an offer.

There are also disadvantages to condo ownership:

- Condos offer less privacy. Visit the unit you're considering at different times of the day and different days of the week to listen for noise.
- As a general rule, the fewer common walls you share with neighbors, the more privacy you have in your unit. Corner units typically sell for a premium, as do top floor units, since no one will be walking on the ceiling above.
- Condominium agreements can be legally complex. Before you buy a condo you should check out three important documents: a Master Deed or Declaration of Covenants, Conditions, and Restrictions (CC and R); the homeowners-association bylaws; and the homeowners-association budget. Restriction covenants tell you what you can do and what you can't do. They are in there to protect the interests of you and the other owners. Review each thoroughly to make sure you know what your rights and responsibilities are.
- Check parking and storage provisions. For example, does your condo deed include a deeded garage or parking space reserved for you, or is parking on a first-come, first-served basis? Are there extra charges for parking, or is parking included in the monthly dues? Are there

provisions for guest parking? Do you have a deeded storage area located outside of your unit? If you need even more storage, is any available and how much does it cost? Find the answers to these questions before you buy.

Keep in mind that many new neighborhoods also have restrictive covenants—a condo is not the only form of home ownership that can restrict your use of the property. Just as with any other real estate purchase, check out all documents thoroughly, and make sure all your questions are answered.

As part of the process, the lender will have the condo association fill out a detailed questionnaire—it's okay to ask for a copy, and the answers will be very insightful!

 Condos in popular vacation spots are often a good investment even if you choose to only use the condo a couple weeks a year. You can usually hire a condo management company to line up renters and deal with maintenance. Just be sure to work the numbers carefully to make sure the rent will cover your mortgage payments and association fees.

 Ask the seller (or agent) for a year-end financial statement for the association. Review it for capital reserves and possible cash-flow problems that could indicate an impending special assessment or increase in the monthly association fees.

MYTH # **30**

Seller Disclosures Are Complete and Accurate.

Fact: You Need to Check *Everything* Yourself

Most states require disclosures to be made by the seller, listing all known problems. Note we used the word "known" in the last sentence: the seller is not obligated to inform you of something he doesn't know and would have no reasonable way of knowing. For instance, if the property has an old oil tank buried in the back, and the owners don't know it exists, they're under no obligation to disclose that information—they can't disclose what they don't know. But if the roof leaks or the furnace isn't working, they are required to disclose those facts.

Disclosures can help you feel more comfortable about a property, but there are a few things you'll need to keep in mind:

- The seller is not obligated to disclose any facts or conditions he is not aware of.
- Disclosures are descriptions of current or past conditions. They in no way imply a warranty against future problems. If the dishwasher works today, works on the day of your final walk-through, and then breaks a month later, the seller isn't obligated to repair or replace the dishwasher. A disclosure only refers to the past or present—it does not guarantee the future.
- Disclosures are designed to list adverse conditions, but "adverse" is open to interpretation. If there's a construction site nearby that creates noise, the seller may not be obligated to disclose that fact. (If the property is near an airport flight path, the seller is not obligated to disclose the noise that results, even though you personally may consider the sound of jets flying overhead to be "adverse.")
- In some states, disclosure statements may not require sellers to disclose problems that are easily observable. If the sidewalk is cracked, the seller may not have to disclose that fact; the assumption is that you will discover it yourself. Disclosures are designed to alert buyers to problems that may not be as easy to detect or identify.

Disclosures can be helpful, but as you can see, it pays to have an independent assessment done so that you'll know exactly what you're getting into. Don't rely solely on a disclosure to tell you everything you want to know.

Investment properties are also excluded from disclosure statement regulations in some states. In those cases, the owner is under no obligation to disclose any problems or defects. If that's the case, make sure you have thorough inspections done by qualified professionals.

Here's a partial list of other things you should check out about a house you're considering. See the Appendix or visit *www.TheMortgage Myths.com* for a complete printable listing.

- School district (boundaries and distance).
- Railroad, highway, industrial, or airport noise.
- Easements—utilities; access to your property and adjoining properties.
- Zoning—residential, commercial, multifamily, and grandfather clauses.
- Restrictive covenants against building fences, outbuildings, parking an RV in the driveway, and so forth, or historic district designations.
- The commute to your workplace—during the times you actually commute!
- The existence of lead paint, radon, asbestos or other nearby toxicity sources (landfills, gas stations, dry cleaners, car wash, etc.).
- Recent repairs—especially drywall or touch-up paint jobs; remodeling may hide problems.
- Sewer and water service.
- Hidden or unrecorded liens against the property.
- Construction liens against the property—(any recent major repairs?).
- Utility bills—(get last 12 months).
- Recent unusual neighborhood events: robberies, burglaries, murders, immediate area foreclosures.

Remember, you'll live in the house. Disclosures only provide a small portion of the information you'll need to know. Don't rely on someone else to check out the house and the neighborhood; you're the best judge of what's right for you, so make sure you check everything yourself. Check the house during the day, during the evening, during the weekend, talk to neighbors . . . check *everything* yourself. The seller is only required to put down what they have to . . . and there are a lot of things you'll want to know that they won't have to or want to disclose.

In real estate circles we have a saying, "Buyers are liars, and sellers are worse." If you read a seller disclosure that has all the "Don't Know" boxes checked, chances are the seller knows a lot more than he's letting on. Check the items yourself, have your inspector focus on the "Don't Know" items, or simply pass on the property.

MYTH # **31**

I Should Buy the Biggest House at a Bargain Price.

Fact: The Smaller Houses in the Neighborhood Control the Value of the Larger Ones

You've probably heard the expression, "Never buy the biggest house in the neighborhood." We're sure there are exceptions to that rule, but they're likely to be few and far between. The value of homes in a particular neighborhood is controlled by the combination of all the homes—the large ones, the small ones, and the ones in between. Appraisers look for what is called "conformity" when assessing a neighborhood. Conformity is an appraisal principle stating that the greater the similarity among properties in an area, the better they will hold their value. In general, conformity assumes that a neighborhood that is reasonably similar in social and economic activity will result in properties that reach their maximum value.

In other words, the more similar the properties, the better chance they'll reach their maximum value. That's why you don't want the biggest house in the neighborhood; it's unlikely to reach its maximum value. (It can be argued and is often true that the smaller houses will carry a higher value due to the presence of larger houses, however.)

The words "a bargain price" may seem like a good thing, but relative to what? If you can buy a 3,000-square-foot home in a neighborhood with similarly-sized homes for $300,000, and you find a deal on a 3,000-square-foot home in a neighborhood filled with smaller homes selling for $280,000, have you found a bargain price? Not necessarily; while it is certainly priced lower than the $300,000 house, its value may also be lower due to the neighborhood it is in.

Your goal is to pay the lowest price you can for a home with the greatest value possible. Price is not an indication of value; it's simply a price. To determine the value of a home, check comparable sales both inside and outside the neighborhood. Make sure you're not fooled by a low price into thinking you're getting a great value—especially if you're looking at the biggest house in the neighborhood.

Stretch yourself, but buy a home in an area where there are larger ones at higher prices. Don't buy the biggest one that will need to come down to meet the norm of the neighborhood; let your smaller home rise to meet the others.

 When you buy a home as an investment property you can often find bargains in smaller houses that have potential for expansion. For example, buying a two-bedroom house and converting unused attic space into a third bedroom may bring the property's value in line with other properties in the neighborhood.

MYTH # **32**

I Should Always Use an Attorney.

Fact: In Most States, Attorneys Aren't Mandatory—and Aren't Needed

While some states require that an attorney review documents before closing (New Jersey, for example, requires an attorney to handle the closing itself), most do not.

Most homebuyers can generally handle routine real estate purchase contracts as long as they read the fine print and understand all the terms. Pay close attention to any clauses, contingencies, or other special considerations that allow you or the seller to back out of the contract, though—if you're in doubt, then do consult an attorney. You can even ask an attorney to only review the items in question, which will decrease your legal fees.

It doesn't happen often, but sometimes attorneys try to prove they earn their fees by requesting changes to standard loan documents. The documentation the lender uses has been reviewed by expert attorneys, and the lender will not look favorably upon changes requested by individual attorneys. The lender is making sure they protect their money. Don't let your attorney nitpick forms that are actually in your best interest, especially the standard conforming forms such as the Mortgage or Note.

It is possible to handle real estate transactions effectively without an attorney; we would never recommend that you do not use an attorney—the choice is yours. If you feel you need an attorney, ask friends or colleagues for recommendations. Feel free to interview the attorneys you're considering—ask about fees, their availability, and their experience. It is by no means accurate to assume that better attorneys charge higher fees; while an attorney's fees may sometimes reflect his or her experience or skills, it is by no means a guarantee of expertise. Get someone who specializes in real estate, not your buddy's divorce lawyer!

In many cases you won't need an attorney—but if you're in doubt, don't hesitate to ask a good one for help.

Like doctors, attorneys specialize in particular areas. Using your divorce attorney to look over paperwork at a real estate closing may not be such a great idea. If you need an attorney, find one who specializes in real estate.

For specific information on states where attorneys are required, check the resource web site at www.TheMortgageMyths.com. You'll find a wealth of other mortgage and real estate information as well.

MYTH # **33**

I Don't Need an Inspection—It Looks Great to Me!

Fact: A Thorough Inspection by an Independent Expert Is a Small Investment

Some inspections are required by state or local law, and others can be negotiated within the offer. Most lenders require a pest inspection; many state or local governments require testing for radon levels, mold, lead paint, and other hazardous items. As a buyer you can—and always should—also require a home inspection be performed by a qualified professional.

Home inspectors evaluate the structure of the house, identifying any issues with the roof, plumbing, electrical systems, heating and air conditioning units, appliances, windows and doors, chimneys, and other components of the property. (Commercial inspectors fulfill the same role on commercial properties.)

If problems are found during the inspection, you have three choices: you can continue with the sale, you can renegotiate the contract, or walk away from the deal! If the problems are minor, most sellers will agree to fix them to your satisfaction so they don't lose the sale. If the problems are major, you can either renegotiate . . . or buy the property knowing that certain repairs need to be made. Or, of course, you can elect to go find another house.

The time period during which inspections must be completed should be noted on the purchase contract. If you're a buyer and you fail to meet the time frame for the home inspection, for instance, the seller is under no obligation to allow you to back out of the contract if a later inspection finds problems. Always make sure your inspections take place in a timely fashion per the agreed-upon time frames on the contract. If they can't be completed within the timeframe, make *sure* to get a written extension!

Anyone can stick the words "Home Inspector" on a business card and perform home inspections. Your home inspector should be certified by the American Society of Home Inspectors (ASHI), the premier home inspection organization in the United States. Why? The type of inspector you have will determine how thoroughly they'll inspect the house.

Here's an extreme example. A neighbor of Terri Murphy's noticed water damage on a second-floor ceiling a month or so after he moved into the home. While he had a home inspection performed before closing, his inspector didn't go into the attic to check for signs of water leakage. Terri recommended he call an ASHI inspector to investigate. The inspector entered the attic, looked around briefly, and said, "I've found your problem. Your buckets are full."

The previous owner obviously knew about the problem and used buckets to catch leaking water! The first home inspector didn't take the time to look in the attic, and missed an obvious (and major) problem.

Keep in mind that no inspector, no matter how thorough, will catch every potential problem. Also, a home inspector isn't an expert on everything. If the home inspector identifies a problem, especially with a major system like a furnace or heat pump, have a specialist or licensed contractor investigate further. The home inspector identifies problems and gives opinions; the home inspector isn't the final word, nor should he or she be.

Also remember you should always conduct a final walk-through inspection as close to closing as possible to make sure the property is in the same condition it was in when you agreed to purchase it. If you can, perform your walk-through the day of closing after the owners have vacated the property so you can make sure no damage occurred during the moving process.

Home inspectors can not only save you money—they can also help you avoid potentially dangerous situations. A customer of Chip's purchased a home without testing the heating system; they bought the home in the middle of summer. When winter rolled around, they found the heat exchanger was cracked and carbon monoxide was leaking dangerously into the home. They were lucky to catch the problem, but a thorough inspection would have caught it ahead of time and saved them from this costly repair.

Tim Kleyla, president of The Mortgage House in Holland, Michigan, recalls a situation with a far worse ending. "One of my clients failed to have a home inspection performed and as a result ended up losing her home," he said. "The roof on the home looked old, but still seemed to be in adequate shape. She chose not to have inspections done, thinking she could save a little money. She moved in … and a few months later it snowed heavily. Water poured into the home as ice buildup forced inside, melted, and ran down the walls. A subsequent inspection revealed the situation had been occurring for years, plus the attic space wasn't properly insulated. The roof needed to be replaced—in addition to other repairs—and the homeowner didn't have the money. She ended up in foreclosure."

Here's the bottom line on inspections: Better to pay a little now than to pay a bundle—possibly even more than you can afford—later.

If your home inspector shows concern over a big-ticket item like the electrical system, plumbing, furnace, central air conditioning unit, roof, or foundation, call a contractor who specializes in that area to come out and take a closer look. Obtain a ballpark estimate for any repairs so you know ahead of time what you're getting yourself into.

MYTH # **34**

I've Seen Enough, I've Found the Home I Love!

Fact: Emotion-Based Transactions Will Cost You Thousands

So, you've been looking at houses for a day or so and have already found the house you want. Do we think that's possible? While it may end up actually being the case, in most cases I'd say no, it's not possible. And even if you have found your dream home, you owe it to yourself to make sure your decision is made rationally and logically—not emotionally.

The average homebuyer looks at between 10 and 15 houses before making an offer on one. Even if you think you've found the perfect house, look at more than 10 houses before you decide to make an offer on *any*. And before you do, go back to that house, and spend time in it.

Look for things you might have missed; walk nearby streets and get a feel for the neighborhood; check out the school system; talk to neighbors if you can. Imagine yourself *living* in the home on a daily basis—is it really right for you and your family? If you think you've found the house you love, you can lose objectivity and easily overlook important items. Or, you may make sacrifices you normally wouldn't make. Be prepared to walk away from a home at any time—*becoming too emotionally invested will almost always cost you money*.

Buying a home is a huge decision, not just from an investment point of view but more importantly from a livability point of view. Your house should meet your present and future needs—it needs to be the right place for you to *live*. We know a couple who bought a house simply because it had a hot tub on the deck; they were so excited by the thought of sipping champagne in mid-winter in their hot tub they ignored the noise from a nearby interstate, the poor condition of the neighbors' homes, the fact their commute would be over an hour . . . they made a purely emotional decision instead of a rational one. You can pay to put a hot tub on your deck—no amount of money will block noise from a nearby interstate highway.

When Chip or Ralph speaks to civic groups, they remind the audience that as soon as you fall in love with a house, you lose. Fall in love with the house *after* it becomes your home—stay objective and make buying decisions based on reason instead of emotion.

Choose a home with your *heart*, but buy the home with your *head*. It's okay to fall in love with a house, especially if you plan on living in the house for the next 10 to 30 years, but don't let your emotions suck you into paying more for the home than you can turn around and sell it for the next day.

MYTH # **35**

It's Okay to Buy—This Area Is Booming.

Fact: Growth and Appreciation Happen Neighborhood by Neighborhood

It's easy to assume that home values are rising rapidly in a city or geographic area—news and media reports tend to focus on cities. A media report that may state, "Home prices in Phoenix, Arizona, are booming." The report is correct: on average, the price of a home in Phoenix is higher this year than it was last year. Does that mean that *every* house in Phoenix has risen in value? Of course it doesn't.

Appreciation happens house by house and neighborhood by neighborhood. No matter how hot the general real estate market is in any city, you can always find neighborhoods where house prices are stagnant—or even declining. No two neighborhoods are the same, and no two houses are the same. Why would their rate of price growth and appreciation be the same?

To determine if a house is likely to appreciate in value, here's what to do:

- Find areas close to colleges, upscale shopping, cultural, and sporting events. You'll notice that people are spending significant sums remodeling older homes.
- Find out what areas have the best schools, and look for available homes within their boundaries—even if you don't have kids!
- Look for areas that are close to where young professionals work and are moving into. When it's time for you to sell and move up, these are the buyers you want to attract.
- If prices in your interest area have steadily increased over the past few years, that's a good sign. Reasonably priced starter homes may be hard to find.
- New areas and subdivisions can be a good way to go. Values will tend to go up in the long term.
- Look for new commercial development. If these companies are investing in the area, it's a sign the area is growing.

And here's what you should watch out for:

- Avoid buying on busy streets and in high traffic areas.
- If the schools don't have a good reputation, this may be an indication the area is going downhill. If so, home values will follow.
- If there are a lot of good deals and concessions available, there's a reason. It's usually not too hard to find out the reasons why if you look around and talk to people in the area.
- If it's a new subdivision of starter homes and you plan on moving in about five years, others who bought at the same time may also want to move. This may put more homes up for sale than the market can handle, and prices can decline (or at least stay flat) in the short term. And if more houses are being built when you want to sell, it'll be tougher for you to sell—your "used" home will be competing against brand-new homes.

If an area or neighborhood that used to be popular starts going downhill, don't buy in on the downward slope thinking that you're getting a bargain. Keep tabs on the neighborhood until you see it begin to pull out of its slump before making an investment.

MYTH # **36**

All Sales Agreements and EMD Requirements Are Standard.

Fact: The Agreement Can Be Written on a Napkin with a $5 Deposit

Most real estate agents use standard, boilerplate sales agreement forms. Why? It's easy, and it saves them time. You can also purchase sales agreement forms at almost any stationery store, bookstore, or find them online. Properly filled out and executed, standard sales agreement forms create a binding contract between two parties.

So does a sales agreement written on a napkin over lunch.

To officially make an offer, all you need is a written contract. A contract is simply a voluntary, legally enforceable promise between two parties to perform some legal act in exchange for consideration. In this case, the legal act will be the transfer of real estate; the consideration will be the purchase price you pay.

You may think or assume you have to use standard forms or agreements, but you don't. (Just because everyone is doing so doesn't mean you have to.)

You can make verbal offers, but you never should. Some oral agreements are enforceable; but most are not. In either case oral agreements can lead to messy and complicated disagreements. Make all your offers in writing, and you avoid any uncertainty, confusion, or misunderstandings.

There are basic elements in a contract:

- ◆ Offer and acceptance.
- ◆ Consideration.
- ◆ Legally competent parties.

♦ Consent.

♦ Legal purpose.

If you make an offer using a real estate agent, the agent will ensure that the offer is written using a valid form, and that it contains appropriate language. Note that the language will be appropriate, but not necessarily *advantageous* to you. It's up to you to make your conditions known on the offer, and consider adding an "Addendum" if necessary, which allows more space to clarify your intentions. Remember that the real estate agent has a vested interest in seeing the transaction completed; you have a vested interest in getting the best possible deal. Therefore, it's up to you to specify the terms that are important to you.

Consideration is a part of any contract. Consideration is both the final price established for the sale, and is also "earnest" money that is put down with the contract. In most cases you'll make a small deposit when you make an offer—typically $500 or $1,000. But, it can be as little as $1 or even no money. Some states require some amount of consideration, but others recognize that your promise to pay (since that's what you're doing when you sign the contract) is consideration in and of yourself.

The intent of consideration is to show your seriousness in making the offer, since if you back out of the contract you could forfeit that earnest money. If you back out due to a contingency that you insert in the contract—for instance, that the sale is contingent upon you qualifying for particular financing terms—and you don't qualify, the contract becomes void and you'll get your earnest money deposit (EMD) back.

Your EMD can also become a powerful component of your offer. A friend made an offer on an income property and made an EMD of $10,000, which was an amount well above the norm in his area. The seller had another offer—and for a higher price—but decided to accept our friend's lower offer because his EMD was such a solid signal of intent, his financial position was strong, and the seller felt very confident he would have no difficulty in obtaining financing.

A real estate sales contract contains the complete agreement between parties. If you make an offer and it's accepted, you can't go back later and request additional concessions or changes. You'll want to be sure your contract contains the exact details of the purchase that you're willing to agree to. Here are key details that should appear on any contract:

- Purchaser and seller names.
- Sales price and terms, including any earnest money deposited.
- How long the contract is good for (usually expressed in hours or days).
- A legal address and description of the land or property, and any covenants or restrictions that apply to the deed.
- Additional items that convey, like appliances, light fixtures, window treatments, outside buildings, and so forth.
- A statement of the kind and condition of the title, and the form of deed to be delivered to the seller.
- The kind of title evidence required, who will provide it, and how many defects in the title will be eliminated.
- A statement of all the terms and conditions of the agreement between the parties, and any contingencies.
- The method that will be used to prorate real estate taxes, rents, fuel costs, and so forth.
- Remedies available in the case of default (by either party).
- Signatures of all pertinent parties.

Most of the above information will appear in standard language on standard contract forms—take the time to read it all to make sure you understand what you're agreeing to. If you're writing your own sales agreement, just make sure you include the items listed above so that your contract will be legally enforceable. If you're confused about anything or have any questions, have an attorney review the contract first. Once you've signed the contract, it becomes a legally binding agreement.

If the other party accepts your purchase agreement without making any changes to it, don't entertain second thoughts that you should have offered less for the property (as the buyer), or asked too little for the property (as the seller). If you reviewed the information thoroughly and chose what was best for you, you made a good decision. Don't worry what the other party received in the transaction.

MYTH # **37**

I Can't Withdraw My Offer—It's Too Late.

Fact: It's Never a Done Deal Until the Fat Lady Sings

You've found the home you love—it's perfect! Better yet, the price is within your means. You've looked at a number of other houses, and you've made a decision based on practical as well as emotional factors . . . so you fill out a sales agreement, make an earnest money deposit (EMD) of $1,000 and your agent heads off to present it the offer to the seller's agent.

You drive home euphoric . . . but when you get home, the message on your answering machine from your boss informs you you're being transferred to another city. You're stuck, right?

No, you're not. An offer isn't a contract until the other party accepts the offer, *and* the acceptance of the offer is communicated back to you. Let's use the same example: you find out you're being transferred, you call your agent, and she calls the seller's agent to withdraw the offer. If the seller's agent hasn't already notified you that the offer was accepted, you're off the hook; plus, your EMD is immediately returned since no contract has been created. (A contract doesn't become a binding contract until both parties sign and execute the contract.)

Let's take it a step further. Say you have a binding contract and you need to back out. You can still do so, but you may lose your EMD. (Depending on the circumstances, some sellers will still return the EMD even if they're not required to do so—but there's no guarantee that will happen.)

Since we're on the subject of earnest money deposits, here's an important point you should keep in mind. "There are no statutory requirements for an EMD," said Amy Tierce. "The EMD can be 10%, $1,000, or even $1. There may be historical practices in place in your locality, but there are no statutory requirements. The key is to craft an offer that is acceptable to the buyer and the seller."

While it is possible that the sellers may attempt to seek damages due to the fact you've backed out of the contract, litigation rarely occurs, and damages are rarely awarded above and beyond the loss of the EMD.

Typically the seller keeps the EMD as compensation. Occasionally the seller may seek additional damages, or even sue for "specific performance" of the contract, but in our experience that seldom occurs.

In the end, the sale hasn't taken place until the final closing has occurred. Either party can back out before that time—it may not be ethical or particularly fair, and there may be a cost to doing so . . . but it can and does happen.

Certainly you can back out of a deal at the last minute. You can leave the bride at the altar. You can have kids and choose not to raise them. Keep in mind that when you sign a purchase agreement, you are entering into a legally binding contract. If you have any doubts, deal with those doubts prior to the day of closing. Ask for the opportunity to review the closing papers at least three days prior to closing.

MYTH # **38**

Beware of Foreclosures— They're a Headache.

Fact: By Doing Your Homework, You Can Be Someone Else's Pain Reliever

Buying foreclosure properties requires more effort and diligence on your part, but the return can make your hard work worthwhile.

Many people don't understand the foreclosure process. Let's take a look at how the foreclosure process works from the homeowner's point of view; we'll pretend you are the homeowner facing financial difficulties.

When you miss a mortgage payment, you're typically sent a letter documenting the missed payment and requesting immediate payment of the past-due amount. Once you've missed several payments, you'll be sent a letter from the bank's lawyer. Receiving a letter from the lawyer means you're in trouble; you haven't just committed an oversight the bank wants corrected but are now considered a serious problem debtor. When you hear from the lawyer, it means the bank has committed resources (in other words, time and money) to try to get you to pay on time.

If you can't reach an agreement with the lawyer, you'll be served with a summons. (The lawyer has very little reason to negotiate, so typically the only agreement you'll be able to reach is that you'll make your loan payments on time—immediately.) After "service," which is the process by which you're physically presented with the summons, the attorney will also file papers with the county courthouse. All other individuals with claims against the property—they're called "junior" obligations—like second mortgages, judgments, or other liens, are served with papers so they have the right to try to protect their interests as well.

It's important to note that if the foreclosing party is negligent in notifying junior lien holders, those creditors have a valid claim for repayment against the eventual new owner of the property. That's why purchasing title insurance when buying foreclosure properties is absolutely essential: you protect yourself against subsequent claims you didn't know about. After all, you don't want to have to be responsible for a lack of attention to detail by the foreclosing party.

To enforce money judgments you have to be served personally. That's one reason foreclosure actions take so long—the homeowner(s) must be tracked down and handed the summons. Often the homeowners won't want to be served and will do their best to avoid it. Each jurisdiction has different laws and rules, but generally speaking if a person can't be located, and all reasonable efforts have been made to find them, a procedure for "publication" is put into place. Publication typically means a public notice is inserted in the classified section of the local newspaper.

Most jurisdictions also require public notice whether or not the homeowner has been served. Public notice allows parties with a legitimate claim to come forward to protect their interests.

After the publication process is complete, the foreclosure action will proceed. If you can't come to an agreement with the bank's lawyer, and can't come up with the funds to pay off the loan, your property will be sold at a foreclosure auction, and you'll be evicted from the property—if you haven't already left, of course.

The foreclosure process is extremely painful for the homeowner. The legal proceedings can take months to complete. The homeowners are subjected to pressure from banks and lawyers, public notice that their home is in the foreclosure process, and the realization that they will soon lose their home.

Now let's look at how the foreclosure auction process works. Foreclosure sales are held anywhere that is centrally located and accessible. The old stereotype of "on the courthouse steps" is often true: if the notice refers to the courthouse steps, it really does mean the auction will be held on the steps outside the courthouse.

In all likelihood you won't be alone on the steps. If you're interested in the property, you should expect others to be as well. The sale begins with a recital of the action by the "referee." (The referee is the receiver, and has the power to execute the sale even without the homeowner's signature.) After the introduction is concluded, the sale begins ... and often is completed within a few minutes. A majority of auctions end with the bank that made the original loan taking legal ownership of the property.

Rules and regulations vary according to locality, but in most cases you'll need to have cash or a cashier's check for at least 10% of the purchase price of the property. You'll also be required to arrange financing and complete the purchase of the property within 30 days. (If you don't manage to get financing, you can lose the 10% you put down, but if you petition the auctioneer, you can sometimes get your deposit returned. There is no guarantee that will happen, though, so you should only bid if you're sure you have adequate financing in place ahead of time.)

You will not have had a chance to inspect the property, except from the outside (and most often just from the curb, since the homeowners won't be likely to want you to step onto their property). The homeowners are under no obligation to let you inside, and neither the bank nor the receiver has the authority to allow you inside. In most cases you'll purchase the property as-is and unseen.

Occasionally the property will be vacant. The homeowner could have abandoned the property ... and possibly a neighbor notified the bank out of concern. The bank may send a crew to board up the house and secure it from vandalism, even though it doesn't officially own the property yet. Some banks will allow you to inspect the property if it is abandoned, but those instances are rare.

The opening bid is usually made by the bank. (It's often called the "upset price.") This price is determined by the amount due the bank and includes the mortgage balance, late payment charges, and all costs incurred in initiating and handling the foreclosure. The bidding is usually opened by a representative of the bank in the event no one else does. The upset price gives you an indication of what the bank needs to get from the property to remain "whole," or put another way, to get their money back.

Bank officials are under no obligation to identify themselves, and occasionally they won't bid at all. It may not seem logical that someone owed money secured by a property will refuse to bid on that property, but it does happen. If the bank doesn't bid, there must be a good reason . . . and that indicates one source of risk for you.

The fact that you can't inspect the house beforehand is a risk: the homeowners could have failed to maintain the property or could even have purposely damaged the property out of anger, frustration, and so forth. Or major environmental problems can be present. Foreclosure properties bought at auction are purchased as-is, and if the bank doesn't bid, that's a signal major problems can and probably do exist.

As the creditor, the bank carries none of the responsibilities of ownership like maintenance, repair, upkeep, and building code compliance. If the bank knows of major problems in these areas, it may simply not bid on the property. As long as the bank doesn't actually own the property it's just another interested party. Once the bank owns the property—which it will if it bids and no one else does—then it assumes all the responsibilities (and the costs) of ownership.

If the bank doesn't bid . . . in all likelihood you don't want the property either. (The problem is you may not know whether the bank has bid or not unless you're familiar with all the parties involved in the auction.)

Banks can only make a claim for the amount of the judgment. If the winning bid is for a greater amount than the judgment, the remaining funds, or "surplus money," go to junior lien holders and if anything else is left the homeowner receives the remainder. Very seldom will there be surplus monies; bidders at the auction are looking for great deals, and are almost always hoping to pay significantly less than market price for the property.

Frequently the amount of the judgment is higher than what investors are willing to pay, especially for a property that is still occupied and they have not had a chance to inspect. If the bank is the high bidder, as often happens, the bank now owns the property. It then becomes "bank owned," and the bank is required to sell the property.

The advantage to buying a property at auction is that you can often pay far less than you would have under normal circumstances. Frequently you can invest in improvements and then down the road sell the home for a much higher price than your cost.

The disadvantages and risks are more numerous. Simply to participate in the auction you must have sufficient funds available (either cash or a cashier's check) to cover 10% of the purchase price. You also must be able to arrange for financing within 30 days to complete the purchase or you risk losing your deposit. You also need a little patience. Most foreclosure sales include a "redemption period" in which the borrower has the right to "cure" the default, or pay off the lender and redeem the property.

Next, you're going to be buying the property as-is, without inspection. The condition of the interior of the home is usually a complete unknown. You'll have to be sure that the price you pay is low enough that you can still afford to make significant improvements or repairs. (If you are lucky enough to be able to inspect the house, try to do so when the utilities are turned on; that will let you check plumbing, heating, and electrical systems.)

Experienced auction buyers assume they will have to make at least some amount of repairs at a minimum: replace all carpet, repaint the interior, replace at least a few of the appliances, and make upgrades to the kitchen and bathrooms. A rehabber we know who has bought hundreds of foreclosure properties says he has always needed to at least replace all the carpet and paint all the walls.

Experienced auction buyers also understand they may have to make major repairs and improvements. Anyone who has bought more than a few foreclosure properties has experienced his or her share of horror stories.

Sometimes the house is in poor shape simply due to neglect; other times, willful destruction has taken place. Occasionally you'll find properties where rooms were gutted, all appliances removed, toilets and sinks had all been torn out . . . In effect, the house can simply be a shell, and thousands of dollars of work and significant amounts of time may be required to return the house to saleable condition.

You're also buying a property where the homeowner (or tenants, if it's a rental property) may not have been evicted yet. Once you're the owner, the responsibility for eviction rests with you and the legal authorities. Of course, you have the law on your side, since you are now the owner of the property, but you still must arrange for eviction. And if you need to make repairs, you'll have to wait until the eviction is completed.

You'll want to buy title insurance if you purchase a house at a foreclosure auction. You may have paid for a title search that came up clean, but you will want to buy title insurance to protect you from what hasn't shown up in the record. Even if it's an illegitimate claim, you'll have to defend against it and the title insurance keeps you from paying those costs out of your own pocket. In addition, if you are found at fault, the company pays the award.

If you decide you wish to buy a foreclosed property at auction, here's some basic advice. First, make sure you have adequate cash reserves to put 10% down. Then, make sure you have financing available so you can complete the purchase within 30 days after the redemption period expires.

Then, estimate your top bid price. You'll want to work backwards from a low market estimate of the home's value. For instance, say you think the house is worth $200,000 on the open market if it's in decent condition. First, estimate a high and a low estimate of possible repair costs. Your low range should include complete repainting, new carpet, and funds for replacing some appliances and doing minor cosmetic repairs. Your high estimate should include those things plus funds for a new heating system, plumbing repairs, kitchen and bath overhauls, and repairs to walls, doors, windows, and so forth. (Your high estimate should take into account as many sources of damage as possible. Hopefully that's not what you'll find, but you can never be sure. And if you don't have unlimited capital at your disposal, you're better off estimating high than low.)

Now factor in time. Estimate how long it will take you to make repairs. Then estimate how long it will take to sell the house once it's in a saleable condition. Remember, every month that passes requires a mortgage payment from you, which eats into your potential profit. Time truly does equal money, and you shouldn't forget to factor in the cost of financing the house while you're repairing it and selling it.

Subtract your estimated repair cost from 90% of the fair market estimate. (You're taking 10% off your estimate to be conservative.) Then subtract the finance cost you'll incur while you repair the house and sell it. The amount that's left is your maximum bid.

You may be thinking there's no way to make money when you factor in all the costs and risks. You're wrong: there is, but only if you enter the transaction with sufficient financial resources at your disposal and with your eyes wide open to the possible risks.

Here's an important note: *Make sure you know where the property is in the foreclosure process.* If it's still in the redemption period, your offer can be trumped by the seller if he or she is able to bring the loan current. If the property is in the sheriff's sale stage, you will become the owner if your bid is the highest.

Buying foreclosure properties at auction can be a great way to obtain properties at bargain prices, but there are definite risks and unknowns. Buying at auction is not for the faint of heart ... and it requires a decent amount of capital in order to repair damage, make improvements, and offset potential risk. There are a number of unknowns involved in buying auction property. If you don't have sufficient financial resources and time to spend managing the repair and renovation process, buying auction foreclosures is a greater risk than you should incur. But if you can, you may turn someone else's nightmare into your dream.

You can get burned buying foreclosure properties at auction if you don't know what you're doing. At auctions, the mortgages, not properties, are sold. You can purchase a $30,000 second mortgage, thinking you're getting a bargain, only to find out later that the second mortgage will be erased when the first mortgage is auctioned off. Do your homework. Check out Ralph's book *Flipping Houses For Dummies* or *Foreclosure Investing For Dummies* for additional details. Spend some time learning the foreclosure process, rules, and regulations in your area, before you begin investing in foreclosures.

MYTH # **39**

I Make Money When I Sell—Not When I Buy.

Fact: You Make Money When You *Buy*—Not When You Sell

Here's the bottom line: while you may actually receive the profits from your house when you sell, the amount of those profits is largely determined by which house you bought and how much you paid. If you make poor decisions when you buy the house, you won't make money when the time comes to sell the house. It's that simple.

You've probably heard that location is everything in real estate. It's true, and if you buy well, you'll sell well. This truism is the cornerstone of real estate investment strategy; here's why.

In less desirable locations, homes are cheaper, and so-called good deals are easier to find. Less desirable locations are often in areas of older and smaller homes, and buying a home there will involve higher upkeep costs and lower appreciation. In other words, the years of mortgage payments and the cost of upkeep will yield less return on your investment when you sell.

The two important keys to remember are, the better the location, the more you can improve both the house and its value. If the overall real estate market heats up, better areas appreciate more. In less desirable areas, you won't be able to get back your investment on anything other than basic improvements, unless you buy at extremely cheap levels.

For example, there are older neighborhoods in nearly every city with small 900-square-foot homes built in the 1940s and 1950s. If they're near a university, downtown, or other desirable location, their value has probably soared. Yet these same types of homes built near an airport or commercial center will sell for thousands less and will be harder to sell.

Recently, Mike and Stephanie found a two-bedroom brick cottage near a private college, close to an upscale shopping area. The house was part of an estate sale and was cosmetically out of date, but they got a good deal on it and were excited at the potential.

Looking at other homes in the neighborhood, Mike and Stephanie had noticed most had already been remodeled or upgraded. (Actually, their home was the least attractive on the street.) It was a great opportunity, and they took advantage of it by painting, restoring the woodwork, and upgrading the kitchen, furnace, and wiring. A few years later, when they outgrew their home, they had accumulated enough equity to put a sizable down payment on their next home.

Mike and Stephanie bought well—which would allow them to sell well. How?

First, they focused on the area. They looked for a neighborhood likely to go up in value, near a college, university, or popular shopping area; an area that would appeal to young professionals who didn't like a long commute, where homes had charm, and where similar-minded homebuyers were moving in and renovating.

Second, they were careful about the money they put into the home. A large percentage of their upgrading required their own labor and cosmetic repairs. The money they did spend went where it would give them the best return: a new furnace, roof, and kitchen.

Third, they realized that eventually the house would be too small and they would have to sell and move to a bigger home. Their plan was to accumulate as much equity as possible, and they kept their eye on what homes were selling for in the area.

They made money when they sold—but only because they made a smart buying decision. In fact, they made money precisely because of how they *bought*—not because of how they sold.

Homeowners and investors make money by *buying* smart.

 If you purchase, fix, and lease the property, you can make money four ways:

1. First, you make money when you buy, purchasing the property below market value.
2. Repairing and renovating the property to bring it up to market standards increases the value of the house and the equity you have in it.
3. As your tenants pay the rent, they pay down the principal on your mortgage, further boosting the equity in the property.
4. Over time, the value of the property rises, further increasing the equity.

MYTH # **40**

My Tenants Will Finance My Investment Property.

Fact: You Still have to Qualify for the Loan

Single-unit rental properties are the easiest way to invest in real estate (other than owning the home you live in.) You can either buy a property, or, if your current home is suitable, buy a new property to live in and start renting your current residence. Many owners of townhouses or condominiums take advantage of this opportunity. They require the least amount of cash, and the least amount of effort on your part. And if you pick the right property in the right location under the right circumstances, you can find yourself in a positive cash flow situation—and your tenants will be making your mortgage payments for you. But you still have to qualify for the loan, and qualification requirements are typically stricter for investment properties than for personal residences.

When you're evaluating a residential rental property, you'll be guided by the same principles you use to evaluate a home you'll live in: location, condition, attractiveness, investment potential, but in addition you'll also evaluate its potential cash flow.

Your goal is to purchase a property where the rental income will exceed your operating expenses. (In some cases a negative cash flow may make sense, but if you're a beginner investor, and you have little access to cash reserves, try to find a property you can rent for more than your expenses.)

Here's an example of a good single-unit rental investment. Some years ago Cheryl bought a small three-bedroom brick ranch in an older neighborhood in a small town for $110,000. The neighborhood was well-established, and most of the owners kept their homes in good repair. The house was also in a good school district. The roof had been replaced a few years previous, and so had the heating system. Cheryl anticipated very little expense in terms of maintenance costs for at least the first few years.

Her target renter was a small family eager to live in a house instead of an apartment—possibly a couple with one child, or a single parent with two children. Fortunately that target market is fairly extensive—a large percentage of families don't have adequate credit or cash to purchase a home of their own.

Her anticipated expenses, including her mortgage, totaled approximately $675. After a survey of rental properties in the area, she determined she could easily rent the home for $775. That net operating income of $1,200 per year may not sound like a lot, but in her mind it was enough to take on the risk of buying the property.

She also saw further potential. The house was located minutes from a local college where parking space was limited. The back of the lot had street access, and she created a parking area for three cars, renting each space for $40 per month to college students. In addition, the property contained a small garage, again at the back of the lot, that she rented as storage space to a local mechanic for $60 per month. Those two additions in revenue increased her net operating income to $2,400, making her much more comfortable with the investment.

Some people buy more expensive houses with the intent to convert them to rental properties, but doing so carries more risk: the average person that can afford to rent a luxury home can probably afford to buy a luxury home. It is possible to make money by renting luxury homes to relocated executives while they purchase a home, but the chances of the property sitting vacant are much greater. If you pursue this option, make sure that the rent you net allows you to cover at least a few months per year worth of vacancies.

Once you've found the right property, you'll still need to qualify for the loan. In many cases the lender will require 20% down. And, most lenders will want to see copies of old leases so they can verify the rental income for the property, along with a breakdown of other costs like taxes, insurance, and so forth. They'll then assume that the property will be vacant for some part of the year—most assume a 75% occupancy rate. Once all the numbers for the property are calculated, the lender will then look closely at your financial situation to determine if your current income and debt levels allow you to cover the payments and expenses for the property. While your tenants may in fact make your payments for you, your lender will want to know that you're capable of making a portion of the payments on your own.

Landlording isn't for everyone. You're responsible for the property, the payments, and often what goes on in the house. Figure out how much you're going to make per month after expenses and then ask yourself, "Will this be worth the added work and worry?" If you can answer "Yes," you may have what it takes to be a landlord. If not, consider hiring a property management company to run it for you.

SECTION 4

The Mortgage Process

MYTH # **41**

The Loan Process Takes a Long Time.

Fact: Experienced Lenders Can Grant Conditional Approval in Under 10 Minutes, and You Can Close in 10 Days or Less Under the Right Circumstances

The average lender requires 2 to 72 hours to grant a conditional loan approval. Better than that, an experienced lender can grant conditional approval within 10 minutes after reviewing your income, debts, proposed down payment, and credit history. (The approval is conditional, of course, because the lender has to take your word that all the information you are providing is accurate and complete.) If you've been preapproved for a loan, most lenders can close in 20 days or less. (Preapproval means all necessary financial documents have been provided to the lender.)

The average loan closing however, takes place between 30 and 60 days after the initial application is made. Sometimes the process is lengthy because of delays caused by the lender or by the borrower; more commonly it's caused because the buyer or seller doesn't *want* to close right away— the buyer may need to sell their current house, or the seller may need to find a new house. (But don't let that fool you into thinking the loan process will have to take that long.)

"We sometimes call it the 20/20 rule," says Jay Capozzoli, a Loan Originator with the Home Loan Center. "Conditional approval is often given within 20 minutes, and loans can usually close within 20 business days of the application." (See Figure 4.1.)

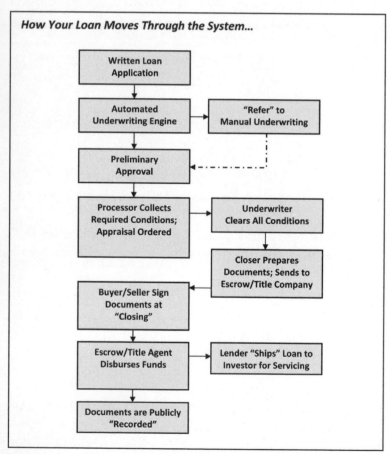

How Your Loan Moves Through the System...

Written Loan Application
↓
Automated Underwriting Engine → "Refer" to Manual Underwriting
↓
Preliminary Approval
↓
Processor Collects Required Conditions; Appraisal Ordered → Underwriter Clears All Conditions
↓
Closer Prepares Documents; Sends to Escrow/Title Company
↓
Buyer/Seller Sign Documents at "Closing"
↓
Escrow/Title Agent Disburses Funds → Lender "Ships" Loan to Investor for Servicing
↓
Documents are Publicly "Recorded"

Figure 4.1 The Loan Process. The loan officer uses a "team" to move your loan through the system to final approval and disbursement of funds.

If you're not in a hurry, your lender can take his or her time. If you are in a hurry, let the lender know. Most lenders will agree to speed up the process if they know failure to do so means they'll lose your business. We recommend getting your financing together first—that way you can ensure that your lender won't cause any delays getting into the home.

Your lender should give you periodic progress reports, too. "A good mortgage broker will make sure you're current on the status of your loan and your closing, and will alert you to any potential roadblocks or changes," says Ruth Faynor. "Stay in close touch with the lender to make sure you can quickly overcome any hurdles if time is of the essence."

Once you've applied for a loan, lenders should provide you with three important documents. (If they don't, don't worry—copies of each are provided in the Appendix and at the resource web site www.TheMortgageMyths.com.)

"The most important booklet you'll receive is *Settlement Costs and You*," says Ruth. "It will help you make sense of closing costs and also the disclosures and terms you'll see on the Good Faith Estimate and Closing Statement. Read it in the beginning so the process isn't foreign to you—you can even take it with you to closing."

The *Consumer Handbook on Adjustable Rate Mortgages* covers Adjustable Rate Mortgages. If you have an interest in an ARM, it should be provided to you by the loan officer.

When Your Home is on the Line explains what could happen if you don't fulfill your mortgage obligations.

"All three booklets are an excellent start in the education process," continues Ruth. "The more you know, the more comfortable you'll be . . . and the more likely your loan will go smoothly."

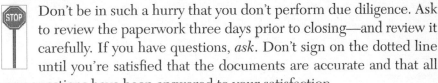

Don't be in such a hurry that you don't perform due diligence. Ask to review the paperwork three days prior to closing—and review it carefully. If you have questions, *ask*. Don't sign on the dotted line until you're satisfied that the documents are accurate and that all your questions have been answered to your satisfaction.

MYTH # **42**

All Applications and Disclosure Forms Are Standard.

Fact: Many Forms Are Lender-Specific—in Order to Protect the Lender

It's true that most real estate forms look similar, at least on the surface. Millions of real estate transactions take place every year, and over time forms have become fairly standardized. That doesn't mean, however, that all forms are alike, even if the intent of the form is the same. Examples of common forms can be found in the Appendix.

Three standard forms are required for all residential transactions:

1. The loan application, or 1003 (called a ten-o-three). (For home equity loans, the lender may use a slightly different application, see Figure 4.2).
2. The Good Faith Estimate (affectionately known as a GFE, see Figure 4.3).
3. The Truth in Lending statement (or referred to as a TIL, see Figure 4.4).

Most loan application forms look the same: they request your name, address, bank accounts, debts, income, employment history, and so forth. Almost all residential mortgage applications will be taken on the 1003 Form (see Figure 4.2). But lenders are not required to use a common form, and some don't. Some lenders may ask for personal or financial information that other lenders do not require. Is that a problem for you? Maybe it is—and maybe it isn't. The only way you'll know is if you read each form thoroughly and make sure you understand what you're signing. Other forms may contain language that's very different from other lenders'. Don't assume that one disclosure form is just like another disclosure form—it may be frustrating to contemplate, but make sure you read each and every

Uniform Residential Loan Application

This application is designed to be completed by the applicant(s) with the Lender's assistance. Applicants should complete this form as "Borrower" or "Co-Borrower," as applicable. Co-Borrower information must also be provided (and the appropriate box checked) when [X] the income or assets of a person other than the Borrower (including the Borrower's spouse) will be used as a basis for loan qualification or [ ] the income or assets of the Borrower's spouse or other person who has community property rights pursuant to state law will not be used as a basis for loan qualification, but his or her liabilities must be considered because the spouse or other person has community property rights pursuant to applicable law and Borrower resides in a community property state, the security property is located in a community property state, or the Borrower is relying on other property located in a community property state as a basis for repayment of the loan.
If this is an application for joint credit, Borrower and Co-Borrower each agree that we intend to apply for joint credit (sign below).

Borrower _____ Co-Borrower _____

I. TYPE OF MORTGAGE AND TERMS OF LOAN

Mortgage Applied for:	[ ] VA [X] Conventional [ ] Other (explain): [ ] FHA [ ] USDA/Rural Housing Service	Agency Case Number	Lender Case Number 0200832

Amount $ 285,000.00	Interest Rate 7.000 %	No. of Months 360	Amortization Type: [X] Fixed Rate [ ] GPM	[ ] Other (explain): [ ] ARM (type):

II. PROPERTY INFORMATION AND PURPOSE OF LOAN

Subject Property Address (street, city, state, & ZIP) 123 Main, ROCKVILLE, MI 49503 County: KENT	No. of Units 1
Legal Description of Subject Property (attach description if necessary) Lot 21, Beanbrook subdivision #3 Section #12, NE Northeast City of Detroit	Year Built

Purpose of Loan: [X] Purchase [ ] Construction [ ] Other (explain): [ ] Refinance [ ] Construction-Permanent	Property will be: [X] Primary Residence [ ] Secondary Residence [ ] Investment

Complete this line if construction or construction-permanent loan.

Year Lot Acquired	Original Cost $	Amount Existing Liens $	(a) Present Value of Lot $	(b) Cost of Improvements $	Total (a+b) $

Complete this line if this is a refinance loan.

Year Acquired	Original Cost $	Amount Existing Liens $	Purpose of Refinance	Describe Improvements [ ] made [ ] to be made Cost $

Title will be held in what Name(s) Christopher J. Wealthy, Katelyn T. Wealthy	Manner in which Title will be held Joint Tenants Joint Tenants	Estate will be held in: [X] Fee Simple [ ] Leasehold (show expiration date)

Source of Down Payment, Settlement Charges and/or Subordinate Financing (explain) Checking Savings Checking Savings, gift

III. BORROWER INFORMATION

Borrower	Co-Borrower
Borrower's Name (include Jr. or Sr. if applicable) Christopher J. Wealthy	Co-Borrower's Name (include Jr. or Sr. if applicable) Katelyn T. Wealthy
Social Security Number Home Phone (incl. area code) DOB (MM/DD/YYYY) Yrs. School	Social Security Number Home Phone (incl. area code) DOB (MM/DD/YYYY) Yrs. School

Figure 4.2 Sample Loan Application (URLA or 1003). This is a partial form. It is a standard national form, and will contain at least four pages. For a full copy of the application, please visit www.TheMortgageMyths.com.
Form provided courtesy of Ellie Mae Corporation.

document. Ask questions if you don't understand, and consult a lawyer or financial professional if you *really* don't understand.

"Homebuyers should ask for a copy of the mortgage instrument or note ahead of time," says Ruth Faynor, "so they can be sure they understand the terms and conditions. Most mortgage instruments *are* standard documents that will have specific information filled in pertinent to your loan. Just be sure the copy you're provided is identical to the note you eventually sign."

Good Faith Estimate
(Not a Loan Commitment)   Date: 01/01/2008

This Good Faith Estimate is being provided by a Mortgage Broker, and no lender has yet been obtained. A lender will provide you with an additional Good Faith Estimate within three business days of receipt of your loan application.

GFE Provided By: RUM CREEK FINANCIAL CORPORATION 137 PEARL ST. NW GRAND RAPIDS, MI 49503 Chip Cummings	Subject Property: 123 Main ROCKVILLE, MI 49503	Borrower(s): Christopher J. Wealthy Katelyn T. Wealthy
Loan Number: 0400548	Interest Rate: 7.000	Type of Loan: Conventional	Base Loan Amt 285,000.00
Loan Program: 30 year fixed	Term: 360	Sales Price: 300,000.00	Total Loan Amt: 285,000.00

The information provided below reflects estimates of the charges you are likely to incur at the settlement of your loan. The fees listed are estimates; actual charges may be more or less. Your transaction may not involve a fee for every item listed. The numbers listed beside the estimates generally correspond to the numbered lines contained in the HUD-1 or HUD-1A settlement statement you will receive at settlement. The HUD-1 or HUD-1A settlement statement will show you the actual cost of items paid at settlement.

Estimated Closing Costs

800	Items Payable in Connection with the Loan				1100	Title Charges		
801 A	Loan Origination Fee @	1.000% +	S	2,850.00	1101	Settlement or Closing Fee	S	200.00
802	Loan Discount Fee @	% +	S		1102	Abstract or Title Search	S	
803	Appraisal Fee		S	325.00	1103	Title Examination	S	
804	Credit Report		S	22.00	1104	Title Insurance Binder	S	
805	Lender's Inspection Fee		S		1105	Document Preparation Fee	S	150.00
806	MI Application Fee		S		1106	Notary Fee	S	
807	Assumption Fee		S		1107	Attorney Fee	S	
808	Mortgage Broker Fee @	% +	S		1108	Title Insurance Fee	S	
809	Tax Servicing Fee		S	21.00	1109		S	
810	Processing Fee		S	200.00	1110		S	
811	Underwriting Fee		S	425.00	1111		S	
812	Wire Transfer Fee		S		1112		S	
813	Flood Certification Fee		S	25.00	1113		S	

Figure 4.3 Sample Good Faith Estimate (GFE). This is a partial form. Federal law states that you must receive a GFE within 3 days of application; however, most lenders will provide one up front upon request.

Form provided courtesy of Ellie Mae Corporation.

Federal Truth-In-Lending Disclosure Statement

Lender/Broker: RUM CREEK FINANCIAL CORPORATION	Loan Number: 0400548	Date Prepared: 01/01/2008
Borrower(s): Christopher J. Wealthy Katelyn T. Wealthy	Property Address: 123 Main ROCKVILLE, MI 49503	

[X] Initial Disclosure estimated at time of application   [ ] Final Disclosure based on contract terms

ANNUAL PERCENTAGE RATE The cost of your credit as a yearly rate.	FINANCE CHARGE The dollar amount the credit will cost you assuming the annual percentage rate does not change.	Amount Financed The amount of credit provided to you or on your behalf as of loan closing	Total of Payments The amount you will have paid after you have made all payments as scheduled assuming the annual percentage rate does not change.
E 7.100 %	E S 400,452.30	E S 282,150.00	E S 682,602.30

Your Payment Schedule Will Be:

Number of Payments	* Amount of Payments	Monthly Payments Are Due Beginning	Number of Payments	* Amount of Payments	Monthly Payments Are Due Beginning
359	1,896.11	06/01/2008			
1	1,898.81	05/01/2038			

Figure 4.4 Sample Truth-In-Lending (TIL) Disclosure. This is a partial form. Federal law states that you must receive a TIL within 3 days of application; however, most lenders will provide one up front upon request.

Form provided courtesy of Ellie Mae Corporation.

Read the loan application, commonly referred to as the ten-o-three (1003), carefully. If you sign an application that contains inaccurate information, even if you weren't the one who fabricated that information, you may be guilty of mortgage fraud. Don't let anyone convince you to claim assets you don't own, to artificially inflate your gross income, or to do anything else dishonest in order to qualify for the loan.

MYTH # **43**

We're Approved: Our Worries Are Over!

Fact: You Can Kill Your Approval Easily—and Unintentionally

Preapproval is a great home buying tool: it lets you know how much house you can afford, allows you to complete transactions more quickly, and lets sellers know that you're not only ready but you're *able* to purchase their home, which enhances your negotiating position.

But, if you were preapproved 30 days ago, your approval may not stand today—most preapproval letters include a time limit under which the approval can be relied upon. More importantly, you could, without realizing it, kill your chances for approval while you're house hunting.

For example, say your current debt-to-equity ratio is 50%; your only debt is your current home, and your outstanding balance is half of the value of your home. (Your debt-to-equity-ratio is one way a lender determines your suitability for a loan.) If in the meantime you purchase a new car and a new boat, and you finance both purchases, your loan approval could go out the window. Or you may decide to leave your job and start your own business; your employment history changes drastically, and the lender may not be as confident about your future income potential.

Your approval can also be unrealistic. "Carefully review the conditions on your approval," said Amy Tierce. "A condition a borrower can't meet is not really an approval. Lenders will sometimes issue commitment letters subject to actions the borrower can't meet—you may think you're approved, but in reality you're not."

Or the loan officer may approve you without verifying that you truly do qualify. "You can't be truly preapproved till the loan officer knows your credit score and your debt to income ratio ... and you can't lock in an interest rate until you have a property address," says Aaron Metaj, president of Apollo Mortgage Corp. "Ask yourself these questions:

- Has the loan officer pulled my credit report?
- Have he reviewed my monthly debts and my monthly income?
- Do I have a signed Sales Contract that's been accepted by the seller?

"If the answer to any of these questions is 'No,' then you're not truly preapproved."

Dave Rodriguez, a loan officer with the Home Loan Center, recalls a situation where a lender had granted "preapproval" without checking whether the couple qualified—an oversight that could have cost them time and money.

"A couple came to me and said, 'We have already been preapproved for a zero-down loan with no PMI for 30 years fixed, and we're already locked in at 5.25. What is your rate—can you beat that package?'

"I asked if the lender had checked their credit score, debt-to-equity ratio, and whether they had a signed contract with a seller. The answer was 'No' to all three questions. I explained that they couldn't truly be preapproved, and that possibly the other lender was simply telling them what they wanted to hear in order to gain their business—and in all likelihood their rate would go up before closing.

"They allowed me to check their credit and debt-to-income ratio, and we determined that the best loan they could qualify for was at a higher rate. They were skeptical, so I recommended they call the lender and ask him to review their qualifications to be sure he could still offer the 5.25% loan ... and he couldn't. (In fact, his offer was worse than the package I had put together.) We closed their loan three weeks later."

Other factors can also play a part. "When a consumer is approved for a loan, they're approved based on the exact information submitted at the time of approval," said Audrey Acquisti, owner of MSource Training and Consulting, providers of training for the real estate and mortgage industries. "If something changes—say they purchase furniture or draw money out of their bank accounts—the loan could be declined because their basic financial situation has changed. Keep in mind that many lenders will, for example, re-pull credit reports the day before a loan is scheduled to close . . . or the lender may call and check employment status."

A change in financial situation can have serious repercussions. "A client applied for a mortgage loan and was laid off from their job two days before closing," Audrey continued, "and that information had to be provided to the lender. The original approval was no longer valid, and the programs (including rates and terms) needed to change—at a significant cost to the borrower."

There are a number of ways you can kill your preapproval. Once you're preapproved, put off making major financial changes (purchases, investments, etc.) or making major lifestyle changes (returning to school, changing jobs, etc.) until *after* you've bought your new home. Don't accidentally kill your loan approval, even if it means waiting another month or two to purchase that new car you've been dreaming of; the wait may well be worth it.

Customers of Chip's were approved for a mortgage, but before the closing they bought furniture for their new home and no longer qualified because of the new debt. The furniture looked great . . . but as it stood, there wasn't going to be a new home to put it in. (Luckily their parents loaned them the money to pay off the furniture, but the closing was delayed while they straightened out the mess.)

"I train my loan originators to prep our customers," said Paco Torch of Torch Mortgage Corporation. "I make sure we caution buyers not to buy or lease anything until the loan closes. In fact, I like to say, 'If you can, don't even breathe until the loan closes.'"

Here's the bottom line: Don't do anything without checking with your loan officer first. A good loan officer won't tell you how to spend your money, but he or she may advise you to wait until the time is right.

 Filing for divorce prior to the day of closing can also throw a wrench in the works, but if you're getting divorced, neither of you is likely to want a joint loan. After the divorce, your situation may improve, as we discussed in Myth #19.

MYTH # **44**

My Interest Rate Is Locked In *and* Guaranteed.

Fact: It Can Change, and You'll Probably Have No Recourse

Locking your interest rate protects you against the possibility of an increase in market interest rates during the period between the lock date and the loan closing. Rates change frequently, and it can be one or two months between the day you apply for a loan and the day your sale closes . . . and rates could have jumped during that time. *Locks are only as good as the loan officer or company that stands behind them.* Only a few states require that the lock from a lender be issued only after the lock has been made with an investor on the other side.

It's important to note that locks should always be provided in writing and are only good for a fixed period of time. Also remember that you can't lock in a rate without a Sales Contract. "A lender who offers to lock a rate before you have a contract isn't really offering you anything," says George Carroll, Senior Loan Officer with The Home Loan Center. "It may seem like a great idea, but he or she has no way of actually locking a rate at that point."

A lock commits the lender to lend at a specified interest rate and points, provided the loan is closed within the specified "lock period." For example, a lender may agree to lock a 30-year fixed-rate mortgage of $200,000 at 7.5% and 1 point for 30 days. The lock lapses if the loan doesn't close within 30 days, and the lender is no longer committed to offer that deal.

A lock imposes a potential cost on the lender, and the longer the lock period, the higher the cost. This cost is in the price quoted to borrowers. The lender who quotes 7.5% and 1 point for a 30-day lock, for example, might charge .875 points for a 15-day lock, and 1.125–1.25 points for a 60-day lock. Why? The charge helps to protect the lender from huge market fluctuations.

Some borrowers elect to "float" the rate, meaning not to lock it, as long as possible. If the market is stable, they hope to benefit from the declining lock price. They may also believe that market rates will decline and they can take advantage of lower interest rates.

We don't recommend that a home purchaser who barely qualifies at today's rate risk a rate increase—if rates jump, you may no longer qualify for the loan. But even if qualification is not an issue, floating past the point where you can change loan providers is risky if you have no way to monitor the market price on the day you finally lock. If the market price on the day you lock is what the loan provider says it is, you are at his mercy. (Some will pad the price just because you have nowhere to go.) On a refinance, you can always change loan providers, so it's a little safer to delay the lock until shortly before closing.

Allowing the price to float on a purchase transaction is safe if you have a way to check the market price on the day you lock. If you originally shopped the lender's web site and found your price there, you can check it again on the lock day. Otherwise, don't float.

Borrowers who are refinancing can monitor the floating interest rate/points quoted to them by the broker against other market information, and if the quote appears out of line they can bail out—after all, you don't *have* to refinance, you just *want* to. Home buyers with a scheduled closing, however, eventually reach the point of no return where it's too late to start mortgage shopping all over again. During a refinancing boom period, when loan processing takes longer, the point of no return might be 45 days rather than the 30 days that might be appropriate in a normal market.

To protect yourself, just don't float past the point where you can bail out and shop elsewhere. Or you should pin down the lender or broker on an objective procedure for determining the market interest rate. One simple and fair rule is that the market rate will be the rate that the lender is quoting to potential new customers on the same day. If you lock only a few days before closing, your rate should be the lender's current float rate. If you lock 15 days before closing, your rate should be the lender's 15-day lock rate on that day. And so on.

One advantage of dealing with a lender or broker who quotes prices on the Internet is that they provide you with the data you need to monitor the rate they give you when you lock.

You're probably wondering what happens if the lock expires before the loan closes. The policy of most lenders is to extend the lock at the same terms if market rates have declined or stayed the same. If rates have risen, however, they will usually only extend at the higher market rate. Lenders may make an occasional exception if they are responsible for delays that cause the lock expiration, but don't count on it. Sorting out who is responsible for which delay is extremely difficult.

Lock expirations are common during a refinance boom when lenders, mortgage brokers, appraisers and escrow agents are swamped with more work than they can handle and many deals simply don't get done on time. During busy periods, lenders will give purchasers a priority. A delayed refinancing can be rescheduled, but failing to complete a home purchase mortgage on time can jeopardize the purchase itself. It could also jeopardize a lender's relationships with real estate brokers, and many depend on agents for borrower referrals.

To minimize the possibility that your lock will expire before you close, select the lock period only after you have asked the loan provider how long the lender's turn-around time is. During a refinance boom, add 15 days to it. In addition, get all your documents available so they can be produced when needed. Be available to answer questions or provide additional documents during the entire period the loan is in process.

Again, a lock is only as good as the lender standing behind the lock. "An individual came to me looking for help," says Tim Wooding. "They thought they had locked in a low interest rate on a 30-year fixed rate mortgage (FRM) to build a new home. The builder wouldn't start the home until the borrower had a commitment letter. They learned they hadn't locked in their financing, and it took almost four months for the lender to finally provide a commitment letter. When they did receive the letter, they found that not only was the loan an ARM instead of a FRM, but there were an enormous amount of fees, so they eventually had to look for other financing. In the meantime they lost time and the home ended up costing more because their original contract with the builder was no longer valid."

If you're comfortable with the rate you're receiving, go ahead and lock. If interest rates fall, you may be disappointed, but the interest you're paying is at least something you rationally decided you were comfortable with at the time you locked. If rates rise, you're protected from paying more than you might be able to afford. And once you lock, always get proof of the lock in writing. If you find out at closing that the interest rate is different from what you thought, what will you do about it at that point? Almost every option available will cost you money.

Interest rates are often negotiable, especially if you have a strong credit history. If you're discussing loans with several companies and prefer one company to another—except for the fact that it charges a slightly higher rate—haggle for the lower rate.

MYTH # **45**

A Preapproval Is a Preapproval.

Fact: Terms and Conditions Can and Do Vary Greatly Between Lenders.

"I'm preapproved!" you exclaim. "My lender says I can borrow up to $200,000!"

Sounds great—but does that mean *all* lenders will agree to lend you $200,000 to buy a new home? No.

Lenders follow different criteria for approving loans, criteria that are based on their business goals, standard practices, and lending experience. (An individual lender's standards may change frequently, too, depending on market and business conditions.) Some lenders allow more leeway on down payments, some allow more leeway when assessing your income, some are more forgiving of credit problems ... the list goes on and on. Lenders are not required to use the same loan approval criteria, and more importantly are not required to "honor" another lender's preapproval. If you've been preapproved by a lender, that preapproval is only applicable to that lender. Don't assume other lenders will also approve you—they may or may not.

So how do you avoid seeking multiple preapprovals? Shop for the right lender before you seek preapproval. Compare terms, rates, conditions, and so forth, until you find the right lender and loan for you. Once you're confident you've found the best potential deal, *then* seek preapproval. Once you've found a home, you can always shop around again, but keep in mind that a different lender will want you to undergo their individual approval process.

Work closely with a reliable loan officer to secure the financing you need. Provide the loan officer with all the paperwork she requests well in advance, so when the time comes to approve the loan, your loan officer won't have to wait for you to send in a key document. Be proactive.

MYTH # **46**

I Have to Let My Lender Escrow Taxes and Insurance.

Fact: Under Certain Conditions, You Can Save by Paying Your Own

Most lenders automatically set up your escrows and may even charge you a fee for the privilege (although usually not!). Escrows are a handy tool, because you don't have to worry about saving up the money for your annual or semiannual real estate tax payments, for example; you make 12 smaller payments throughout the year (as part of your mortgage payment) that covers your annual tax fee. Escrows are a very convenient way to make sure you have sufficient funds to cover your taxes and insurance. Keep in mind if you're putting less than 20% down, escrows are mandatory (except for some subprime mortgages).

Escrow accounts can include amounts for taxes, insurance, PMI, special assessments, condo association dues, environmental fees, or amounts to cover back taxes.

Do you have to allow the bank to set up and manage your escrow account? Not always—and there is at least one reason why you shouldn't.

Banks do not pay interest on money deposited in an escrow account for real estate purposes. If your escrow account contains significant sums of money throughout the year, you can't earn any interest on those funds. If you set up your own escrow account, you can receive interest. If your taxes and insurance are high, you may have thousands of dollars in an escrow account at any given time—so why not get a return on that money?

Different escrow agents offer different programs and terms—you can shop for the escrow agent that's right for you. Most will charge a small fee for the service; compare that fee to what your lender will charge to make sure you're getting a good deal. Also keep in mind that you'll be responsible for making monthly payments directly to the escrow agent; you'll need to discipline yourself to make those payments. Making payments shouldn't be a problem, though—you shouldn't be buying the house if you can't afford to make your monthly principal, interest, and escrow payments, regardless of who you're writing the checks to. We recommend setting up a separate savings account to pay your escrows from.

Remember that if your homeowners policy covers items like expensive paintings or jewelry, your insurance premium may be high, and that amount will be included in your escrow account.

If you are a first-time homebuyer, don't waive tax escrows. Escrows help you maintain the financial discipline you may still be developing, and you don't want to get off to a rocky start!

Shop around and compare terms and services—you may find you can save money while you meet your financial obligations to the lender, the insurance company, and the government.

 Never waive the property tax and insurance escrow unless you have enough money in the bank to cover a full year's expenses. Many homeowners get behind on their taxes and insurance payments and lose their homes in foreclosure because they used that money for another purpose.

MYTH # **47**

I'm Self-Employed—Getting Approved Will Be Tough.

Fact: Some Programs Are Designed for Business Owners and Employees on Commission

If you're self-employed your income history may vary greatly, and future income can be hard to predict. As a result, getting loan approval can be more difficult

Lenders consider you self-employed if you own 25% or more of the business that employs you. If you have a full-time job and own a business that you operate part-time, you're not considered self-employed, but the additional income from your business can help you qualify for a loan.

Self-employed borrowers typically are required to provide extensive documentation to the lender. Why? The secondary mortgage market requires greater levels of documentation because, quite frankly, it's potentially easier for borrowers to embellish verifications or exaggerate income if they are self-employed. In addition to the normal documentation you'll need to furnish, you may be required to furnish complete income tax returns from the previous two years, a balance sheet from your business for the previous two years, and a year to date profit-loss statement. If you work on commission, the lender typically needs W-2 forms and tax returns for the previous two years; then, your income will be averaged over those two years. (Many lenders will also want to see that your income is increasing, and that the massive commission you received two quarters ago isn't a fluke.)

Pulling together the required documentation may be tough, especially if you aren't the greatest bookkeeper in the world. If that's the case, consider a no-doc loan. No-doc stands for "no documentation" and means exactly what it says: you qualify for the loan based on your credit history and on your verbal statements of income, debt, and so forth. No-doc loans typically are more expensive than full documentation loans and require higher credit scores, but they're definitely an option you should look into if you're self-employed.

You can also use creative financing techniques. For instance, you could get a 75% mortgage, put down 10%, and have the lender—or even the seller—carry the other 15% of the purchase price in a second mortgage. (This type of mortgage is called 75/10/15 financing.) It may be easier—and require less documentation—for you to qualify for a 75% mortgage, you will avoid private mortgage insurance (PMI), and you may have an easier time qualifying for the loan because the interest rate and points required could be lower.

Also consider seller financing. Many sellers require little (or in some cases no) documentation—many won't even run a credit check. If the rate and terms are right for you, you may also save money, especially on closing costs. Or, if because of your business you have a good relationship with a local banker, you may be able to take out a commercial loan to purchase the home, using the home (and possibly other assets) as collateral.

If you're currently a full-time employee and are considering starting your own business—that you'll work at full-time—it makes sense to purchase a home first. The qualification process for borrowers who are not self-employed requires less paperwork and documentation.

When you're self-employed, the loan officer may try to estimate your income using previous federal income tax returns, or may ask you to self-report your income. Be careful with self-reported income. Self-reporting does not mean you can make up numbers. Provide accurate information.

MYTH # **48**

The House Needs Repairs—We'll Do Them Later.

Fact: Repairs Are Cheaper if Done in Advance, and an Escrow Account Won't Protect You

Two weeks ago your offer to purchase a house was accepted, and you just had a home inspection performed by an ASHI certified home inspector. So far so good . . . but the home inspector feels the septic system isn't functioning properly. You're heartbroken, because you simply love the house . . . but then the seller offers to set aside $2,000 to repair the septic system. He even agrees to put it in escrow, so you know the funds will be available when you need them. Your problem is solved! Now you can still close on time, and you'll have the money to make repairs later.

Your problem isn't solved—it may be just beginning.

Escrow accounts intended to hold funds for house repairs are in principal a great idea; they ensure money to pay for the repairs in question is available to you. (In this case the seller places the funds in the escrow account, and those funds are controlled and disbursed by the escrow agent, so the buyer doesn't have to worry about the seller failing to meet the obligation.) And in some cases everything works out fine . . . but what if the repairs cost more than is in the escrow account?

If that happens, you may have no recourse. The additional funds come out of your pocket.

If a house needs repairs completed, you have two basic options. One is to require the homeowner to make the repairs and to allow you to have those repairs inspected before the closing will take place. If the repairs aren't made, or aren't made to your satisfaction, the contract is no longer valid and you don't have to purchase the house.

The other method is to place funds in an escrow account and make repairs later. This is a less preferable option for one major reason: how do you know exactly what the repairs will cost? A contractor can provide an estimate of the cost, but what if the problem turns out to be more extensive than originally thought? A customer purchased a home with septic system problems—when he went to make repairs, he learned one septic field had been placed on top of another field. The cost was more than double what was originally estimated, and he had no recourse at that point.

Some buyers request the seller place 150% of the estimated cost in the escrow account to cover contingencies, with excess funds later returned to the seller, but 150% may not be enough to cover the actual cost.

Have any major repairs completed before you purchase the house. It's cheaper, and you'll rest easier knowing the seller will be the one worrying about how much the repairs will cost—not you.

When buying investment properties or foreclosures at below market value, don't nitpick flaws in the house. Many times you're getting a great deal because the homeowner doesn't want to deal with cleaning, painting, recarpeting, and installing replacement windows and a new roof. Factor the cost of repairs into your total investment in the property, and if you can still earn 20 percent or more, it's a good deal. If you can't, then consider asking the homeowner to cover the more costly repairs.

MYTH # **49**

Personal Profiling Is Part of the Approval Process.

Fact: The Lender Only Cares about Repayment

The Fair Housing Act forbids lenders from discriminating based on race, sex, age, and other forms of discrimination. For that reason alone, lenders do not use any form of racial profiling during the loan approval process.

In addition, most lenders use an Automated Underwriting (AU) system to take applications and process loan approvals. The AU system does not request information about an applicant's race; the underwriter is not privy to that information (and more importantly, really doesn't care).

What does the lender care about? The lender is only concerned with whether or not you can you repay the loan. The lender will evaluate your credit history and your personal financial information to gauge whether you're capable of repaying the loan, and whether you appear willing (based on how you've handled credit in the past) to repay the loan.

When it comes to your heritage, background, or lifestyle, the lender doesn't care. Remember, loan officers and mortgage brokers only get paid if they make the loan—they have no incentive whatsoever to use any type of personal profiling, because they want and need to make loans in order to make a living!

 When you're selling a house, the only color you should see is "money green." Don't take into account a purchaser's race, sex, background, or lifestyle. Sellers can and do face stiff penalties for wearing their racism on their sleeves. Everyone has an equal right to housing—live by that rule.

SECTION 5

It's Closing Time

MYTH # **50**

Someone Else Decides the Closing Date and Location.

Fact: You Can Close Anytime and Almost Anywhere

Often your lender, real estate agent, or title company representative will set the closing date, typically to take place at a real estate office, lawyer's office, at a title company, or at an escrow agency. Why? Because they have busy schedules, and they hope to fit you into a nice slot in their schedules.

Does that mean you have to accept the appointment time and location? Of course you don't. You can close at your house if you want, or at a restaurant, or in the park . . . the closing is not dependent on the location; the closing is only dependent on the appropriate parties and appropriate documents being present. If the appointment set works for you, great; if not, ask for a different one. As long as the right people attend and the right documents are on hand, you can close anywhere, and at any time.

But you should understand your closing may be delayed. "Not closing on time is the biggest disillusionment most consumers face," says Patrice Yamato. "The consumer must supply information and the originator must process information in a timely fashion. Plus, many of the key players aren't employed by the originator, like the title company, REALTOR®s, inspectors ... many pieces have to come together for a closing to take place on time.

"Make sure you know who the go-to person is for your mortgage," she recommends, "and stay in touch. A good mortgage company will keep you current on any factors that may jeopardize your closing date."

Just make sure you're available to close. "A colleague of mine worked with a couple on a home purchase," explains Ruth Faynor. "He assumed they understood the process, and he called to let them know the loan would close at 1 P.M. on Thursday. Thursday came and all the parties were present ... except the homebuyers. They assumed the loan officer and REALTOR® signed on their behalf, so to celebrate their purchase they'd gone on vacation."

 In some markets the closing is controlled by the seller's agent or attorney. If you know someone in the business, or you prefer working with a particular title company, let the seller and his agent know up front, and see if you can agree to a change of venue.

MYTH # **51**

Why Do I Need Title Insurance—I Can't Even Select the Provider

Fact: Insurance Is a *Must*, and Only You Get to Pick the Provider

If you need a mortgage, you must purchase title insurance because all mortgage lenders require it for an amount equal to the loan. Title insurance lasts until the loan is repaid. Just as with private mortgage insurance (PMI), you pay the premium, except this time you make a single payment made at the time of closing. Title insurance protects against loss arising from problems connected to the title to your property. Before you purchased your home it may have gone through several ownership changes, and the land on which it stands might have gone through many more. There may be a weak link at any point in the title chain that could pop up to cause problems. For example, someone along the way may have forged a signature when transferring title, or there may be unpaid real estate taxes or other liens that exist on the property. Title insurance covers the insured party (you) for any claims and legal fees that arise from those types of problems.

Title insurance protects against losses arising from events that occurred prior to the date of the policy. Coverage ends on the day the policy is issued and extends backward in time for an indefinite period. Property and life insurance works exactly the opposite way: those policies protect against losses resulting from events that occur *after* the policy is issued, for a specified period into the future.

The title insurance required by the lender protects the lender up to the amount of the mortgage, but it doesn't protect your *equity* in the property. To cover your equity you'll need an owner's title policy for the full value of the home. In many areas, sellers pay for owner policies as part of their obligation to deliver good title to the buyer. In other areas, borrowers must buy it as an add-on to the lender policy. We recommend purchasing an owner's title policy because the additional cost, above the cost of the lender policy you have to get, is relatively small.

Protection under an owner's policy lasts as long as the owner or any heirs have an interest in or any obligation with regard to the property. When you or they sell, however, the lender will require the purchaser to obtain a new policy. The new policy protects the lender against any liens or other claims against the property that may have arisen since the date of the previous policy—in other words, against something *you* may have done.

For example, if the contractor you failed to pay for remodeling your bathroom places a lien on your home, you're not protected by your title policy, because the lien was placed after the date of the policy. You'll probably be required to get the lien removed before you can sell the property. But in the event the lien hasn't been removed and a search has failed to uncover it, the new lender will be protected by a new policy.

You can shop around for title insurance. Unlike mortgage insurance, where the carrier is always selected by the lender, borrowers can select the title insurance carrier. Few do, however. Most leave it up to one of the professionals with whom they're dealing: their real estate agent, their lender, or their attorney. This means that competition and marketing among title insurers is largely directed toward these professionals who can direct business—not towards consumers.

In many states, insurance rates are regulated. But in others, it can pay to shop around. It's difficult to generalize because market conditions vary state by state, and sometimes within states. We would certainly suggest shopping around in states that don't regulate title insurance rates: Alabama, the District of Columbia, Georgia, Hawaii, Illinois, Indiana, Massachusetts, Oklahoma, and West Virginia.

You'll waste your time shopping in Texas and New Mexico, because these states set the prices for all carriers. Florida also sets title insurance premiums, but not other title-related charges, which can and do vary.

In the remaining states it may or may not pay to shop. Insurance premiums are the same for all carriers in "rating bureau states": Pennsylvania, New York, New Jersey, Ohio, and Delaware. These states authorize title insurers to file for approval of a single rate schedule for all carriers through a cooperative entity. Yet in some there may be flexibility in title-related charges. More promising are "file and use" states—all those not mentioned above—that permit premiums to vary between insurers. For an up-to-date list of state requirements, go to the resource site at www.TheMortgageMyths.com.

Some builders will insert a clause in the sales contract requiring you to use their service provider, but no law states you must accept that term. We've also heard of instances where real estate agents require that their service provider be used (and some attempt to charge a fee as well.) Again, no law requires you to use the builder's or the real estate agent's service providers, so if you don't want to, simply refuse to do so.

It's a good idea to ask an informed but disinterested person whether it pays to shop in the area where the property is located. Just keep in mind that the people likely to be the best informed are also likely to have an interest in directing your business in a direction that's to their advantage.

If you're buying a foreclosure property or other investment property, take a look at the title work early in the process. A title company may be willing to provide you with a title commitment that shows the current publicly document information about the property, for no charge, in the hopes of gaining your future business. You can also take a trip down to the county clerk or register of deeds office to research the title work, mortgage, and deed on your own.

 If you don't recognize the title company, or are asked to close in an unusual location—ask for a "Closing Protection Letter." These are issued by the insurer to cover the closing agent, and protects you by insuring the proper disbursement of funds!

MYTH # **52**

It's Cheaper to Close at the End of the Month.

Fact: You'll Pay the Same Amount, So Close on Your Schedule

Some homeowners try to save money by closing at the end of the month. Their reasoning goes like this: "Okay, if I close at the end of April, then my payments won't start until the first of June, and I'll save a whole month's worth of payments."

Sounds good . . . but it's not accurate.

Once your loan closes, you're paying interest on the loan—each and every day. While it is true your first payment may not be due for 30 days, you'll still be charged interest during that 30-day period, and often you'll pay that interest at your closing (this interest payment is often called "prepaid interest.") So if your first payment isn't due for 30 days, you may be asked to make a prepaid interest payment covering those 30 days. If your first payment isn't due for 10 days, your prepaid interest payment will cover those 10 days.

There is absolutely no advantage to closing on different dates—in the end you'll pay the same amount in principal and interest. On almost all mortgages, payments are typically due on the first of the month; the only exceptions are home equity loans, bridge loans, second mortgages, and seller financing. Otherwise your payments will be due on the first of the month, so no amount of "closing date maneuvering" will save you money.

Instead of trying to save money (since you can't), focus on picking a closing date that fits your schedule—like when you'll be ready to move.

 We recommend that most buyers close on a deal at the beginning of the month. That way you won't have your first house payment due for approximately 40–50 days. When you move into a new place, you can usually use that 40–50 day grace period.

 On some government-insured loans it *is* cheaper to close at the end of the month, as a seller or on a refinance, due to the way *they* calculate interest. Check with your lender to find out if you will be charged a full month's interest, regardless of the closing date.

MYTH # **53**

I Can't Review Documents in Advance.

Fact: You Can Review All Documents at Least One Day Prior to Closing

You should review at least three forms in advance of closing: The HUD-1, the Mortgage or Deed of Trust, and the Note.

The HUD-1 or "Uniform Settlement Statement" is used for all residential real estate loan transactions, and itemizes all the charges and expenses incurred by the buyer and the seller.

The HUD-1 statement is a standard national form that settlement agents (like title companies or attorneys) are required to use to close the transaction. The rules require you to be furnished a copy of the HUD-1 statement at least one day before settlement, but that sometimes doesn't happen. There could be delays due to inefficiency on the part of the lender, the title company, or simply because last-minute items like repairs haven't been completed, and so they are unsure of last-minute charges. Many times the title or settlement agent will simply tell you it isn't ready—but that's not good enough. Tell them you won't close until you've had a chance to review it at least the day before. While they may complain or argue, it's in their best interest for you to close on time, and if you push hard enough, they'll do whatever is necessary to get a copy to you on time. Real estate agents and sellers dislike delay as much as you do, and the last thing the title company wants to do is admit to an agent that documents weren't ready on time—they risk losing business and referrals in the future.

Always ask for a copy of the statement ahead of time so you can review it before you go to the closing. Once you're at the closing you'll feel pressure to hurry up and complete the transaction. You're much better off taking the time to review it completely for accuracy and to make sure no agreements or terms have changed. If there are any differences, be sure to ask for a clarification. Even though many HUD-1 statements detail transactions involving hundreds of thousands of dollars, you would be surprised how often mistakes are made. Review your statement carefully for any errors. We recommend you go so far as to check all the mathematical calculations, too—mistakes can and do happen, even on the simplest items.

"As a consumer I would want to know what I'm going to sign at the time of closing," said Audrey Acquisti. "Over the years real estate professionals have grown accustomed to creating a 'signature assembly line' and closing the loan as quickly as possible. Borrowers should ask for documents in advance—never sign a document you've never seen, and never sign a blank document."

If for some reason you don't get a copy ahead of time and you decide to look the document over at closing, it will be hard to resist the temptation to hurry . . . but take the time to review it thoroughly even if (and they will be, believe us) the other parties are impatient. Think of it this way: it's your money, it's your investment, and it has to be right for you. If they grow impatient . . . that's too bad. It's as simple as that.

Also watch for junk fees; for example, we've even seen title companies charge a fee for, believe it or not, e-mailing documents.

In addition to the HUD-1 statement, you'll also want to inspect the mortgage or the deed of trust (different states use different instruments) and the note.

At a minimum, here's a list of items you'll want to check for accuracy on these documents:

- Name (full and complete for all borrowers).
- Property address.
- Amount of the mortgage (and purchase price).
- Interest rate.
- Term.
- Legal description of the property.
- Social security number(s).
- ARM adjustment parameters (if applicable).
- ARM index (if applicable).
- HUD-1 closing costs versus your initial GFE.
- Payment amount (principal and interest).
- Pre-payment penalties.

We've included copies of several of these standard forms in the Appendix and on the resource site at www.TheMortgageMyths.com for your review. Take the time to understand them—the more you know about the process the smoother it will go.

STOP Don't wait until the day of closing before you review documents. Some closings can take longer than three hours because one of the parties decided to wait until the actual closing to read every document word for word. If you have no choice, that's fine, but you're better off notifying the closing officer several days in advance and reviewing the documents beforehand.

MYTH # **54**

The Seller's Home Warranty Protects Us.

Fact: It's a Sales Tool and Rarely Pays Off

Home Warranty. Those words sound comforting, don't they? Buying a home is stressful and filled with uncertainty . . . a warranty sounds great, right? Plus, if you have a warranty, why pay for a home inspection? If something goes wrong, you're still covered!

Many sellers highlight the fact they include a home warranty; real estate agencies and home warranty insurers claim homes sell significantly faster when a home warranty is included. That may be true, but that doesn't mean a home warranty will pay off if there's a problem.

No two seller's home warranty policies, like any other insurance policies, are alike. Individual insurers, and individual policies, cover different items for different periods of time. For example, many policies cover appliances like stoves or refrigerators for one year after the home is purchased; most will not cover major structural items like roofs, foundations, and floor joists.

No home warranty policy covers everything. For example, a customer of Chip's bought a home with a warranty. They moved in, and three months later the ceiling showed discoloration. The seller had painted over previous water stains. A "normal" roof leak was covered by the home warranty; in this case, the water leak was caused by a family of raccoons living in the attic. Because the leak was caused by the raccoons, the warranty didn't cover the damage or the repairs.

Tim Kleyla shared his own experience with an insufficient warranty. "I was 24 years old and had decided it was time to purchase my first home. When I saw the house I eventually purchased I was sold the minute I walked in. The REALTOR® was very excited to inform me that the home included a home warranty. The home was about 60 years old—everything appeared in good working order, just very old.

"The following year when summer rolled around, on went the air. It was fantastic! Ninety degree-plus temps outside with high humidity ... the weather was brutal. In the middle of this lengthy heat wave—out went the air.

"We called the local repairman and with much humor in his voice he told me that he would like to take it back to the shop.

"I asked, 'To work on?'

' "No,' was his reply, 'to show it to the guys at the shop—it's so old I've never seen one like this before.'

' "Oh,' I said.

'"Yup,' he continued, 'There's nothing I can do to help you out ... and by the way when you put in a new air conditioning unit you'll want to replace the furnace as well, because the new air handler will kill that dinosaur in a week.'

'"Oh.'

"He left and I called the warranty company. They sent out their man to take a look. His job was to determine if it was a warrantable condition. I told them that I had already had someone look at it and determined it was a lost cause. They told me that they had to have their guys take a look and see what they could do.

"Their team came out and decided that it would be able to get it going again ... a charge by the way that I had to pay. And in fact they did get it going again—for a few more weeks. So I called them back and they came out again. Same process, same charge.

"It limped along until just after both the warranty (such as it was) and the unit itself expired at the end of the year. They then told me that they would be happy to replace it with a new one, and added that, 'By the way, you may want to replace that furnace as well, since a new air handler will kill an old furnace like that in a week.'

"Three years later we finally got a new air conditioner and furnace from the first dealer—which we paid for, of course."

The cost of a policy varies according to factors like the size and age of the home, but the average home warranty policy costs between $400 and $500. Many also carry a co-pay charge; if a professional comes to the house to fix a problem, you may be responsible for the first $40 to $60 of the charge.

You can also purchase a buyer's home warranty if you like; the terms and coverage are similar, but if you purchase your own, you will at least be able to specify what is and is not covered.

Here's the bottom line: if you're considering purchasing a home that offers a seller's warranty, don't be tempted to skip inspecting the home using an ASHI-certified inspector. The warranty will not cover all items—peace of mind will come from having a thorough inspection performed and requesting repairs where necessary, not from having a seller's warranty policy that may or may not cover you if there's a problem later.

Although no home warranty provides 100% coverage for every repair, we always recommend that sellers purchase a home warranty to offer with their house and that buyers insist on a warranty—or pay for one—at the time of purchase. Like any insurance policy, shop around and read the warranty so you know what you're getting.

MYTH # **55**

The House Will Be in Move-In Condition.

Fact: Always Inspect Before Closing

Think about the last time you moved: were you completely focused on making sure the house or apartment was left in spotless condition? We're guessing you weren't, even if you did take the time to do so anyway. Moving is stressful, complicated, and tiring ... the last thing anyone wants to do is give the house the white-glove treatment before leaving.

If you're lucky, the house will be in perfect condition for you to move in. In all likelihood, though, it won't. And why take the chance? Inspect the house before closing, preferably the day of closing after the seller has vacated the property. If the house is full of trash, or the yard looks like the moving truck cyclone just passed through, and you close on the house ... the responsibility for cleaning up is yours.

A friend of ours bought a house some years ago, and he performed the walk-through and found a boat in the yard, tools in the basement, empty boxes in the garage ... stuff was everywhere. He talked to the seller, and the seller said, "I'm sorry ... I got really behind and haven't finished cleaning up. Once we're through with closing I'll come out and clean everything up—I promise."

As you can guess, the seller never showed up. Our friend called him a number of times and heard the same excuses. After a few weeks he cleaned everything up on his own. A month later the seller showed up to pick up his tools and boat—our friend didn't argue over the boat, but he kept the tools for his "trouble." "After all," he reasoned, "Anything left on the premises after closing is mine, right? The trash was obviously mine . . . so now the tools are, too."

You may not wish to go that far, but make sure you inspect the house before you close. You'll have no recourse after the closing if the house isn't in the right condition.

 Consider adding a clause to the purchase agreement that $1,000 will be held in escrow until the house is vacated, broom-clean, and free of all debris. This provides the previous homeowner a little extra motivation to do the right thing.

MYTH # **56**

It's All Triple-Checked and Ready to Go!

Fact: Mistakes Still Happen, So Check Everything Again

It's closing day, and everyone is excited. You're excited because you're moving into the house of your dreams. The sellers are excited because, well, because they're selling. The real estate agent is excited because he or she doesn't receive a commission until the sale is complete. As a result, the closing feels more like a celebration than a legal transaction.

It's okay to celebrate, but first take care of business. You'll sign a number of important documents, and it's possible that one or more of the documents may contain errors. If the title company representatives, loan officers, lawyers, and so forth, have been busy, they may have finished processing the paperwork at the last minute—and mistakes happen even if everyone involved has the best of intentions.

What should you do? Check everything. And we do mean *everything*. Again, request copies of the HUD-1 statement the day before, and make sure it's accurate . . . including the math. Make sure that legal descriptions are accurate and thorough, names and Social Security numbers are accurate, loan documents are accurate, condo or co-op agreements are accurate and complete, the survey and lot lines are accurate—take the time to check *everything* thoroughly. If you do miss a problem, in all likelihood you can correct the problem later, but it may take time and money to correct. It's always easier and cheaper to correct any problems or mistakes before all the documents are signed.

Mistakes do happen. In one case, documents were signed with the wrong legal description of the property; the seller had actually "sold" his neighbor's house.

You can bet most of the other participants will spend more time "celebrating" than reviewing documents, so take it on yourself to be the "official" document inspector. You'll be glad you did, especially if catching a mistake saves you time, money, or avoids headaches later. Also make sure any agreements (like the refrigerator conveying) are in writing—if they're not, it's too late to fix the problem after closing.

And while you're at it, make sure you've taken care of all the details in terms of inspections, surveys, and other legwork. (See Myth #33 for a full discussion of inspections.) Tim Kleyla recalls a client who bought a piece of property adjoining land owned by the state. The buyer intended to build as far back from the road as he could; Tim recommended he have an initial survey performed to site the house. The buyer refused, feeling he could save $150 by skipping the survey.

"Halfway through construction," Tim said, "an official came to the building site and asked him to put the state's 100-foot pine trees back up! The owner had cleared the wrong piece of property, and he had cut down more than a dozen trees owned by the state!"

It gets worse. The charge was $5,000 per day until the trees were back! "Forget the question of how you put 100-foot trees back after they've been cut down," Tim continued. "The owner was in a panic. Eventually he and the state came to a compromise: he gave up twenty-two of his twenty-five acres in exchange for the trees."

Check all your documents before closing, and follow the advice of real estate professionals: when they recommend you perform inspections or surveys, remember they're looking out for you and your best interests.

A few days prior to closing is the time to read documents word for word and request corrections. On the day of closing, you should only need to check to be sure corrections were made and that the 1003 (loan application) contains no misrepresentations. Don't wait until the day of closing to get picky.

I Need Homeowners Insurance to Cover the Entire Purchase Price.

Fact: You Only Need to Cover the Loan Amount or Replacement Value

Insurance is designed to protect you from financial catastrophe. Home-owner's insurance covers you from perils like fire, vandalism, theft, lightning, and windstorms. If, for example, your house burns to the ground, insurance will protect you from loss.

Your lender will require you to maintain coverage equal to the cost of rebuilding the home at current prices, or to at least cover the remaining balance on your mortgage. The cost of rebuilding the home is based on the square footage of the home, not on the amount you paid for the home.

You also don't need coverage for your land—land doesn't burn. If your home will cost $250,000 to rebuild and your lot is worth $50,000, you don't need $300,000 worth of coverage, because your land won't need to be replaced (even though it may be a little scorched).

If your home is located in a flood plain, you may be required—or you may simply want—to purchase flood insurance. Flood insurance is offered through the National Flood Insurance Program under the oversight of the Federal Emergency Management Agency (**FEMA**).

While many lenders will allow you to only maintain coverage equal to the outstanding balance of your mortgage, most experts recommend you maintain coverage that will allow you to rebuild your home at current prices. The incremental cost is small compared to how much you may have to spend if your coverage is not sufficient. You may also wish to add coverage for earthquakes, hurricanes, or other natural disasters

Either way, start shopping in advance. Get three quotes from different agents well before closing, and inform your loan officer which one you selected.

 If you compare homeowner's insurance to health insurance or auto insurance, you'll see homeowner's insurance is a real bargain. So don't skimp. In many localities, you can't close on a house unless you have a sufficient insurance to cover at least the purchase price.

MYTH # **58**

I Need Credit Life Insurance to Protect Myself.

Fact: Credit Life Is One of the Worst Ways to Protect Your Investment

The advertising pitch usually sounds something like this: "If something happens to you, make sure your loved ones can stay in your home—credit life insurance will protect your home and your loved ones. If something bad happens to you, make sure nothing bad happens to your home, too."

If you put it that way, it sounds reasonable, right? In fact, though, purchasing credit life insurance is a mistake. It's typically much more expensive than a standard term life insurance policy, and its value decreases over time as you pay down the mortgage on your home. Why do we compare it to term life insurance? Because that's really what it is; unlike whole life insurance policies, which carry a cash value that grows over time, credit life insurance only lasts until the house is paid off (or until you quit making the payments on the insurance policy.) There is no residual cash value to the policy.

Here's how it works: you buy a policy that covers the outstanding mortgage on your home. Each month you make monthly payments towards the policy. Let's say your monthly credit life insurance payment is $50, and your mortgage is for $200,000 over 30 years. Twenty years from now your payment will still be $50, but you may only owe $130,000 . . . and that's all the insurance will pay out if you die. In effect you keep paying the same amount for a lower and lower benefit—and the premiums are high relative to standard term life insurance.

A couple of years ago a 46-year-old friend took out a credit life insurance policy on a house with a mortgage of $285,000. His payments were nearly $550 per year. Then he shopped around and learned he could get a 20-year term life insurance policy for $1,000,000 for a little over $800 per year. He nearly tripled his coverage—and if he does pass away in 15 years, his beneficiaries will receive the entire $1,000,000 . . . not the outstanding balance on his mortgage.

If you have dependents, you need some form of life insurance. If you want to protect your home, it makes sense to avoid purchasing expensive (and limited) credit life insurance—instead find a solid term life policy that will not only pay off your mortgage but will also leave additional funds for your family.

Yes, you do need to provide for you dependents . . . but not through a credit life policy.

 If you have dependents and you don't have life insurance and disability insurance, now is the time to buy these important policies. If you're the primary breadwinner and you die or can't work enough to cover the house payments along with other bills, you're likely to lose your home.

MYTH # **59**

My House Payment Will Never Change.

Fact: It *Will* Change, So Be Prepared

If you have a fixed-rate mortgage, your principal and interest payments won't change; those payment terms were established when you got the loan. (If you have an adjustable-rate mortgage (ARM), your payments will change based on the terms of the loan and the index to which your rate is tied.)

But your payment can and probably still will increase over the life of your loan if you include escrow payments for taxes and life insurance. Tax rates typically increase over time, and so do assessment values; if you're currently putting $50 per month into an escrow account to cover a $600 annual bill, and your taxes rise to $900, your monthly payment will increase by $25 to cover the difference. If your insurance premiums increase, so will the monthly escrow amount.

Each year, you will receive an "Annual Escrow Disbursement" statement that details all of the deposits and payments made in/out of your account by the servicer. Review this carefully for errors, and note how they will collect any "shortages." Usually, the shortage is spread out over the next twelve months to make it easier to absorb.

Chip made a loan to a couple, and a year after they closed the home was reassessed at a considerably higher amount. Due to the increase in real estate taxes their payments went up over $400 per month. A dramatic change like that can sometimes occur after a construction loan converts to a conventional loan, since the value of the home is lower during the construction phase, and thus the tax is lower.

While your principal and interest payment won't change on a fixed-rate mortgage, you can bet your taxes and insurance costs will eventually increase over time . . . and as a result so will your monthly mortgage payment. Be prepared!

 Don't assume that a property tax assessment is carved in stone. If the county tax assessor comes up with an assessment with which you disagree, file a dispute. You *can* fight City Hall, and you can often win.

SECTION 6

The Refinance Game

MYTH # **60**

Never Refinance Until the Rate Is 2% Lower.

Fact: Look at the Cost Versus the Return, Not the Rate

The "2% rule" has become a mantra for some—many think that there must be at least a 2% difference between their present interest rate and a new loan's interest rate before the loan makes sense. While the 2% rule is handy, it is nothing more than a quick way to determine how quickly you'll recover the cost of refinancing a loan. In general it takes two years to recover your costs if you refinance if there's a 2% differential in the interest rates—and that's really all the 2% rule is good for.

There are great reasons to refinance your mortgage, but the calculations aren't as simple or obvious as the 2% rule. As you can probably guess, whether refinancing makes sense is based on your individual situation, not on a general rule.

In order to actually save money, you have to stay in your house longer than the "break-even period"—the period over which the interest savings cover the refinancing costs. The greater the difference between the new interest rate and the rate on your existing loan, the shorter the break-even period will be. The more it costs to obtain the new loan, the longer the break-even period will be. While the 2% rule is an easy rule of thumb to follow, what's more important is your actual savings and break-even point; not a rule of thumb.

Keep in mind the break-even period is not the cost of the new loan divided by the reduction in the monthly mortgage payment. Among other things, that calculation doesn't allow for the difference in how rapidly you pay off the new loan as opposed to the old one. Let's say that in 1997 you took out an 11%, 30-year fixed rate loan; it now has a $100,000 balance with 21 years left before you pay it off. You want to refinance into a 7% 15-year loan at a cost of $3,750. Here's how it breaks down:

- Monthly payment on the old loan = $1,019
- Monthly payment on the new loan = $899
- Reduction in monthly payment = $120
- $3,750 divided by $120 = 31 months

This basic calculation says that you break even in 31 months. However, because of the shorter term and lower rate on the new loan, in 31 months you would owe $7,041 less than you would have owed on the old loan. So, the rule of thumb in this case seriously overstates the break-even period. Taking account of differences in the loan balance, you would actually be ahead of the game in 12 months, as shown below (see Figure 6.1).

- Savings in monthly payment: $120 for 12 months = $1,440
- Plus lower loan balance in month 12: $2,620
- Equals total saving from refinance: $4,060
- Less refinance cost: $3,750
- Equals net gain: $310

The basic rule of thumb (dividing the upfront cost by the reduction in mortgage payment) gives you a sense of the true break-even period only if the term on your new loan is close to the unexpired term on your old loan. If there's a big difference in the term, the rule of thumb isn't as accurate.

The rule of thumb also ignores other factors that affect the break-even period. These include the time value of money, taxes, and differences in the cost of mortgage insurance between the old and new mortgage.

A reputable lender or mortgage broker will be glad to help you work through the different scenarios so that you fully understand the

The Refinance Game:

Outstanding loan balance is $90,000; Original term of 30-years at 9.50%, with 12 years remaining "— Does it make sense to refinance at 6.50%?

	Payment	Balance In 12 months	In 36 months
9.50% loan	$1,049.81	$85,775.83	$76,018.65
6.50% refi	$ 568.86	$88,994.06	$86,775.58

Extra 12 years of payments at $568.86 = $81,915.84
6.50% refinance over remaining 12 year term:
    $901.73 = $148.08 _real_ savings per month.

If cost of refinance = $6,000
    Real break even period is 41 months!

Bottom line: Don't bother refinancing if it is for short-term. Better solution: do a cash-out refinance, and leverage the equity! Remember, it's not about the rate—it's about cash flow and return on equity!

*Original loan balance of $124,850.

Figure 6.1 Does Refinancing Make Sense?

break-even period and the financial ramifications of different loan terms, or you can use the calculators provided on our resource site at www.TheMortgageMyths.com.

If the purpose of the refinance is to reduce costs, as opposed to raising cash, you should refinance if your total costs are lower with the new mortgage than with your current mortgage, over the period you expect to have the new mortgage.

Let's say you have a $320,000 loan balance, at 6.25%, with 25 years to go. Your potential new loan is at 5.25% for 30 years, with cash payments of 2 points (2% of the loan balance, or $6,400) plus $2,200 for other settlement costs. You're assuming you'll keep the new mortgage for 5 years.

Here's how it works out:

1. Upfront costs consisting of points and settlement costs are $8,600 on the new loan, $0 on the old one.

2. Monthly payments of principal and interest are $106,024 on the new loan and $126,657 on the old one. (These numbers are calculated by multiplying the monthly payments by 60, since we're looking at a 5-year period.)

3. Lost interest is $7,057 on the new loan, $7,216 on the old one.

The last item is the interest you would have earned on up front and monthly payments if you had saved the money you're spending at 2.24%. (Loan officers sometimes claim that borrowers don't understand lost interest. Most borrowers *do* understand that money they spend could have earned interest if they hadn't spent it and had invested it instead.) Lost interest, however, can easily be excluded from the analysis by setting the savings rate to zero.

There are two cost offsets:

1. Tax savings on interest and points is $23,469 on the new loan, $25,753 on the old one. (A tax rate of 25.5% is used in this calculation.)

2. Reduction in loan balance is $25,122 on the new loan, $31,198 on the old one. In both cases, these were calculated from the original balance of $320,000.

Deducting the cost offsets from the costs, your new mortgage has a net cost of $73,089 as compared to $76,922 for the old one. Refinancing would save you $3,833 over 5 years. Your break-even period is 39 months.

Refinancing costs you money out of pocket, since there are settlement costs involved. Many borrowers who refinance choose to finance those settlement costs into the loan. The result is added cost to the mortgage if you don't pay closing costs in cash. If you use this option, you'll find that it reduces the gains from refinancing. This is largely because you have to pay interest on the costs at the mortgage rate. If you had financed the settlement costs of your new 30-year loan in the example we just went through, the net gain from the refinance would have dropped from $3,833 to $1,240, while the breakeven period would have increased from 39 to 53 months.

Financing the costs, furthermore, can flip the loan amount above 80% of the property value, which triggers PMI. If you're already paying PMI, it will likely raise the PMI premium.

Any reputable mortgage lender or mortgage broker will walk you through the different break-even scenarios using all the costs involved—if you're not comfortable doing the math yourself, ask for help. If the lender won't walk you through the exercise, find another lender.

Remember, a mortgage is a financial planning tool, not a debt. Before you refinance, make sure it really saves you money and that it fits into your overall financial plan.

 Consider using a refinance calculator to determine whether refinancing will pay off for you; you can find one at our web site, www.TheMortgageMyths.com. Simply plug in your numbers and you'll see the breakeven date; if you plan on living in the home past the breakeven date, refinancing makes sense.

MYTH # **61**

I Should Never Refinance Into a Higher Interest Rate.

Fact: A Higher Rate Might Save You Thousands in the Long Run

All things being equal, refinancing into a higher rate doesn't make sense. If you've had a 30-year, 6% fixed mortgage for a year or two, it makes no sense to refinance into a 7% 30-year fixed mortgage if all you're accomplishing is getting a new mortgage. There are, however, situations where refinancing, even into a higher rate, can make a lot of sense.

You may, for instance, decide to consolidate credit card debt into a refinanced mortgage. The argument for debt consolidation—and it's a good one—is that it will reduce interest costs. The interest rate on a second mortgage is usually well below the rates on credit cards, and mortgage interest is also tax-deductible as long as your debt doesn't exceed the value of the home. As you can see in Figure 6.2, the savings on interest can be substantial.

Consolidation, however, does have disadvantages that should be considered. Perhaps the most important, at least for some borrowers, is

The Debt Game:

When (if ever) does it make sense to refinance into a higher interest rate? To kill off those other pesky debts!

Before:

Debt	Balance	Rate	Payment
Mortgage	$90,000	6.50%	$1,021.96
Auto	$14,000	7.25%	$338.63
Credit Card	$8,500	12.00%	$255.00
Credit Card	$3,800	14.25%	$114.00
Total	$116,300		$1429.59

After:

Debt	Balance	Rate	Payment	Savings
Mortgage	$121,300	7.50%	$713.20	*$716.39 per month!*

If you were to maintain the same payments as before, the mortgage would be paid off in just *7 years!*

Figure 6.2 Does a Higher Rate Make Sense?

that consolidation will convert unsecured debt into debt secured by their home. If a financial problem in the future makes it impossible to service credit card debt, you can always choose to stop paying; your credit will be negatively affected, but if you can continue to service your first mortgage, at least you won't lose your home. If you've consolidated all your debt and secured it with your home, discontinuing payments is disastrous.

Another disadvantage of consolidation is that the new second mortgage may affect your ability to refinance your first mortgage if a good opportunity to do so appears. When a first mortgage is paid off, an existing second mortgage automatically becomes a first mortgage. This makes it impossible to replace the old first mortgage with a new one unless the second mortgage lender provides the refinancing lender with a written statement indicating a willingness to subordinate the second mortgage to a new first mortgage. Many second mortgage lenders will do this, charging fees that range from minor to unbelievably high, but some won't do it at all.

If you're paying for mortgage insurance on your first mortgage, adding a second mortgage will probably extend the period over which you must pay. Under prevailing rules for terminating mortgage insurance, the balance of the first mortgage must be paid down to a lower level if there is a second mortgage.

If the second mortgage results in your total mortgage debt exceeding the value of the property, you may lose your mobility. Let's say you're offered a better job in another city that would require you to relocate. If you owe $120,000 on a $100,000 house, selling the house means finding $20,000 in cash to pay off both mortgages. If you can't find the cash, the only way to relocate is to default, which would prevent you from buying a house in your new location.

So—those are the disadvantages you should be aware of. The fact remains, though, that if the situation is right, refinancing, even into a higher rate, could be a great move for you, especially if you feel your job is secure and your financial situation is solid. Why pay 15% interest on a credit card if you can pay 7% instead . . . and get a tax break, too?

"The most popular reason to refinance into a higher mortgage rate is due to higher rates on credit cards or home equity lines," said Dave Acquisti. "If you're tired of watching the rates go up and up, refinancing into a higher mortgage, even at a higher rate than your original first mortgage, may result in lower overall interest payments across all of your debt. Refinancing and pulling all your debt into one loan can make perfect sense, especially if you'll be eliminating 21% or 24% credit card debt.

"In addition, if you plan to be in the home for some period of time and you have an ARM, refinancing into a fixed-rate mortgage may be your best bet."

 Refinancing often makes sense when homeowners need to consolidate high-interest debt, even if it means taking on a mortgage with a higher interest rate. Add up your monthly payments both before and after refinancing: If your total monthly payments after refinancing are lower, refinancing may be your best option, even if the result is a mortgage with a higher interest rate.

Even at a higher rate, the FHA's 95% LTV cash-out option could be much cheaper than a lower-rate conventional loan with extra PMI costs.

MYTH # **62**

I'm Not Allowed to Pay Extra—There's a Prepayment Penalty.

Fact: Most Penalties Only Kick in Under Extreme Circumstances

Prepayment penalties have become more common in recent years. Why? Because mortgage refinance rates have been at an all-time high—and few mortgages run to term. (Some homeowners buy houses every few years, requiring a new mortgage each time.) Prepayment penalties are typically focused on the first three to five years, because the lender makes money from downstream activities like selling the mortgage on the secondary market and on servicing the loan. (For example, charging a high fee when your payment is late.) Prepayment penalties help lenders maintain profit levels in case homeowners don't hold the mortgage for very long.

On the flip side, some lenders offer a lower interest rate if a prepayment penalty is included in the loan. (If you don't read your loan documents carefully, you might not even realize a prepayment penalty is included.)

Normally, prepayment penalties focus on paying off the loan in full, not on making extra payments. If you make one or two extra payments a year, or add $100 to each payment to help pay down the principal balance more quickly, your lender is unlikely to care.

Generally the prepayment penalty only kicks in if you pay more than 20% of the principal off within the prepayment penalty period, and most states limit the period to 3 years or less. In some cases the prepayment penalty can be what's called a "3-2-1": the first year the penalty is 3%, the 2nd year it's 2%, and the 3rd year 1%. Or the penalty can be a 3-1-1, where

Here's an example of a prepayment penalty calculation for a $100,000 loan balance:

Penalty Period	Extra Charge
0–12 months	$3,000
13–24 months	$2,000
25–36 months	$1,000

Figure 6.3 Prepayment Penalty. Note: Prepayment would be slightly less in months 1–36 due to the declining principal balance. Penalty is calculated on outstanding balance at time of payoff, not original loan balance.

the first year penalty is 3%, followed by 1% penalties the following two years. Here's a look at how it works (see Figure 6.3).

If you're retiring the mortgage (either due to refinancing or because you're selling the house), many lenders will waive the prepayment penalty if you refinance with them, or have a clause that states the penalty is waived if you sell the home. While the lender may lose a little money when you retire the original mortgage, they'll hope to make it up by maintaining you as a borrower on another loan.

If you can't get the prepayment penalty waived, contact the lender and ask under what circumstances waivers are granted, and who has the authority to grant those waivers. Then plead your case, including threatening to take your business elsewhere. While the lender doesn't have to agree, many will. If the lender doesn't agree, make sure the savings you'll receive by financing with another lender at least partially offsets the cost of the prepayment penalty.

Be especially careful of prepayment penalties when buying and selling investment properties over the short term. If you plan on buying and selling a house in a matter of three to six months, and you take out a $200,000 mortgage with a 3 percent early payment penalty, the loan could cost you $6,000 when you pay it off early—and that may represent a good chunk of your profit.

MYTH # **63**

Reverse Mortgages Are a Bad Idea.

Fact: For Older Borrowers, It Can Be a Great Financial Planning Tool

Reverse mortgages make great sense, for example, for persons on a fixed income. Many experts recommend that a reverse mortgage be a part of every individual's retirement plan, and they're growing in popularity. According to the National Reverse Mortgage Assn., there were over 90,000 reverse mortgages done in 2006—more than double from the previous year. Atare Agbamu, president of Think Reverse LLC, is one of the country's leading experts on reverse mortgages. Here's what he recently had to say:

"You can't eat equity—equity isn't cash.

"Costs for retirees aren't fixed—they're variable. And they tend to increase. But many retirees are on a fixed income; what do they do when their expenses are greater than their income? For many the best option is to consume the equity in their home.

"Traditionally there are two ways to consume a home's equity. Either you sell the house, in which case you need another place to live, or you refinance, in which case you have a mortgage to pay. For a person on a fixed income, having a mortgage isn't a wise thing to do—it's yet another payment that has to be made.

"A reverse mortgage allows you to take some of the equity in your house and convert it into cash for monthly expenses—and still live in the house. If you're currently 62 years or older, the assumption today is that you'll live for 100 years. At 62, you can get between 57 and 60% of the equity in your house.

"Here's the problem: many people who would be better off with a reverse mortgage end up with a refinance—people on fixed incomes end up in a cash flow crunch and lose their houses. With a reverse mortgage, that can't and won't happen. Currently the average mortgage broker or mortgage lender doesn't know about reverse mortgages, and therefore doesn't recommend them.

"The central lending risk is shifted to the lender, unlike a mortgage, where the risk is borne by the borrower. Before FHA stepped in with an insurance program to back the reverses, there were few lenders willing to participate because they didn't want the risk involved. Now the FHA backs the reverse mortgage lenders, eliminating the risk and making it more attractive for lenders to participate.

"There are several ways you can take money out. A tenure reverse mortgage provides a fixed amount of cash for as long as you live. Under the term option, you receive a fixed amount of cash for a fixed period of time: for 5 years, 10 years, etc. Or you can take a lump sum, or a mix of tenure and a credit line.

"Here's an important point: Generally I don't advise clients to take reverse mortgages if they have a short-term need for cash or if they plan to move soon—the ideal person is someone who wants to stay in the house for the rest of their lives; he or she will receive income from the home and will be guaranteed a place to live.

"Reverse mortgages are anti-predatory loans because of the safety measures built in. A third-party steps in to advise you on the product, in effect serving as an information arsenal that helps you make a rational decision. Reverse mortgages require full disclosure of all fees, including fees that will exist over the life of the loan. There's a limit on what lenders can make—2% of the value of the loan—with no hidden fees. No reverse mortgage lender has an advantage in terms of rate, because Fannie Mae controls the rate: you'll get the same rate everywhere in the country. All rates are the same. Best of all, even if you run out of the equity in your house, you can still live there.

"When the borrower dies, the loan becomes due and payable. The lender will send a due and payable notice to the estate, and the estate has up to three months to respond. They can pay off the loan or they can sell the house and use the proceeds to pay off the loan. The only time the lender can take the property is if no one responds to the notices. Between death and payment, you can have up to one year to make the payoff."

Here's the key: On a cost-value basis, there is absolutely no comparison in the forward mortgage industry in terms of value and safety for an elderly person. Reverse mortgages are a new pillar of our retirement plans, especially in an age where retirement finance has become an uncertainty. In the past, if you worked for a company for 40 years you received a gold wristwatch and a fixed retirement. Today, major corporations are getting out of the 'retirement business' and have replaced pensions with 401(k)s, but the average person in the U.S. currently has less than $25,000 in their 401(k). Most people's largest asset is their home, and reverse mortgages allow you to tap that asset and still live in the asset. You made all the mortgage payments; why not enjoy the benefits of those payments?

As people become more conscious of reverse mortgages, it will create a radical change in personal finance and in how people view their equity in their homes; many will choose to take out less equity from their homes now because they'll plan to use it later. A reverse mortgage is a product with huge implications for our future in the 'new retirement world.' It's really the only thing that we can count on—even 401(k)s can lose value if the stock market dips.

Here's another important point. Reverse mortgages are considered to be loan proceeds, so the "income" is not taxed. Your estate can also use any accumulated interest to offset the estate liability. For people with a huge estate, the best thing to do is to weigh it down with reverse mortgage debt—you enjoy the benefits of the cash, tax-free, and your estate isn't taxed later.

Still think reverse mortgages are a bad idea? In some cases they can be the solution to an otherwise insurmountable problem. One of Chip's most gratifying professional experiences occurred at a closing. The lady who was closing on the loan was crying—not because she was sad, but because she was thankful she could keep her home. She was living on a fixed income, and her house had deteriorated and needed major repairs. She had a lot of equity in the home but couldn't qualify for a mortgage due to her low fixed income. Her children helped her get a reverse mortgage; not only could she pay for repairs, but she also received extra monthly "income" from the home . . . and she now could stay in the home for the rest of her life. She never thought she could keep her home, but with a reverse mortgage, she did.

If you have a home you would like to keep in the family, consider setting up a reverse mortgage with the relative you plan to leave the house to. Consult an attorney to set up the necessary paperwork and calculate the monthly amounts your relative needs to pay you. For more about reverse mortgages, check out *Reverse Mortgages For Dummies* written by our friend Sarah Lyons.

MYTH # **64**

My Terms May Change If the Loan Is Sold.

Fact: Loan Terms Will Remain the Same No Matter Who the Check Is Made Out To

Mortgages given by lending institutions are regulated and governed by consumer protection laws. Once you've gotten a mortgage, the terms—interest rate, the length of the loan, and so forth—can't change, even if the loan is sold on the secondary market. The basic terms of your mortgage remain in force until the loan is satisfied.

In fact, *you should assume your loan will be sold on the secondary market.* Some lenders typically sell between 75% and 100% of their loans, while others prefer to keep the loans within their portfolio (in other words, in-house). If your loan is sold, it's of no consequence to you; the only change will be that you'll write your check to a different institution and mail it to a different address. Even that may not change; some loans are sold, but the original lender maintains "servicing" of the loan: receiving payments, mailing statements, dealing with late payments, and so forth.

Your monthly payment can and probably will change over time, though. If your lender is escrowing for taxes or insurance, and those rates increase, your monthly payment will increase. Or if you're currently paying PMI but in the future you are no longer required to do so because your outstanding balance is lower than 80% of the home's value, your premium will decrease. But your interest rate and term (including ARM adjustment rules) can't and won't change.

You may think you'll be able to walk into your local branch and make your mortgage payment, but in most cases you can't—your loan will be sold on the secondary market.

Who owns your loan is, really, immaterial. All that matters is that you're happy with the loan you have—once you have the loan, your terms won't change.

 Although the terms of your loan may not change, the loan servicer who handles your payments may change. Whenever your loan changes hands, keep a close watch on your mortgage statements and credit report. We've seen plenty of homeowners with bruised credit because a loan servicer posted payments to the wrong account.

MYTH # **65**

Refinancing is Easy—I Already Qualify.

Fact: You Might Not Qualify, and You May Have to Make Repairs in Order to Qualify

Many homeowners assume refinancing a current mortgage—especially with the same lending institution—will be a done deal. "After all," they reason, "I already own the home, and I've made my payments on time . . . there's no way they won't approve me."

While we wish that were true, it's not. Just because you qualified a few years ago for a loan doesn't mean you can qualify for a loan of a similar size (or larger size) today. Your financial situation may have changed drastically: You may have taken on more debt, your income may have decreased, or your credit record may be less solid than it was . . . any number of changes to your financial position can have occurred. While it's certainly to your credit that you've been on time with your mortgage payments, that is by no means the only criteria the lender will use to determine whether you qualify for a new loan.

We explained this fact to a friend, and he said, "Wait a minute—the lender will let me keep my old loan, but they won't make a new loan? I'm the same guy and it's the same house . . . why isn't approval automatic?"

For one thing, the lender can't "take away" your old loan just because your financial situation has changed. The lender can only cancel the mortgage if you enter the foreclosure process—as long as you make payments on time, the lender can't decide you're no longer a good credit risk. (Nor will they care—again, as long as the payments are made on time, they really could care less.) But, a lender can decline to offer you a new mortgage if the level of risk appears to be too high based on your current financial status.

In order to refinance, you may also have to make repairs to your home if major problems exist. If you wish to refinance and take some of the equity out of the home, the house will need to appraise at or above a certain level . . . and if the condition has deteriorated, the appraisal amount may not be sufficient for the lender to make the loan. In order to qualify you'll need to make the necessary repairs.

Or your situation may have changed, making qualification more difficult. A customer of Chip's financed a second home, then two years later wanted to refinance. In the meantime, he had turned the house into a commercial enterprise by running his business out of it, and because it no longer qualified as a residence, it fell under different underwriting terms. (The printing presses in the living room gave it away!)

One exception to this rule is an FHA "streamline refinance." If you are refinancing an FHA loan and just want a lower rate (or even a shorter term), then under this program, you don't have to qualify! That's right—as long as you have been making the payments, and not increasing your loan amount (over what you owe plus any of the costs involved), then it's a done deal! Check with your loan officer or an FHA-approved lender to see if you qualify.

Don't assume you automatically qualify for refinancing, especially if your financial situation has changed. The typical lender won't qualify you under your old conditions—the lender is only interested in your current situation.

 Don't stop making your monthly mortgage payments because you're in the process of refinancing and paying off your existing mortgage. Keep making the payments until you close on your new loan.

If you have an ARM that recently has (or will) reset to a higher rate, and the higher payments have led to difficulties, ask about the new FHA*Secure* program, designed to help borrowers with subprime loans or who are facing possible foreclosure.

MYTH # **66**

Refinancing: Better than Home Equity or Construction Loans.

Fact: Refinancing Could Be and Often Is Much More Expensive

When someone asks for advice on whether or not to refinance a mortgage, the first question Chip asks is, "Why do you want to refinance?" So, if *you're* considering refinancing, why do *you*?

If you're looking for a lower interest rate, a shorter-loan term, or to convert an adjustable-rate mortgage into a fixed-rate mortgage, then whether or not it makes sense is based on some straightforward math calculations. You'll evaluate the costs of refinancing, the savings you'll enjoy, and you'll calculate whether refinancing is a good deal for you or not. (See Myth #60 for an overview of evaluating the benefits of refinancing.)

If you're interested in refinancing so you can take cash out of the home, you'll assess the possibilities differently. First, you'll evaluate the costs of refinancing and the savings you'll enjoy. If, for example, interest rates are flat (or even have risen), refinancing is not likely to offer any savings on your original loan terms. If that's the case, refinancing is a bad option, and you're better off getting a home equity line or a construction loan. Why? Most home equity lines require little in terms of closing costs, and allow you to draw money out as you need it—which means you'll only be charged interest when you draw the money out, not all at once. A few years later, if interest rates have fallen, you might decide to refinance your first mortgage and your home equity line into a new mortgage that offers savings that offset the costs of a new mortgage.

A few years ago a customer asked to borrow $2,000. Chip asked him the purpose of the loan, and he said he wanted to buy new furniture, and borrowing against his home seemed like a good idea. After Chip explained the closing costs involved, he referred him to a local furniture store that financed the purchase internally—and for a lot less than an equity loan would have cost. (In his case the closing costs would have been 200% of the original loan amount!)

Refinancing a mortgage requires an approval process, closing costs, and so forth; it's expensive and time consuming. Getting a construction loan, or better yet a home equity line, is relatively inexpensive. If refinancing doesn't offer long-term savings, don't make the mistake of spending money you didn't have to.

 Always compare the full cost of the loan over the expected life of the loan to determine how much the loan will cost. See Myth #12 for step-by-step instructions on how to calculate the cost of a loan.

 A Home Equity line of credit is a great safety net—set it up *before* something goes wrong and you need it!

MYTH # **67**

Low Inflation Means Low Appreciation.

Fact: Inflation and Appreciation Are Not Related

Homes appreciate for a wide variety of reasons: the housing market where the house is located, the neighborhood, the initial price paid for the home, the age of the home, the quality of nearby schools, an imbalance in supply and demand, improvements made by the homeowners, etc. We could list dozens more reasons, but none would involve inflation.

Inflation is the tendency or trend where prices and wages rise. Simply put, if prices rise by 4%, the inflation rate is 4%. Does that mean your home's value will also rise by 4%? It might—and it might not (see Figure 6.4).

If inflation rates are low, your house could still appreciate dramatically. If you live in certain parts of New York, California, Florida, Arizona, or a number of other areas where home prices have exploded, you're also aware that inflation rates have stayed relatively low. Low inflation didn't mean low appreciation—far from it.

More reliable economic indicators are mortgage interest rate levels, wage rate levels, supply and demand levels, but even these indicators don't tell the whole story. Whether a home will appreciate in value has much more to do with its location and local market conditions than it ever will with inflation rates. To find out about local conditions, ask real estate agents for information or contact the local REALTOR® association office. While they can't necessarily tell you which areas are hot, per se, they can

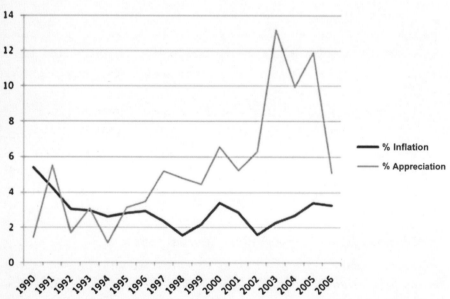

Figures based upon Q4 statistics, and provided by the U.S. Bureau of Labor and Statistics and Office of Federal Housing Enterprise Oversight.

Figure 6.4 Inflation versus Appreciation. Although there are dips, the rate of appreciation consistently outpaces the rate of inflation.

give you specific information about appreciation rates, they can compare the home price changes between different neighborhoods, and they can give you a good sense of local trends.

Instead of using a macroeconomic indicator like inflation rates to try to predict whether a home will rise in value, focus on local events, local conditions, and the local market—those are your best indication of where housing price trends in your area will go.

 Basing a trend on anything less than 5 years is a questionable practice. Home values typically rise 5 to 10 percent on average over the course of 20 to 40 years, but it's not uncommon to for property values to drop over the course of a few years. Stay in a house for 20 to 30, and you're likely to see it double or triple in value.

MYTH # **68**

I Have to Live There at Least Three Years to Break Even.

Fact: Look at the Rate of Return of the Cost—Not Just Time

Your home is, first and foremost, where you live. Your home is also an investment; for many it's the biggest investment they'll ever make. It's natural—even admirable—to want to make money from that investment. It's also natural to think about how long it will take to make money, and as a result, many homeowners think in terms of time, not in terms of return.

If that seems confusing, think about it this way: If you want to make money from your home, or if you want to refinance and you're deciding whether it makes good financial sense, or if you're considering adding on to your house and you want to know if it's a good financial move ... what matters most is what return you'll receive and how long it takes to get that return. If you spend $20,000 on a new kitchen, and immediately increase your home's value by $30,000, that's a great return in very little time. If you spend $20,000 and your home's value increases by $20,000, there's no real return—you're breaking even.

What you should care most about is the rate of return you'll receive on an investment, and not on how long it takes to break even. Let's use a different example: Say you're considering adding a new bedroom to your house. The cost of the addition is $15,000. You're willing to do some of the work yourself to save costs. Based on sales of comparable properties in your area you determine the addition will add $20,000 in value to your home. You'll make a $5,000 profit on a $15,000 investment, which is a 33% return. Outstanding!

Your rate of return though, depends on when you sell the home and actually receive your profits—while you're living in the home, you've only made a "paper" profit. If you sell tomorrow, your return is 33%. If you sell in 10 years, your return is 3.3% because the money you invested has been tied up in the home for that length of time. (On the other hand, you get to enjoy the use of the new bedroom, and your enjoyment is certainly valuable, too.)

You can save money another way too. When you buy a home as a residence, you'll typically be asked to sign a statement (called a homestead exemption) indicating you intend to live in the home for 12 months. Terms and rates on owner-occupied properties are lower than for investment properties, so to prove owner occupation government agencies sometimes check utility bills, driver's license records, and other documents to verify where you reside. Some investors try to claim a homestead exemption on two different properties; don't be tempted to do so, because it's likely that someone will check.

In the end, whenever you consider an investment, look at the rate of return, and decide if it makes sense based on your financial goals.

 Your break-even point on a house has more to do with the deal you made when you purchased the property. As mentioned previously, you make your money when you buy a property. Many investors make 20% or more the day they purchase the property. Buy smart, and you profit on the day of purchase.

MYTH # **69**

Refinancing Is a Cheap Way to Get Cash.

Fact: If You're Not Careful, Refinancing May Be the Most Expensive Way to Get Cash

If you've paid down your mortgage, or if your home's value has risen in the past few years, you could have significant equity you can tap. ("Equity" simply means the difference between your home's value and the outstanding balance on your mortgage—if your home is worth $300,000 and you only owe $200,000, you have $100,000 in equity in the home.)

"First take the time to look at what the cash will be used for," advises Tim Wooding. "If it will be used to make an investment, like purchasing an income property, it may be a great use of your capital. If it's to be used for a vacation, it probably isn't the best use of your capital."

So, if you want to convert the equity in your home into cash, first ask yourself why. Why do you need the cash? If you want to pay down other debt, pay medical expenses, pay college tuition, or make improvements to add value to your home . . . it may be the right choice to make. If you want to spend the money on a major vacation, on the other hand, you may want to think twice: your home equity is, in effect, an asset similar to owning shares of stock or having money in the bank. Don't blow it frivolously.

If you have decided you want to remove some amount of equity from your home, there are two main ways to do so. One is to refinance your original mortgage. Say you own a $300,000 home and you only owe $100,000 on your mortgage; you could refinance that loan, borrowing $200,000, using $100,000 to pay off your original mortgage, and pocketing the other $100,000. Many people choose this option, but there are at least two main disadvantages: you'll pay closing costs on the new loan, and you'll start making interest payments on the higher loan balance immediately, and for the life of the new loan.

Another option is to take out a home equity loan. A home equity loan doesn't affect your first mortgage, and doesn't require an extensive documentation or approval process because the risk to the lender is largely covered by the value of your home. There are two subtypes of home equity loans: a home equity loan and a home equity line of credit. The main difference is that proceeds from a home equity loan are distributed immediately; if you take out a $100,000 home equity loan, you get those funds immediately—and you start making payments on the full amount immediately. A home equity line is a line of credit up to a maximum amount. If you take out a $100,000 home equity line, that amount is available to you, but you don't have to draw it all (or any of it) out at any given time. You use it when you need it or want it. If you only need $10,000 today, great—draw $10,000; you'll only make payments on that $10,000, not on $100,000 as you would if you had a home equity loan. A home equity line is almost always the better choice, because even if you'll eventually need to use the entire line of credit available, you can phase your spending in over time and avoid unnecessary interest payments. In addition, as you pay off your home equity line, you can withdraw from your available balance as many times as you like.

Here's a simple way for you to decide between refinancing and getting a home equity loan if you want to take equity out of your home. Refinancing makes sense if you'll save money on the transaction. For example, if you currently have a 9% mortgage, and you can refinance into a 6% mortgage, refinancing and taking cash out of the home is very likely to be your best choice: Not only do you receive the cash you want, but you also lower your interest costs over the life of the loan. If you can't save money by refinancing, a home equity line is your best option: You avoid closing costs, you can qualify more easily, and you'll only make interest payments when you actually draw from your home's equity.

In some cases refinancing is the more expensive option. A customer was referred to Chip because she had struggled to get financing to buy a manufactured home; so in order to purchase the home her parents paid cash for the house and then took a lien on the house assuming their daughter could refinance once she was in.

One problem with this approach was that refinancing guidelines typically require 12 months "seasoning," so she would need to wait 12 months before refinancing. She was also limited on how much she could borrow, because mortgage refinancing is typically limited to a 90% loan to value ratio (LTV), so she could only borrow up to 90% of the value of the home. Her solution—an expensive one—was to get an FHA refinance, which allowed up to 95% LTV, but as a result she also needed MIP (the FHA version of mortgage insurance)—and under FHA guidelines, for a minimum of five years. While she was able to purchase the home, in this case refinancing was far from the cheapest way to do so.

Regardless of which way you decide to get the cash, remember to make your payment ratios comfortable. As mentioned previously, when you add on the extra payment, keep the total amount of all your payments below 50% of your income!

 Set goals, communicate your goals to the loan officer, and then sit back and listen. Many homeowners only pay attention to the monthly payment and as a result miss the big picture—the long term. Loan officers are trained to look far into the future to determine just how much that loan will cost you.

 Make sure that your back debt-to-income ratio is still 50% or less when you add up any new loan payments.

MYTH # **70**

My Escrows Are Already Set Up.

Fact: Escrows Are Rarely Transferable

What is an escrow? An escrow is legally defined as a legal arrangement where an asset, usually money, is delivered to a third party called an escrow agent to be held in trust pending a contingency or the fulfillment of a condition or conditions in a contract. Upon that event occurring, the escrow agent will deliver the asset to the proper recipient; otherwise the escrow agent is bound by his or her fiduciary duty to maintain the escrow account.

In plainer language, an escrow agent holds money as a third party and distributes it to the appropriate parties. If you've purchased a fairly expensive item from an eBay auction, an escrow agent may have been involved: the seller sent money to the escrow agent, and the agent held the funds until the buyer received the item. In real estate terms, escrows are most often used to hold funds for taxes and insurance—each month a portion of your monthly mortgage payment goes into escrow, and at the end of the year is used to pay your real estate taxes. If your total real estate tax bill will be $900, a monthly payment of $75 ($900 divided by 12 months) is added to your principal and interest payment to cover the yearly tax bill.

Lenders typically prefer to escrow for real estate taxes and hazard insurance—that way they know the bills will be paid. For example, maintaining adequate hazard insurance is a loan requirement, so it makes sense for the lender to want every assurance you'll maintain hazard insurance over the life of the loan, and having the escrow agent pay the bill is more reliable than trusting every homeowner to do so. In fact, in most cases the lender will simply assume you'll agree to escrow those funds, and will set the loan up that way automatically.

If you buy a new home, you'll need to set up escrows (keep in mind the lender will do it for you).

For an FHA refinance with the same lender, FHA asks the lender to "net out" the escrows so setting up a new escrow account won't be necessary. (In fact, many times the same lender will try and net escrows out for you even if it's not an FHA loan.)

If you're offered seller financing, and you wish to escrow for taxes and insurance, you'll need to make arrangements with an escrow agent yourself.) Escrows are almost never transferable. There may also be a small fee associated—it will show up on your HUD-1 statement. It's almost impossible to avoid the fee and the need to set up new escrow accounts, and it really isn't worth the effort to try. Spend your time focusing on saving money in other areas, like by shopping aggressively for the right loan in the first place.

[STOP] If you receive seller financing, enter language into the agreement stating that a licensed servicer will be managing the escrow accounts and paying your property taxes and insurance on time. Also insert language that you will receive the necessary forms at the end of the year indicating the total interest you paid and the total in property taxes and insurance. You'll need this information to file your income tax returns.

SECTION 7

Short of Cash? Creative Financing Solutions

MYTH # **71**

I Can't Use a Gift for a Down Payment.

Fact: You Can Use a Gift Even If It Was Given to You 10 Minutes Ago

When you apply for a loan, most lenders will ask for between two and three months' worth of documentation: W-2 statements, bank statements, and so forth. One of the things a lender looks for is the appearance of a large cash deposit in your bank account; the presence of a large deposit may indicate you've received a loan from a friend or relative that you'll use toward your down payment. The lender wants to determine if you've borrowed money for your down payment because that's additional debt you'll have (and that you may not have declared), and the lender needs to take that debt into account in determining whether you're financially capable of handling the loan.

As a general rule, lenders want borrowers who put less than 20% down to meet the down payment requirement with funds they have saved as opposed to gifts from family and friends. Lenders typically check bank statements and other financial records for up to 60 days (2 bank statements) prior to your application to ensure the funds are yours—and they try to determine the source of any large deposits recently made. If you've recently received a large bonus, cash from the sale of an asset, or tax refund, the lender will want to see documentation indicating the source of that large deposit.

If a relative or friend is willing to make a gift to help you with a down payment, and it occurs less than 60 days before you apply for a loan, they may be asked to furnish a "gift letter." A gift letter is a letter from a relative (or a party with whom a strong relationship has been established) stating that the amount given has been *gifted* to the buyer and that the funds are not a loan that must be repaid.

Currently, gifts of up to $11,000 per year, per person, can be received with no tax consequences to the donor or the recipient. In fact, a couple with two sets of parents could obtain $44,000, receiving $11,000 from each parent. If the couple were to bridge the closing over two calendar years (for example, closing in January of the next year), the couple could accept $44,000 in December and another $44,000 in January, for an $88,000 down payment—all tax-free.

Keep in mind a gift letter will *definitely* be required if you're lucky enough to receive gifts that large!

Gifts can also come from nonprofit entities (government agencies) or even churches. Make sure you document the transfer of the funds: copies of the checks, the gift letter, and deposit slips showing the exact amount of the gift deposited into the account.

A real estate agent called asking Chip to help her client who had been renting a condo for 12 years. In order to keep living there she needed to purchase the unit because the condo association had changed their bylaws to no longer allow renters.

He met with the buyer: she had no cash for a down payment; she had no credit history because she paid all her bills in cash; she was a single mother with two children; and she had long-term employment but was only making $6.47 per hour. We cut her costs as low as possible and convinced the seller to pay some of the closing costs, but even that wasn't enough.

Her church stepped in and made a cash gift to help her purchase the condo. The church had a program in place to help parishioners in need, and since it was a 503(c) organization, the gift was legal and met underwriting requirements.

For the first time in her life the buyer owned property. She was crying at the table at closing and struggled to sign the forms because she was so emotional. Thanks to her church she went from being afraid of being homeless to being a homeowner.

A sample of a gift letter that you can use is included in the Appendix, or available on the resource website at www.TheMortgageMyths.com.

"Creative financing options" can go too far. Ralph recently was involved in a case in which a couple had agreed to purchase a home for nearly double what it was worth. They were going to pay $3,500,000 for a $1,850,000 house, cash out $1,650,000, give 25 percent of that to the guy who put the deal together, and use the rest of the money to renovate the property—all without the knowledge of the lender. "Creative financing" that misrepresents the situation to the lender is a form of mortgage fraud.

MYTH # **72**

A Biweekly Mortgage Simply Changes My Payment Schedule.

Fact: A Biweekly Mortgage Saves You Money and Reduces the Term of Your Loan

A homeowner with a biweekly mortgage pays half the monthly principal and interest payment every 2 weeks, which results in an extra monthly payment every year. (52 weeks per year divided by 2 weeks = 26 half-payments per year, which is the equivalent of 13 monthly payments rather than 12. You don't make two payments per month, you make a payment every two weeks.)

Because of the extra month's payment, a biweekly mortgage pays off earlier than a monthly mortgage will because the 13th payment is applied entirely to the principal balance (see Figure 7.1).

The biweekly mortgage confuses a lot of people because they mistake the interest payments made over the life of the loan with the interest rate.

To get the benefit of a biweekly payment structure, simply add 1/12th of your principal amount to your payment each month:

Program	Payment	Balance in 12 months	In 60 months
30-yr Fixed	$632.07	$98,882.24	$93,610.81
+ 1/12 pmt	$684.74	$98,231.04	$89,888.47

Loan is paid off in the 24th year, saving **$44,244.90**

Figure 7.1 Monthly versus Biweekly Payment. Note: Calculated on $100,000 loan at 6.5%.

Total interest payments paid over the life of a loan depend on the rate, on the amount borrowed, and on how rapidly the loan itself is paid off. Converting a conventional loan to a biweekly doesn't change your interest rate. What it does is use the extra payments you make every year to reduce the principal balance, which in turn reduces your total interest payments.

The loan is paid off early, just as it would have been if you had begun with a mortgage carrying a shorter term. (In fact, borrowers taking out a new loan who are attracted to the accelerated repayment schedule on a biweekly are usually better off with a conventional loan having a shorter term. For example, 15- and 20-year loans often carry lower rates than 30-year loans, while a borrower taking a 30-year biweekly will pay the 30-year rate, even though a 7% biweekly pays off in about 23 years.)

If you already have a 30-year mortgage and are attracted by the prospect of paying it off early, there is nothing wrong with converting it to a biweekly, but it will cost you. (After all, no lender will do the work of converting your existing loan into a biweekly without being compensated for their effort.)

If you don't already have a biweekly mortgage, there are easy alternatives that will cost you nothing. If you regularly receive a bonus at the end of the year, for example, make it a habit to send your lender an additional check equal to the amount of the bonus, marked "additional principal," along with your regular check for the normal monthly payment. Keep in mind that if you make an extra payment equal to 1/12 of your regular monthly payment at the end of each month, you will pay off the balance just as you would with a biweekly. (Remember though, your total payment probably includes an escrow amount for taxes and insurance, so you don't need to include escrow amounts in the equation.) You start reducing the balance (and interest on that balance) with the first additional payment.

There is one problem: the alternative approaches we just mentioned require self-discipline on your part—which you may or may not be able to stick with. Having a third party set up the procedure, and then legally obligating yourself to making the additional payments, forces the discipline on you. If you think about it, this "enforced discipline" is the only service you receive when you purchase a biweekly deal from a third party.

Whether you need that enforced discipline, only you can decide—but you can save money and pay off your loan earlier with a biweekly mortgage. We recommend that you don't buy a biweekly plan; some companies will charge up to $500 or more up front, plus a monthly fee. Calculate your own payment and create your own biweekly plan at no cost instead.

 Don't get overly obsessed with paying down your mortgage. Focus on paying down bad debt first. Pay down your credit card balances, pay off your car loan, then pay into your retirement account, and *then* start thinking about paying a little extra toward the principal on your mortgage. Remember, home mortgage interest is tax-deductible. Interest on credit card debt and auto loans is not.

Don't let someone sell you a "biweekly" payment program on your existing mortgage—be disciplined and do it yourself!

MYTH # **73**

Seller Financing Is Risky and Expensive.

Fact: Seller Financing Is No More Risky than a Traditional Loan If You Do Your Homework, and You Can Often Save Money on the Deal

Seller financing is an important and popular tool that can help buyers purchase a property they could otherwise not be able to buy. Sellers are sometimes willing to become "banks" for the buyer, taking payments just as a bank would until the loan is paid off. In all other respects the transaction is the same as through traditional financing—the deed is transferred to your name, and you simply make your payments to the seller instead of to a bank. Seller financing can be used for all or part of the loan; the seller can do a "seller second" for a small percentage of the total loan amount.

More and more sellers are offering financing because the rate of return they can get is better than through income-producing investments like CDs, money market accounts, or other "safe" investment vehicles. It's easy to understand if you think about it: a seller will be much happier receiving 7% interest on the mortgage he offers you than he will be receiving 2% or 3% from a money market account.

For buyers, seller financing can be a cheaper alternative. You won't pay loan fees or PMI premiums, and in many cases the credit checks and underwriting requirements are much lower. (Some sellers won't even check your credit—we have a friend who owns four seller-financed investment properties, and his credit was never checked.) In general, the closing costs involved in seller financing are much lower than with traditional financing, too: you won't pay points or loan origination fees, for example.

Why would the seller be willing to finance your purchase of their property? It's important that you understand the seller's side of the transaction—that will help you understand that seller financing isn't risky or unsafe. The seller may be willing to offer financing if:

- The property type is difficult to finance through traditional third-party lenders.
- The property has been on the market for 90 or more days.
- An "as-is" closing is required because the property is in need of repairs.
- The owner has not met minimum holding time or title "seasoning" requirements required by traditional lenders.
- An immediate closing is required due to imminent foreclosure or other financial burdens.
- A quick closing is preferred by seller to free up investment capital.
- The seller wants long-term interest income.

The last reason listed is very common. Put yourself in a seller's shoes for a second: Say you've owned a rental property for a number of years and you've paid off the mortgage. You enjoy the monthly income you receive from rental payments but you're not interested in being a landlord anymore—it's too much trouble. By selling the property and offering owner financing, you still get monthly income—but you avoid all the duties of being a landlord since that's now the new owner's role. In addition, you've avoided any capital gains taxes that might be due if you sold the property outright.

Here's why seller financing can be advantageous to you as a buyer.

- You can often put little or no money down. Some sellers will require 10, 20, or 30% down, but many will accept less than 10%, especially if their goal is to receive monthly income from the property in the form of mortgage payments.
- You'll face lower credit requirements. As we said, some sellers won't check your credit at all. Most will simply make sure you've had no bankruptcies or foreclosures in your past.
- Sellers won't require you to have an underlying (qualifying) income. If it's an investment property you're buying from the seller, a traditional lender will expect you to have sufficient income to cover at least some of the monthly payments on the property in case it's vacant for a period of time. Sellers *assume* your income will be derived from rent payments. As long as the rent you will receive covers the monthly payments, the typical seller won't ask about your monthly income from other sources.
- The terms can be more flexible. You and the seller agree on terms—you can decide on any terms you're comfortable with and can both agree to. Price, interest rate, terms, and any other loan requirements are all up for negotiation. If you have unusual needs, you and the seller may be able to reach an agreement that a traditional lender won't be willing to make. For instance, let's say you work on commission, and at year-end you always receive a lump-sum payout. If the seller agrees, you could make lower monthly payments for eleven months of the year, and a larger payment on the twelfth month. Most banks won't even consider that option.

- Closing costs are lower. Sellers don't usually ask for points, loan application fees, origination fees, and so forth. The seller isn't covering advertising costs, overhead, or other costs that a lending institution has to cover.
- You'll complete less paperwork. Sellers don't answer to a bureaucracy, so the only paperwork you'll complete is what's absolutely necessary for the transaction to be legal in your locality.
- The sale can take place much more quickly. We've known people to close on a property within a few days of signing a contract.
- When it comes time to sell or refinance, you may be able to get a "discount" from the seller, whereas that will not be possible with a traditional lender.

Some sellers will ask for a balloon note—they want monthly payments for a certain number of years, and after that they'd like to cash out. Situations like that are common when the owner is nearing retirement age. If the owners are in their early sixties, for instance, they're probably not concerned about receiving mortgage payments for the next 30 years; 5 or 10 years may be long enough.

When the balloon payment is due, you'll simply get traditional financing (or use another creative financing method).

Keep in mind that the loan agreement you reach can have unusual requirements. It's not uncommon to buy a property using owner financing and find a clause in the contract stipulating you can't sell the property for at least five years—the owner wants to be sure he receives mortgage payments for at least five years before receiving the balance of the principal. Make sure you're comfortable with whatever agreements you reach.

Also make sure that you perform a title search to ensure you know what liens may be against the property. In one case a borrower on a land contract had been making payments for over 10 years, and when they tried to pay off the land contract found out the seller hadn't been making timely payments to the underlying lender, so as a result even if they paid off the seller they couldn't get title to the property.

And make sure you know who the underlying debtors are, and make sure you record any second loans or underlying land contracts so the seller can't go out and use the property as collateral.

If you want or need seller financing, and the sellers of a house you're considering aren't offering financing, they're unlikely to entertain the idea unless you put the request in writing as a part of your offer to buy the property. Think about it: if you're selling a property, and a person casually asks if you're interested in financing it, you're likely to say no. If their request comes with an attractive offer on the property, and you haven't had many offers, you may be more willing to at least look at the possibility.

Make the request a part of your offer, and if you'd like, feel free to be present when your agent presents the offer. (You have the legal right to be present whenever an offer is made on your behalf.) That way you can answer any questions the sellers may have.

 Although seller financing is a great way to buy and sell a house, a loan servicer should be brought into the deal to handle the payments, process necessary payment documentation for filing taxes, and pay property taxes and insurance out of the escrow account on time. Some banks will handle this for a fee.

MYTH # **74**

Government Loans Are Only for Low-Income Borrowers.

Fact: Government Loans Are for Anyone Who Meets the Criteria

Although some FHA-subsidized programs are intended to assist low-income families, the FHA's goal is to insure lenders on housing loans made to borrowers who do not meet the conventional down payment requirements or other conditions of traditional mortgages. The loans are insured by the Department of Housing and Urban Development (HUD), so the lender is protected against the borrower's default and can offer more flexible terms and competitive interest than some borrowers may be able to obtain elsewhere. The borrower must have a satisfactory credit record, the down payment that is required (or funds that have been gifted for use as a down payment), the cash needed for closing, and an income sufficient to meet the monthly mortgage payments without difficulty. In fact, citizenship is not a requirement for obtaining an FHA loan as long as the borrower will reside in the property.

VA loans are also not restricted to low-income buyers; a veteran of the U.S. armed forces can qualify for a VA loan, often enjoying lower interest rates, a low or no-down-payment requirement, no prepayment penalty, and no cap on the size of the loan (although the loan is limited to what the applicant is able to afford, of course).

Keep in mind, income from non-vets and nonspouses can't be counted for a VA loan. Customers of mine could qualify for a VA loan based on their combined incomes, but were not due to be married until September—and they wanted to purchase the home in July. In order to qualify, they needed to get married before they could close on the home!

Is an FHA loan or VA loan your best bet? Find out what the terms are for your individual financial situation, compare those terms with conventional financing, and make the best choice for you.

 FHA financing is the financing of choice for first-time home buyers. You won't need a huge down payment, and interest rates are typically competitive. The government secures these loans in order to encourage home ownership, so take advantage of the generous offer.

MYTH # **75**

No Bank Will Finance Us.

Fact: There Are Loan Programs to Fit Almost Everyone's Financial Situation

Here's the bottom line: If you have income, you can get a loan. If you can pay it back, we can find a loan for you. Loans are no longer one size fits all, and neither is the loan approval process.

Many customers are told by one lending source they can't obtain a loan and believe it's the final word on the subject. "I have already talked to my bank," they may say, "and I was told me I couldn't obtain financing for a new home."

Unfortunately, a large number of potential homebuyers—and current homeowners—don't really understand how the lending industry works. Many have the impression that all loans come from a single pool of money.

But the lending industry is more specialized than almost any other business sector. Sadly, most lending avenues are not presented to the clients depending on the bank or lending institution they had originally contacted. For example, if a potential client goes to their current bank, that bank may only offer conforming loans. If the client does not meet the bank's conforming guidelines, the bank has no other option than to deny the loan. Sometimes that denial may be due to bruised credit and/or derogatory records, but it also can happen simply because of a situation unique to the applicant, such as:

- "I'm self-employed and cannot verify my income."
- "I had an issue with a medical problem which kept me from work. Now I have a few collections associated with my credit."
- "I don't have bad credit, because I don't have *any* credit."

Because every individual is unique, the number of unique situations is virtually limitless, and many lending institutions aren't set up to handle those situations.

But there is good news. Many specialized organizations focus on specific and unique customer circumstances, with programs like:

- One day out of bankruptcy.
- Low credit scores.
- 100% financing.
- High debt-to-income ratios.
- Stated asset loan programs.

The list goes on and on. Institutions that focus on customers with less than perfect situations fall under the blanket title of "nonconforming lenders." Because they do not conform to rigid guidelines, their rules are more conducive to obtaining a loan.

These nonconforming loans are typically not offered by a credit union or bank. Keep in mind a bank's goal is to place you within their set of loans. If you rely on their expertise, you may not be made aware of the other options available to you and assume you can't get a loan.

Nonconforming lenders use a variety of approval methods. Typically lenders want documentation of your financial history: items like bank statements, pay stubs, W-2 forms, and so forth. Some loan types require lots of documentation—others, almost none. (That's why they're called "no-doc," meaning "no-documentation" loans.)

Here's a summary of the main methods of loan approval:

- *Full Documentation.* Both income and assets are disclosed and verified, and income is used in determining the applicant's ability to repay the mortgage. "Formal" verification requires the borrower's employer to verify employment and pay, and the borrower's bank to verify deposits. "Alternative" documentation, designed to save time, accepts copies of the borrower's original bank statements, W-2s, and paycheck stubs.

At one time, full documentation was the rule, and it remains the standard. In recent years, however, other documentation programs have grown in use.

- *Stated Income, Verified Assets.* Income is disclosed, and the source of the income is verified, but the amount itself is not verified. (You list how much you make, and your employer verifies that you are indeed employed, but they do not verify the amount you make.) Assets are verified and must meet an adequacy standard, such as six months of stated income and two months of the expected monthly housing expense in reserve. This program is also frequently called "NIV" for No Income Verification.
- *Stated Income, Stated Assets* (SISA). Both income and assets are disclosed but not verified. However, the source of the borrower's income is verified.
- *No Ratio.* Income is not disclosed or verified, and expense ratios are not calculated to use in qualifying the borrower. The standard rule

that the borrower's housing expense cannot exceed some specified percent of income is ignored. Assets are disclosed and verified.

◆ *No Income.* Income is not disclosed, but assets are disclosed and verified and must meet an adequacy standard.

◆ *No Income, No Assets* (NINA). Neither income nor assets are disclosed. This is usually called a "no-doc" loan, because you're not providing any documentation to the lender. The loan will be approved based entirely on your credit history, the property in question, and the Loan to Value ratio. In the industry, we also call this the "Liar's Loan."

◆ *Limited Income, Stated Assets* (LISA). Income is disclosed, and assets are verified.

While these categories are fairly well established in the lending market, there are many differences between individual lenders with respect to the details of each program. For example, under a stated income program, a lender may or may not require that an applicant sign a form authorizing the lender to request the applicant's tax returns from the IRS in the event the borrower defaults. Or lenders can differ in the amount of assets they require you to have.

Recent market conditions have also limited the availability of some of these types of loans in the marketplace. With the subprime "crash," several nonconforming investors have tightened up their guidelines, or eliminated programs altogether. Keep looking! New creative programs come out every day to meet market demands. Check with several mortgage brokers to find out the current options.

Why are there so many different documentation programs? Lenders realized that many consumers who were potential homeowners were kept out of the market by excessively rigid documentation requirements. It also dawned on lenders that documentation could be viewed as a risk factor that could be priced or offset by other risk factors. (In other words, the less documentation you provide the more risk the loan may carry, but if the lender prices the loan high enough, it's worth it to the lender to take on that risk.) If a borrower has solid credit and is putting 25% down, for example, why should the lender worry too much about documentation?

Full documentation carries the least risk to the lender, a no income/no asset (a no-doc loan) carries the most risk, and the others fall somewhere in between. If the documentation level is riskier, the lenders will charge you more, will require a risk offset, or will do both. The typical risk offsets are large down payments and high credit scores—the more risk, the more down payment the lender will want, and also the higher the credit rating they'll expect you to have.

A good lender or mortgage broker can help you determine the right strategy and the best program for your individual situation. In many cases, the best way to increase your chances for approval is to increase the amount of your down payment; a larger down payment reduces the amount of risk the lender incurs and makes it more likely your loan will be approved.

Many homebuyers use money from their IRA, Keogh, or 401(k) plans to make a larger down payment. You can withdraw up to $10,000 penalty-free for a down payment and/or closing costs. (To be a valid nontax transaction, the money must be used to close the home before the 120th day after it is withdrawn.)

And, you can use one or more relatives' IRAs up to a $10,000 maximum. If you have a Roth IRA, you can withdraw funds penalty-free and tax-free if you're a first-time buyer.

You can also use tax-free gifts towards your down payment. Gifts of up to $11,000 per year, per person, can be received without any tax consequences. As mentioned earlier, a couple with two sets of parents could obtain $44,000—$11,000 from each parent. If the couple were to bridge the closing over two calendar years (for example, closing in January of the new year), the couple could accept $44,000 in December and another $44,000 in January, for an $88,000 down payment—tax-free.

If you find you don't have enough income and down payment strength to qualify for a loan, here are some other possibilities for raising cash:

- Sell an asset such as a car, boat, or motorcycle.
- Put a lien on an asset. Borrow against a car, a boat, a life insurance policy, stock, certificates of deposit, or other personal property. (Be careful not to create more long-term debt in the process, though.)
- Refinance an asset such as personal property (either free and clear or with existing debt on it) to free up cash.

- Receive a gift letter for the down payment or closing costs from a relative.
- Barter a service, using sweat equity as either part of the down payment or closing costs. For example, a roofer may make roof repairs in lieu of using the seller's cash for repairs.
- Forgo a vacation and work instead. This could generate extra income. If a bonus is in your future, now might be a good time to request it. You may even be willing to take a little less for the privilege of receiving the bonus early.
- Use a co-borrower or cosigner to help reduce the loan amount for which the borrower needs to qualify.
- Have the seller or other third party place extra funds with the lender in a pledged account to add extra collateral to the loan and therefore reduce the lender's risk.

If your debt level is too high to qualify for a loan, here are some possibilities for reducing your overall debt:

- Pay off a debt. Use cash or another asset to alleviate the debt or sell an asset that has debt against it.
- Pay down a debt. Because the secondary market views long-term debt as anything that can't be paid off in ten months, you could pay down the debt below that point. Lenders can choose to be more restrictive on what's considered long-term debt, so check with the lender.
- Refinance a high-rate loan into a lower rate and payment.
- Consolidate your loans. Doing this may allow you to take several high-rate loans and wrap them into one lower-interest-rate loan, and even lower the monthly payments by extending the loan term.
- Destroy credit cards and close the account. (You should ask the lender if and how this might benefit the borrower's ability to qualify first, though. Before changing a cash or debt position, the borrower should consult the lender to see how what's proposed could help or hurt his or her credit picture.)

Mortgage brokers work with hundreds of different lenders; they can offer a wide variety of programs in one-stop shopping, and they're highly motivated, because they don't get paid unless they find a loan for you. A good mortgage broker can help you find the right program for your needs, especially if she takes the time to explore options.

A customer of Chip's wanted to buy a home but thought he couldn't qualify. He worked on a golf course as a groundskeeper, so his employment was stable but his income was relatively low. After talking with him, Chip learned he qualified for a VA loan because he had served in the Coast Guard (many people don't realize that service in the Coast Guard qualifies for a VA loan). Chip also learned his son received subsidy payments from the state due to a disability; the son lived with his customer, he was the custodian of record for the son, and as a result they could count those funds as income. Even though he thought he'd never qualify, he was able to purchase a home—with no money out of his pocket.

There are many different paths and avenues you can take to finance a new home or refinance an existing loan into a new loan. Some paths are obvious—many are not. Find out about all the resources and options that your bank has to offer. If you're working with a broker, ask what lenders they represent.

Above all, don't ever assume that one rejection is the final word. You may not have exhausted all possible options, or possibly with a little tweaking and adjusting your denial can become an approval. Make sure to use all resources available in the lending market.

At the same time, make sure you stay within your financial limits. Ensure your back ratio is less than 50%—make sure all your monthly payments, including your mortgage payment, car payments, credit card payments, and so forth—are less than 50% of your gross monthly income. While a subprime lender may be able to help you qualify for a loan, make sure you don't borrow more than you can afford.

 One way to always succeed at getting what you want is to take the Ralph Roberts's "No" means "Know" approach. "No" actually means that the other person doesn't "Know" enough to say "Yes." If you are turned down for a loan, find out why and then take steps to eliminate that reason. Once all the reasons for denying you a loan are gone, the only remaining answer is "Yes." Be persistent.

MYTH # **76**

A Lease-Option Plan Is Always a Bad Idea.

Fact: A Lease-Option Can Save You a Lot of Money Under the Right Circumstances

Would you like to buy a home (or investment property) but you don't have enough cash for a down payment?

If you answered "yes," a lease with option to purchase can make it possible. Before you jump in, though, it's important to understand the pros and cons of lease-options to maximize your benefits.

A lease-option is a combination real estate rental, sales, and finance technique. It's a property lease for a fixed time period, such as 12 or 24 months, with an option for the tenant to buy the property at an agreed option price at any time during the lease term.

In general, the lease-option technique is one of the quickest and least expensive methods available to investors for buying and selling real property. The purchaser is not required to conform to the various underwriting guidelines that banks and other lenders require. The seller, unlike an underwriter working for a mortgage company, typically requires little in the way of documentation. In most cases the seller providing the financing doesn't care where the money for a down payment comes from as long, as it comes from *somewhere*. To the seller, cash is cash.

Buyers like lease-options because little upfront cash is required. Sellers also like lease-options because they provide the necessary cash flow to pay the mortgage and property taxes—from a tenant who has a vested interest in treating the property well and who is likely to buy it.

A lease-purchase is different from a lease-option because it *obligates* the tenant to purchase the property at the end of the lease. With a lease-option the tenant has the right, but *not* the obligation, to purchase the property.

In both cases the tenant normally pays above-market rent and in return receives a monthly rent credit toward the down payment. Of course, both a lease-option and a lease-purchase obligate the seller to sell the property on the agreed terms.

Advantages of lease-options for buyers include:

- A small amount of upfront cash is required. The amount of upfront cash needed to acquire a home or other property on a lease-option is usually small; often just a few thousand dollars for the first month's rent plus nonrefundable option consideration. This option money is in lieu of a security deposit.
- The monthly rent credit builds a down payment. The unique characteristic of a lease-option is the rent credit toward the buyer's down payment. Typically, the rent credit is 10% to 100% of the monthly rent, depending on how motivated the seller is to sell. The higher the rent credit percentage, the greater the probability the tenant will buy.
- The "tenant" can try out the property before buying. Another special lease-option benefit for the tenant is the ability to try out the property before buying. If it turns out to be undesirable, the tenant hasn't tied up a large amount of cash in a home that might be difficult to resell.
- You can control property with very little cash. Buyers enjoy great leverage; they have the ability to control a property and profit from its potential market value appreciation with very little cash. Lease-option buyers gain this unique advantage.
- Longer terms mean greater profitability. Although most residential lease-options are for short terms, like one or two years, smart buyers seek lease-options with the longest possible term. They hope the property will appreciate over the long term.

A lease option is a great idea if you're new to the area and you're not sure if the home or neighborhood will be suitable for you. One couple moved to the area and didn't have the funds to purchase the property outright, so they lease-optioned the home for a two-year period, made payments for those two years, and decided the commute was a little too far for them. They decided to purchase a home elsewhere.

And, they made a little money, too. Instead of simply walking away from the home, they took advantage of the fact the property had appreciated by selling the lease-option to another party. In effect they would have had to pay to walk away, but instead they walked away, and with money in their pocket. While they didn't end up buying the home, a lease option was still a great idea.

Keep in mind that sellers typically try to collect the maximum amount of option money they can. They assume the more the buyer or tenant has invested in their property, the better they will take care of it. And, if the buyer decides not to exercise their option, the seller keeps the option money and the house.

As a buyer, your goal will be to pay as low an option premium as possible. Why invest more than you have to? Then, if the property appreciates in value, when you exercise your option your profits will be greater. In effect you can build equity in the house while you're leasing it.

Here's an example of a lease-option. A buyer has signed a lease-option agreement for a single-family house that gives him the right to purchase it at any time during the next twelve months. (He doesn't have to buy the house; he simply has the right to buy the house.) He agrees, if he chooses to, to purchase the house for $100,000, and he gives the seller a $2,000 option premium. If the seller gives the buyer $100 in credit towards the purchase of the house, at the end of the 12-month option period the buyer would have accrued a total of $1,200 in credit that could be applied toward the purchase price. (If the seller wanted to be more generous and offer the buyer $200 per month in credits, he or she could simply increase the price of the house by a corresponding amount.)

If the buyer exercises his option at the end of the 12-month period, his purchase price for the house is $98,800. If he doesn't exercise the option, the seller keeps the credit towards the purchase and the option premium (if the original lease-option contract is written that way, of course).

Always make sure to record a memo of lease option at the county recorder's office showing there is a lease option on the property; that way anyone looking to buy the property or finance against it will have to go through you (since you have first right of refusal).

A lease-purchase (or land contract) works in a similar way, except that the buyer has entered into a contract to purchase the house; he simply hasn't completed that purchase. If the lease-purchase contract is for 12 months, at the end of 12 months he must purchase the home or he is in default. The seller keeps the option premium and any credits he's accrued.

In short, the lease-option technique is similar to a purchase option in that it grants the right to investors to purchase property at a predetermined price within a predetermined period of time. The lease-option technique, however, combines the basic lease or rental agreement with an option to purchase contract.

Here's the bottom line: Lease-options provide greater flexibility in structuring transactions while simultaneously reducing your level of risk. If you see a sign that says FOR SALE OR RENT, or you're looking at a rental property and there's a real estate sign in the yard, in almost every case you can get a lease option for nothing down.

STOP Lease-option agreements can be a great way to purchase your first home, but have an attorney look over the paperwork and check the title first. Because the paperwork isn't going through normal channels, the property may not be inspected and appraised and the title may have hidden problems. A second set of eyes can protect you from making an expensive mistake.

MYTH # **77**

I Can't Make My Payments, So I'll Lose My Home.

Fact: Your Lender Has Every Interest in Working with You If You Face Financial Difficulties

Once you get behind, it's hard to catch back up—and the lender knows it.

With the huge increase in credit over the past few years, and creative ARM interest rates now resetting all over the place, delinquencies and foreclosures are reaching record numbers across the country. It's all we hear in the news! But you don't have to become part of those statistics.

Borrowers who have financial difficulties may find themselves in a situation where they know they can't continue making their mortgage payments. If that happens to you, your best bet is to come up with a game plan *before* you become delinquent. Then talk to your lender, explain your situation, and offer alternatives. (It's always easier and more effective to ask for help before there's a major problem—if you take the initiative and step forward your lender will be much more likely to work with you.) Here are the major components of a plan you'll present to your lender:

- ◆ Document your loss of income or the reason you're facing financial difficulty. This will also position you to demonstrate to the lender that your inability to pay is involuntary, in case that's necessary later on.
- ◆ Estimate your equity in the house. Your equity is what you could sell it for after sales commissions and paying off your mortgage. This step will help you develop a strategy for dealing with the lender.
- ◆ Determine realistically whether your financial reversal is temporary or permanent. A temporary reversal is one where, if you are provided payment relief for up to 6 months, you will be able to resume regular payments at the end of the period and repay all the payments you missed within the following 12 months. Prove your case that the reversal is temporary in writing.

If you can't meet these conditions, your financial reversal is considered permanent by the lender. If the change in your status is permanent, it means that you can resume regular payments only if the payment is permanently reduced. This requires modifying the loan contract by reducing the interest rate, extending the term, or both.

Keep in mind the position of the lender. While some actions you can take on your own, such as selling your house, other actions have to be negotiated with the lender. You will always be more successful—in any negotiation—if you know where the other party is coming from and understand their position.

The lender's main objective is to minimize their loss, of course. The action that minimizes loss to the lender depends on the equity you have in your house, on whether your financial reversal is temporary or permanent, and on whether or not you are dealing in good faith with the lender.

Let's say you have substantial equity in your house. If you do, the least costly action to the lender may be foreclosure. While foreclosure is expensive, the lender is entitled to be reimbursed from the sales proceeds for all foreclosure costs plus all unpaid interest and principal. If you have enough equity, the lender can be confident they won't lose any money on the deal.

While foreclosure makes the lender whole, it's a financial disaster for you. Your equity is gone, you incur the costs of moving, and your credit is ruined. You should always avoid foreclosure, even if it means selling your house.

If your financial problems are temporary—and you can persuade the lender they are temporary—the lender may be willing to provide payment relief (or a "forebearance"). The lender will probably prefer to keep your loan rather than to foreclose on it. The burden of proof is on you in this situation to demonstrate that the relief will really work, though.

If your financial problems are permanent, sell the house before you begin accumulating delinquencies. In a high-equity situation, there is little hope that the lender will agree to modify the loan contract, so don't waste your time even trying. Focus instead on making a bad situation better and get out while you can. If you sell, at least you'll retain your equity and your credit rating.

If you have little or no equity, and your financial problems are temporary, it will be easier to persuade the lender to offer payment relief. With no equity, the foreclosure alternative is more costly to the lender.

If your financial problems are permanent, the lender probably will be willing to accept either a "short sale" or a "deed in lieu of foreclosure." With a short sale, you sell the house and pay the lender the sales proceeds; with a deed in lieu of foreclosure the lender takes title to the house. In both cases your debt obligation usually is fully discharged. (It does appear on your credit report, but it's not as bad a mark as a foreclosure.) The lender who can get all or most of his money back in these ways probably will not be willing to modify your original loan contract. Remember, no lender wants or needs to do you a favor; they just want their money. (Wouldn't you?)

If your equity in the house is negative (you owe more than the house is worth) but you want to remain there, the lender may give you payment relief, or make a contract modification if necessary to make the payment manageable. With negative equity, these may be the least costly options for the lender.

"I went to the dentist and the hygienist was crying," said Paco Torch, president of Torch Mortgage Corporation. In his fourteen-year lending career Paco has also written policies and procedures for federal law and is a certified trainer for the NAMB. "I asked her what was wrong. She explained that her husband just been laid off because his company was going out of business, and she was afraid they'd lose their home. After I calmed her down, I told her to call her mortgage company immediately to explain the situation. She called, and the lender agreed to cut the payments in half for six months while her husband found another job. In my experience most mortgage lenders will work with you; as long as you have a good payment record and you talk to them up front, they'll help you out. After all, they don't want the house back—they have a vested interest in trying to help you."

In August 2007, President Bush and the FHA announced a new program designed to help delinquent borrowers who have been victims of higher payments due to ARM resets. If you were comfortably making your payments before the increase, you may be entitled to refinance through FHA—even if you're currently delinquent!

The program, called FHA*Secure*, is designed to run through December 2008, and will save an estimated 240,000 people per year from foreclosure. If you fit this category, this program can save you thousands in lost equity and payments—and probably save your home!

Here's the key: if you're having financial difficulties, start working on a plan to solve the problem as early as you can, and talk to your lender early on. Don't wait until it's too late!

 When you're facing foreclosure, you have several options:

- **Reinstate the loan.** If you owe relatively little in back payments and can obtain financial help from family and friends, this is usually the best option.
- **Negotiate with the lenders for a forbearance.** Again, if you have a fairly solid financial future and have experienced a temporary setback, the lender may agree to a forbearance and may provide a realistic payment schedule.
- **Sell the property.** When you can't afford the mortgage payments and probably won't be able to afford the payments

in the near future, selling the property and getting your equity out of it is usually the best move.

- **Refinance the mortgage.** If you have substantial equity built up in your property, you may be able to refinance your way out of foreclosure by taking out a mortgage to consolidate your outstanding debt.
- **Sell short.** You may be able to convince the lender to accept less than full payment of the loan, especially if the loan is insured.
- **Sell to an investor.** If you have some equity in the home—but not enough time to market and sell the property before losing it in foreclosure—consider selling it to an investor. The investor may allow you to rent back the property or offer you a lease-option agreement.
- **Take out a second mortgage.** If you can't negotiate a forbearance and don't have the cash available to reinstate the mortgage, you may be able to take out a second mortgage from a private lender to reinstate the first mortgage. (However, you then have two mortgage payments.)
- **Offer a deed in lieu of foreclosure.** Negative equity is a good sign that you may benefit by offering the lender a deed in lieu of foreclosure. With a deed in lieu of foreclosure, you give the property deed to the lender, and the lender forgives any remaining debt. (Lenders do not always agree to such deals, but it's definitely worth asking.)
- **File for bankruptcy.** Filing for bankruptcy typically only delays the inevitable—and leaves you with additional attorney fees to pay and a serious blemish on your credit report.
- **Rent It Out.** If you can't sell it, and are going to lose it, then your best option may be to rent it out and try to cover the costs. Rent something in the meantime that is more cost effective.
- **Do nothing.** Doing nothing is the worst course of action. You lose any equity you have built up, your credit rating takes a serious blow, and you lose the house anyway. Take action—the sooner the better.

Many localities have a mandatory redemption period after the foreclosure sale that provides you with additional time to take action. In some cases, the redemption period lasts as long as six to twelve months. During this time you still have control of the house; no one can kick you out or evict you. You may still be able to sell your house and cash out some of the equity in it. Know your rights.

Many states and localities have developed funds or programs to assist people facing foreclosure. Similar to the FHASecure program, they will help save your home and get you back on track.

We have been blessed to assist thousands of people with their dream of homeownership. It is our hope that you have discovered a whole new insight as to how the industry works, and by taking the right steps, how you to can beat the Mortgage Myths—and save thousands on your home financing.

Best wishes, and we look forward to hearing about your success!

Appendix

All forms and required disclosures, as well as various calculators and other resources, can be found at www.TheMortgageMyths.com. These are current as of date of publication. As these forms and disclosures tend to change periodically, any updates can be found at that same resource web site.

All forms and disclosures provided by Greatland Corporation (www .Greatland.com).

Consumer Handbook on Adjustable Rate Mortgages

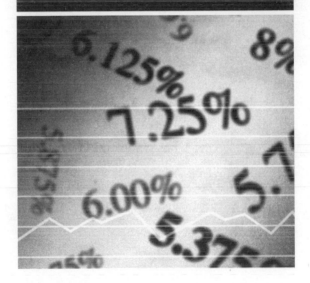

This booklet was originally prepared in consultation with the following organizations:

- American Bankers Association
- America's Community Bankers
  (formerly the National Council of Savings Institutions
  and the U.S. League of Savings Institutions)
- Comptroller of the Currency
- Consumer Federation of America
- Credit Union National Association, Inc.
- Federal Deposit Insurance Corporation
- Federal Reserve Board's Consumer
  Advisory Council
- Federal Trade Commission
- Independent Bankers Association of America
- Mortgage Bankers Association of America
- Mortgage Insurance Companies of America
- National Association of Federal Credit Unions
- National Association of Home Builders
- National Association of Realtors
- National Credit Union Administration
- Office of Special Advisor to the President for
  Consumer Affairs
- The Consumer Bankers Association
- U.S. Department of Housing and
  Urban Development

With special thanks to Fannie Mae.

The Federal Reserve Board and the Office of Thrift Supervision prepared this booklet on adjustable-rate mortgages (ARMs) in response to a request from the House Committee on Banking, Finance and Urban Affairs (currently, the Committee on Financial Services) and in consultation with many other agencies and trade and consumer groups. It is designed to help consumers understand an important and complex mortgage option available to homebuyers.

We believe a fully informed consumer is in the best position to make a sound economic choice. If you are buying a home and looking for a home loan, this booklet will provide useful basic information about ARMs. It cannot provide all the answers you will need, but we believe it is a good starting point.

PEOPLE ARE ASKING . . .

"Some newspaper ads for home loans show surprisingly low rates. Are these loans for real, or is there a catch?"

Some of the ads you see are for adjustable-rate mortgages (ARMs). These loans may have low rates for a short time—maybe only for the first year. After that, the rates may be adjusted on a regular basis. This means that the interest rate and the amount of the monthly payment may go up or down.

"Will I know in advance how much my payment may go up?"

With an adjustable-rate mortgage, your future monthly payment is uncertain. Some types of ARMs put a ceiling on your payment increase or interest-rate increase from one period to the next. Virtually all types must put a ceiling on rate increases over the life of the loan.

"Is an ARM the right type of loan for me?"

That depends on your financial situation and the terms of the ARM. ARMs carry risks in periods of rising interest rates, but they can be cheaper over a longer term if interest rates decline. You will be able to answer the question better once you understand more about ARMs. This booklet should help.

Mortgages have changed, and so have the questions that consumers need to ask and have answered.

Shopping for a mortgage used to be a relatively simple process. Most home mortgage loans had interest rates that did not change over the life of the loan. Choosing among these fixed-rate mortgage loans meant comparing interest rates, monthly payments, fees, prepayment penalties, and due-on-sale clauses.

Today, many loans have interest rates (and monthly payments) that can change from time to time. To compare one ARM with another or with a fixed-rate mortgage, you need to know about indexes, margins, discounts, caps, negative amortization, and convertibility. You need to consider the maximum amount your monthly payment could increase. Most important, you need to compare what might happen to your mortgage costs with your future ability to pay.

This booklet explains how ARMs work and some of the risks and advantages to borrowers that ARMs introduce. It discusses features that can help reduce the risks and gives some pointers about advertising and other ways you can get information from lenders. Important ARM terms are defined in a glossary on page 11. And a checklist at the end of the booklet should help you ask lenders the right questions and figure out whether an ARM is right for you. Asking lenders to fill out the checklist is a good way to get the information you need to compare mortgages.

2

WHAT IS AN ARM?

With a fixed-rate mortgage, the interest rate stays the same during the life of the loan. But with an ARM, the interest rate changes periodically, usually in relation to an index, and payments may go up or down accordingly.

Lenders generally charge lower initial interest rates for ARMs than for fixed-rate mortgages. This makes the ARM easier on your pocketbook at first than a fixed-rate mortgage for the same amount. It also means that you might qualify for a larger loan because lenders sometimes make the decision about whether to extend a loan on the basis of your current income and the first year's payments. Moreover, your ARM could be less expensive over a long period than a fixed-rate mortgage— for example, if interest rates remain steady or move lower.

Against these advantages, you have to weigh the risk that an increase in interest rates would lead to higher monthly payments in the future. It's a trade-off—you get a lower rate with an ARM in exchange for assuming more risk.

Here are some questions you need to consider:

- Is my income likely to rise enough to cover higher mortgage payments if interest rates go up?

- Will I be taking on other sizable debts, such as a loan for a car or school tuition, in the near future?

- How long do I plan to own this home? (If you plan to sell soon, rising interest rates may not pose the problem they do if you plan to own the house for a long time.)

- Can my payments increase even if interest rates generally do not increase?

HOW ARMs WORK: THE BASIC FEATURES

The Adjustment Period

With most ARMs, the interest rate and monthly payment change every year, every three years, or every five years. However, some ARMs have more frequent rate and payment changes. The period between one rate change and the next is called the "adjustment period." A loan with an adjustment period of one year is called a one-year ARM, and the interest rate can change once every year.

The Index

Most lenders tie ARM interest-rate changes to changes in an "index rate." These indexes usually go up and down with the general movement of interest rates. If the index rate moves up, so does your mortgage rate in most circumstances, and you will probably have to make higher monthly payments. On the other hand, if the index rate goes down, your monthly payment may go down.

3

Lenders base ARM rates on a variety of indexes. Among the most common indexes are the rates on one-, three-, or five-year Treasury securities. Another common index is the national or regional average cost of funds to savings and loan associations. A few lenders use their own cost of funds as an index, which gives them more control than using other indexes. You should ask what index will be used and how often it changes. Also ask how it has fluctuated in the past and where it is published.

The Margin

To determine the interest rate on an ARM, lenders add to the index rate a few percentage points called the "margin." The amount of the margin may differ from one lender to another, but it is usually constant over the life of the loan.

Index rate + margin = ARM interest rate

Let's say, for example, that you are comparing ARMs offered by two different lenders. Both ARMs are for 30 years and have a loan amount of $65,000. (All the examples used in this booklet are based on this amount for a 30-year term. Note that the payment amounts shown here do not include taxes, insurance, or similar items.)

Both lenders use the rate on one-year Treasury securities as the index. But the first lender uses a 2% margin, and the second lender uses a 3% margin. Here is how that difference in the margin would affect your initial monthly payment.

Home sale price $ 85,000
Less down payment   - 20,000
Mortgage amount $ 65,000

Mortgage term   30 years

FIRST LENDER
One-year index = 8%
Margin = 2%
ARM interest rate = 10%
Monthly payment @ 10% = $ 570.42

SECOND LENDER
One-year index = 8%
Margin = 3%
ARM interest rate = 11%
Monthly payment @ 11% = $ 619.01

In comparing ARMs, look at both the index and margin for each program. Some indexes have higher values, but they are usually used with lower margins. Be sure to discuss the margin with your lender.

4

CONSUMER CAUTIONS *

Discounts

Some lenders offer initial ARM rates that are lower than their "standard" ARM rates (that is, lower than the sum of the index and the margin). Such rates, called discounted rates, are often combined with large initial loan fees ("points") and with much higher rates after the discount expires.

Very large discounts are often arranged by the seller. The seller pays an amount to the lender so that the lender can give you a lower rate and lower payments early in the mortgage term. This arrangement is referred to as a "seller buydown." The seller may increase the sales price of the home to cover the cost of the buydown.

A lender may use a low initial rate to decide whether to approve your loan, based on your ability to afford it. You should be careful to consider whether you will be able to afford payments in later years when the discount expires and the rate is adjusted.

Here is how a discount might work. Let's assume that the lender's "standard" one-year ARM rate (index rate plus margin) is currently 10%. But your lender is offering an 8% rate for the first year. With the 8% rate, your first-year monthly payment would be $476.95.

But don't forget that with a discounted ARM, your initial payment will probably remain at $476.95 for only 12 months—and that any savings during the discount period may be made up during the life of the mortgage or be included in the price of the house. In fact, if you buy a home using this kind of loan, you run the risk of . . .

Payment Shock

Payment shock may occur if your mortgage payment rises very sharply at the first adjustment. Let's see what would happen in the second year if the rate on your discounted 8% ARM were to rise to the 10% "standard" rate.

ARM Interest Rate	Monthly Payment
1st year (w/discount) @ 8%	$ 476.95
2nd year @ 10%	$ 568.82

As the example shows, even if the index rate were to stay the same, your monthly payment would go up from $476.95 to $568.82 in the second year.

Suppose that the index rate increases 2% in one year and the ARM rate rises to 12%.

ARM Interest Rate	Monthly Payment
1st year (w/discount) @ 8%	$ 476.95
2nd year @ 12%	$ 665.43

5

That's an increase of almost $200 in your monthly payment. You can see what might happen if you choose an ARM because of a low initial rate. You can protect yourself from large increases by looking for a mortgage with features, described next, that may reduce this risk.

HOW CAN I REDUCE MY RISK?

Besides offering an overall rate ceiling, most ARMs also have "caps" that protect borrowers from extreme increases in monthly payments. Others allow borrowers to convert an ARM to a fixed-rate mortgage. While they may offer real benefits, these ARMs may also cost more, or may add special features such as negative amortization.

Interest-Rate Caps

An interest-rate cap places a limit on the amount your interest rate can increase. Interest caps come in two versions:

- Periodic caps, which limit the interest-rate increase from one adjustment period to the next; and
- Overall caps, which limit the interest-rate increase over the life of the loan.

By law, virtually all ARMs must have an overall cap. Many have a periodic cap.

Let's suppose you have an ARM with a periodic interest-rate cap of 2%. At the first adjustment, the index rate goes up 3%. The example shows what happens.

ARM Interest Rate	Monthly Payment
1st year @ 10%	$ 570.42
2nd year @ 13% (without cap)	$ 717.12
2nd year @ 12% (with cap)	$ 667.30
Difference in 2nd year between payment with cap and payment without = $ 49.82	

A drop in interest rates does not always lead to a drop in monthly payments. In fact, with some ARMs that have interest-rate caps, your payment amount may *increase* even though the index rate has stayed the same or declined. This may happen when an interest-rate cap has been holding your interest rate down below the sum of the index plus margin. If a rate cap holds down your interest rate, increases to the index that were not imposed because of the cap may carry over to future rate adjustments.

6

With some ARMs, payments may increase even if the index rate stays the same or declines.

The following example shows how carryovers work. The index increased 3% during the first year. Because this ARM limits rate increases to 2% at any one time, the rate is adjusted by only 2%, to 12% for the second year. However, the remaining 1% increase in the index carries over to the next time the lender can adjust rates. So when the lender adjusts the interest rate for the third year, the rate increases 1%, to 13%, even though there is no change in the index during the second year.

ARM Interest Rate	Monthly Payment
First year @ 10%	$ 570.42
If index rises 3% . . .	
2nd year @ 12% (with 2% rate cap)	$ 667.30
If index stays the same for the 3rd year @ 13%	$ 716.56
Even though the index stays the same in 3rd year, payment goes up $ 49.26	

In general, the rate on your loan can go up at any scheduled adjustment date when the lender's standard ARM rate (the index plus the margin) is higher than the rate you are paying before that adjustment.

The next example shows how a 5% overall rate cap would affect your loan.

ARM Interest Rate	Monthly Payment
1st year @ 10%	$ 570.42
10th year @ 15% (with cap)	$ 813.00

Let's say that the index rate increases 1% in each of the next nine years. With a 5% overall cap, your payment would never exceed $813.00—compared to the $1,008.64 that it would have reached in the tenth year based on a 19% interest rate.

Payment Caps

Some ARMs include payment caps, which limit your monthly payment increase at the time of each adjustment, usually to a percentage of the previous payment. In other words, with a 7½% payment cap, a payment of $100 could increase to no more than $107.50 in the first adjustment period, and to no more than $115.56 in the second.

7

Let's assume that your rate changes in the first year by 2 percentage points but your payments can increase by no more than 7½% in any one year. Here's what your payments would look like:

ARM Interest Rate	Monthly Payment
1st year @ 10%	$ 570.42
2nd year @ 12% (without payment cap)	$ 667.30
2nd year @ 12% (with 7½% payment cap)	$ 613.20
Difference in monthly payment = $ 54.10	

Many ARMs with payment caps do not have periodic interest-rate caps.

Negative Amortization

If your ARM includes a payment cap, be sure to find out about "negative amortization." Negative amortization means that the mortgage balance increases. It occurs whenever your monthly mortgage payments are not large enough to pay all of the interest due on your mortgage.

Because payment caps limit only the amount of payment increases, and not interest-rate increases, payments sometimes do not cover all of the interest due on your loan. This means that the interest shortage in your payment is automatically added to your debt, and interest may be charged on that amount. You might therefore owe the lender more later in the loan term than you did at the start. However, an increase in the value of your home may make up for the increase in what you owe.

The next illustration uses the figures from the preceding example to show how negative amortization works during one year. Your first 12 payments of $570.42, based on a 10% interest rate, paid the balance down to $64,638.72 at the end of the first year. The rate goes up to 12% in the second year. But because of the 7½% payment cap, your payments are not high enough to cover all the interest. The interest shortage is added to your debt (with interest on it), which produces negative amortization of $420.90 during the second year.

Beginning loan amount = $ 65,000
Loan amount at end of 1st year = $ 64,638.72
Negative amortization during 2nd year = $ 420.90
Loan amount at end of 2nd year = $ 65,059.62 ($ 64,638.72 + $ 420.90)
(If you sold your house at this point, you would owe almost $ 60 more than you originally borrowed.)

8

To sum up, the payment cap limits increases in your monthly payment by deferring some of the increase in interest. Eventually, you will have to repay the higher remaining loan balance at the ARM rate then in effect. When this happens, there may be a substantial increase in your monthly payment.

Some mortgages include a cap on negative amortization. The cap typically limits the total amount you can owe to 125% of the original loan amount. When that point is reached, monthly payments may be set to fully repay the loan over the remaining term, and your payment cap may not apply. You may limit negative amortization by voluntarily increasing your monthly payment.

Be sure to discuss negative amortization with the lender to understand how it will apply to your loan.

Prepayment and Conversion

If you get an ARM and your financial circumstances change, you may decide that you don't want to risk any further changes in the interest rate and payment amount. When you are considering an ARM, ask for information about prepayment and conversion.

Prepayment. Some agreements may require you to pay special fees or penalties if you pay off the ARM early. Many ARMs allow you to pay the loan in full or in part without penalty whenever the rate is adjusted. Prepayment details are sometimes negotiable. If so, you may want to negotiate for no penalty, or for as low a penalty as possible.

Conversion. Your agreement with the lender may include a clause that lets you convert the ARM to a fixed-rate mortgage at designated times. When you convert, the new rate is generally set at the current market rate for fixed-rate mortgages.

The interest rate or up-front fees may be somewhat higher for a convertible ARM. Also, a convertible ARM may require a special fee at the time of conversion.

9

WHERE TO GET INFORMATION

Before you actually apply for a loan and pay a fee, ask for all the information the lender has on the loan you are considering. It is important that you understand index rates, margins, caps, and other ARM features such as negative amortization. You can get helpful information from advertisements and disclosures, which are subject to certain federal standards.

Advertising

Your first information about mortgages probably will come from newspaper advertisements placed by builders, real estate brokers, and lenders. Although this information can be helpful, keep in mind that the ads are designed to make the mortgage look as attractive as possible. These ads may play up low initial interest rates and monthly payments, without emphasizing that those rates and payments later could increase substantially. So get all the facts.

A federal law, the Truth in Lending Act, requires mortgage advertisers, once they begin advertising specific terms, to give further information on the loan. For example, if they want to show the interest rate or payment amount on the loan, they must also tell you the annual percentage rate (APR) and whether that rate may go up. The APR, the cost of your credit as a yearly rate, reflects more than just a low initial rate. It takes into account interest, points paid on the loan, any loan origination fee, and any mortgage insurance premiums you may have to pay.

Ads may play up low initial rates. Get all the facts.

Disclosures From Lenders

Federal law requires the lender to give you information about ARMs, in most cases before you apply for a loan. The lender also is required to give you information when you apply for a mortgage. You should get a written summary of important terms and costs of the loan. Some of these are the finance charge, the APR, and the payment terms.

Read information from lenders—and ask questions— before committing yourself.

Selecting a mortgage may be the most important financial decision you will make, and you are entitled to all the information you need to make the right decision. Don't hesitate to ask questions about ARM features when you talk to lenders, real estate brokers, sellers, and your attorney, and keep asking until you get clear and complete answers. The checklist at the back of this booklet is intended to help you compare terms on different loans.

10

GLOSSARY

Adjustable-Rate Mortgage (ARM)

A mortgage for which the interest rate is not fixed, but changes during the life of the loan in line with movements in an index rate. You may also see ARMs referred to as *AMLs (adjustable-mortgage loans)* or *VRMs (variable-rate mortgages).*

Annual Percentage Rate (APR)

A measure of the cost of credit, expressed as a yearly rate. It includes interest as well as other charges. Because all lenders follow the same rules when calculating the APR, it provides consumers with a good basis for comparing the cost of loans, including mortgages.

Buydown

With a buydown, the seller pays an amount to the lender so that the lender can give you a lower rate and lower payments, usually for an early period in an ARM. The seller may increase the sales price to cover the cost of the buydown. Buydowns can occur in all types of mortgages, not just ARMs.

Cap

A limit on how much the interest rate or the monthly payment may change, either at each adjustment or during the life of the mortgage. Payment caps don't limit the amount of interest the lender is earning, so they may cause *negative amortization.*

Conversion Clause

A provision in some ARMs that allows you to change the ARM to a fixed-rate loan at some point during the term. Conversion is usually allowed at the end of the first adjustment period. At the time of the conversion, the new fixed rate is generally set at one of the rates then prevailing for fixed-rate mortgages. The conversion feature may be available at extra cost.

Discount

In an ARM with an initial rate discount, the lender gives up a number of percentage points in interest to give you a lower rate and lower payments for part of the mortgage term (usually for one year or less). After the discount period, the ARM rate will probably go up depending on the index rate.

Index

The index is the measure of interest-rate changes that the lender uses to decide how much the interest rate on an ARM will change over time. No one can be sure when an index rate will go up or down. To help you get an idea of how to compare different indexes, the following chart shows a few common indexes over an eleven-year period (1994–2004). As you can see, some index rates tend to be higher than others, and some more volatile. (But if a lender bases interest-rate adjustments on the average value of an index over time, your interest rate would not be as volatile.) You should ask your lender how the index for any ARM you are considering has changed in recent years, and where the index is reported.

11

Margin

The number of percentage points the lender adds to the index rate to calculate the ARM interest rate at each adjustment.

Negative Amortization

Amortization means that monthly payments are large enough to pay the interest and reduce the principal on your mortgage. Negative amortization occurs when the monthly payments do not cover all the interest cost. The interest cost that isn't covered is added to the unpaid principal balance. This means that even after making many payments, you could owe more than you did at the beginning of the loan. Negative amortization can occur when an ARM has a payment cap that results in monthly payments not high enough to cover the interest due.

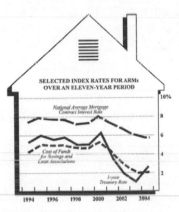

SELECTED INDEX RATES FOR ARMs
OVER AN ELEVEN-YEAR PERIOD

National Average Mortgage
Contract Interest Rate

Cost of Funds
for Savings and
Loan Associations

1-year
Treasury Rate

Points

One point is equal to 1 percent of the principal amount of your mortgage. For example, if the mortgage is for $65,000, one point equals $650. Lenders frequently charge points in both fixed-rate and adjustable-rate mortgages in order to increase the yield on the mortgage and to cover loan closing costs. These points are usually collected at closing and may be paid by the borrower or the home seller, or may be split between them.

12

MORTGAGE CHECKLIST

Ask your lender to help fill out this checklist.

	Mortgage A	Mortgage B
Mortgage amount	$ _____	$ _____

Basic Features for Comparison

	Mortgage A	Mortgage B
Fixed-rate annual percentage rate (the cost of your credit as a yearly rate, including both interest and other charges)	_____	_____
ARM annual percentage rate	_____	_____
Adjustment period	_____	_____
Index used and current rate	_____	_____
Margin	_____	_____
Initial payment without discount	_____	_____
Initial payment with discount (if any)	_____	_____
How long will discount last?	_____	_____
Interest-rate caps:		
periodic	_____	_____
overall	_____	_____
Payment caps	_____	_____
Negative amortization	_____	_____
Convertibility or prepayment privilege	_____	_____
Initial fees and charges	_____	_____

	Mortgage A	Mortgage B
Mortgage amount	_____	_____

Monthly Payment Amounts

	Mortgage A	Mortgage B
What will my monthly payment be after 12 months if the index rate:		
stays the same	_____	_____
goes up 2%	_____	_____
goes down 2%	_____	_____
What will my monthly payment be after 3 years if the index rate:		
stays the same	_____	_____
goes up 2% per year	_____	_____
goes down 2% per year	_____	_____

Take into account any caps on your mortgage and remember that it may run 30 years.

Revised: 2005

EQUAL HOUSING
OPPORTUNITY

ITEM 2196 (0510)

GREATLAND ■
To Order Call: 800-530-9393 □ Fax: 616-791-1131

Buying
Your
Home

Settlement Costs and
Helpful Information

WELCOME

A HUD GUIDE

TABLE OF CONTENTS

I. INTRODUCTION

II. BUYING & FINANCING A HOME

    A.   Role of the Real Estate Broker 3

    B.   Selecting an Attorney 3

    C.   Terms of the Agreement of Sale 4

    D.   Shopping for a Loan 5

    E.   Selecting a Settlement Agent 8

    F.   Securing Title Services 8

    G.   RESPA Disclosures 9

    H.   Processing Your Loan Application 10

    I.   RESPA Protection Against Illegal Referral Fees 11

    J.   Your Right to File Complaints 12

III. YOUR SETTLEMENT COSTS

    A.   Specific Settlement Costs 12

    B.   Calculating the Amount You Need at Settlement 16

    C.   Adjustments to Costs Shared by Buyer and Seller 17

    D.   HUD-1 Settlement Statement 18

IV. APPENDIX

    Consumer Information on Home Purchasing
and Related Topics 22

I. INTRODUCTION

CONGRATULATIONS! You have decided to buy a new home. This booklet will help you take this big financial step by describing the home buying, home financing, and settlement process. Lenders and mortgage brokers are required by federal law, the Real Estate Settlement Procedures Act ("RESPA"), to give you this booklet. You should receive it when applying for a loan, or within three business days afterwards. Real estate brokers frequently hand out this booklet as well.

You probably started the home buying process in one of two ways: you saw a home you were interested in buying or you consulted a lender to figure out how much money you could borrow before you found a home (sometimes called pre-qualifying). The next step is to sign an agreement of sale with the seller, followed by applying for a loan to purchase your new home. The final step is called "settlement" or "closing," where the legal title to the property is transferred to you.

At each of these steps you often have the opportunity to negotiate the terms, conditions and costs to your advantage. This booklet will highlight such opportunities. You will also need to shop carefully to get the best value for your money. There is no standard home buying process used in all localities. Your actual experience may vary from those described here. This booklet takes you through the general steps to buying a home, to eliminate, as much as possible, the mysteries of the settlement process.

II. BUYING & FINANCING A HOME

A. Role of the Real Estate Broker

Frequently, the first person you consult about buying a home is a real estate agent or broker. Although real estate brokers provide helpful advice on many aspects of home buying, **they may serve the interests of the seller, and not your interests as the buyer.** The most common practice is for the seller to hire the broker to find someone who will be willing to buy the home on terms and conditions that are acceptable to the seller. Therefore, the real estate broker you are dealing with may also represent the seller. However, you can hire your own real estate broker, known as a buyer's broker, to represent your interests. Also, in some states, agents and brokers are allowed to represent both buyer and seller.

Even if the real estate broker represents the seller, state real estate licensing laws usually require that the broker treat you fairly. If you have any questions concerning the behavior of an agent or broker, you should contact your State's Real Estate Commission or licensing department.

Sometimes, the real estate broker will offer to help you obtain a mortgage loan. He or she may also recommend that you deal with a particular lender, title company, attorney or settlement/closing agent. You are not required to follow the real estate broker's recommendation. You should compare the costs and services offered by other providers with those recommended by the real estate broker.

B. Selecting an Attorney

Before you sign an agreement of sale, you might consider asking an attorney to look it over and tell you if it protects your interests. If you have already signed your agreement of sale, you might still consider having an attorney review it. An attorney can also help you prepare for the settlement. In some areas attorneys act as settlement/closing agents or as escrow agents to handle the settlement. **An attorney who does this**

will not solely represent your interests, since, as settlement/closing agent, he or she may also be representing the seller, the lender and others as well.

Please note, in many areas of the country attorneys are not normally involved in the home sale. For example, escrow agents or escrow companies in western states handle the paperwork to transfer title without any attorney involvement.

If choosing an attorney, you should shop around and ask what services will be performed for what fee. Find out whether the attorney is experienced in representing home buyers. You may wish to ask the attorney questions such as:

◆ What is the charge for negotiating the agreement of sale, reviewing documents and giving advice concerning those documents, for being present at the settlement, or for reviewing instructions to the escrow agent or company?

◆ Will the attorney represent anyone other than you in the transaction?

◆ Will the attorney be paid by anyone other than you in the transaction?

C. Terms of the Agreement of Sale

If you receive this Booklet before you sign an agreement of sale, here are some important points to consider. The real estate broker probably will give you a preprinted form of agreement of sale. You may make changes or additions to the form agreement, but the seller must agree to every change you make. You should also agree with the seller on when you will move in and what appliances and personal property will be sold with the home.

◆ **Sales Price.** For most home purchasers, the sales price is the most important term. Recognize that other non-monetary terms of the agreement are also important.

◆ **Title.** "Title" refers to the legal ownership of your new home. The seller should provide title, free and clear of all claims by others against your new home. Claims by others against your new home are sometimes known as "liens" or "encumbrances." You may negotiate who will pay for the title search which will tell you whether the title is "clear."

◆ **Mortgage Clause.** The agreement of sale should provide that your deposit will be refunded if the sale has to be canceled because you are unable to get a mortgage loan. For example, your agreement of sale could allow the purchase to be canceled if you cannot obtain mortgage financing at an interest rate at or below a rate you specify in the agreement.

◆ **Pests.** Your lender will require a certificate from a qualified inspector stating that the home is free from termites and other pests and pest damage. You may want to reserve the right to cancel the agreement or seek immediate treatment and repairs by the seller if pest damage is found.

◆ **Home Inspection.** It is a good idea to have the home inspected. An inspection should determine the condition of the plumbing, heating, cooling and electrical systems. The structure should also be examined to assure it is sound and to determine the condition of the roof, siding, windows and doors. The lot should be graded away from the house so that water does not drain toward the house and into the basement.

Most buyers prefer to pay for these inspections so that the inspector is working for them, not the seller. You may wish to include in your agreement of sale the right to cancel, if you are not satisfied with the inspection results. In that case, you may want to re-negotiate for a lower sale price or require the seller to make repairs.

◆ **Lead-Based Paint Hazards in Housing Built Before 1978.** If you buy a home built before 1978, you have certain rights concerning lead-based paint and lead poisoning hazards. The seller or sales agent must give you the EPA pamphlet "Protect Your Family From Lead in Your Home" or other EPA-approved lead hazard information. The seller or sales agent must tell you what the seller actually knows about the home's lead-based paint or lead-based paint hazards and give you any relevant records or reports.

You have at least ten (10) days to do an inspection or risk assessment for lead-based paint or lead-based paint hazards. However, to have the right to cancel the sale based on the results of an inspection or risk assessment, you will need to negotiate this condition with the seller.

Finally, the seller must attach a disclosure form to the agreement of sale which will include a Lead Warning Statement. You, the seller, and the sales agent will sign an acknowledgment that these notification requirements have been satisfied.

◆ **Other Environmental Concerns.** Your city or state may have laws requiring buyers or sellers to test for environmental hazards such as leaking underground oil tanks, the presence of radon or asbestos, lead water pipes, and other such hazards, and to take the steps to clean-up any such hazards. You may negotiate who will pay for the costs of any required testing and/or clean-up.

◆ **Sharing of Expenses.** You need to agree with the seller about how expenses related to the property such as taxes, water and sewer charges, condominium fees, and utility bills, are to be divided on the date of settlement. Unless you agree otherwise, you should only be responsible for the portion of these expenses owed after the date of sale.

◆ **Settlement Agent/Escrow Agent or Company.** Depending on local practices, you may have an option to select the settlement agent or escrow agent or company. For states where an escrow agent or company will handle the settlement, the buyer, seller and lender will provide instructions.

◆ **Settlement Costs.** You can negotiate which settlement costs you will pay and which will be paid by the seller.

D. Shopping for a Loan

Your choice of lender and type of loan will influence not only your settlement costs, but also the monthly cost of your mortgage loan. There are many types of lenders and types of loans you can choose. You may be familiar with banks, savings associations, mortgage companies and credit unions, many of which provide home mortgage loans. You may find a listing of some mortgage lenders in the yellow pages or a listing of rates in your local newspaper.

◆ **Mortgage Brokers.** Some companies, known as "mortgage brokers" offer to find you a mortgage lender willing to make you a loan. **A mortgage broker may operate as an independent business and may not be operating as your "agent" or representative.** Your mortgage broker may be paid by the lender, you as the borrower, or both. You may wish to ask about the fees that the mortgage broker will receive for its services.

◆ **Government Programs.** You may be eligible for a loan insured through the Federal Housing Administration ("FHA") or guaranteed by the Department of Veterans Affairs or similar programs operated by cities or states. These programs usually require a smaller downpayment. Ask lenders about these programs. You can get more information about these programs from the agencies that run them. (See Appendix to this Booklet.)

◆ **CLOs.** Computer loan origination systems, or CLOs, are computer terminals sometimes available in real estate offices or other locations to help you sort through the various types of loans offered by different lenders. The CLO operator may charge a fee for the services the CLO offers. This fee may be paid by you or by the lender that you select.

◆ **Types of Loans.** Loans can have a fixed interest rate or a variable interest rate. Fixed rate loans have the same principal and interest payments during the loan term. Variable rate loans can have any one of a number of "indexes" and "margins" which determine how and when the rate and payment amount change. If you apply for a variable rate loan, also known as an adjustable rate mortgage ("ARM"), a disclosure and booklet required by the Truth in Lending Act will further describe the ARM. Most loans can be repaid over a term of 30 years or less. Most loans have equal monthly payments. The amounts can change from time to time on an ARM depending on changes in the interest rate. Some loans have short terms and a large final payment called a "balloon." You should shop for the type of home mortgage loan terms that best suit your needs.

◆ **Interest Rate, "Points" & Other Fees.** Often the price of a home mortgage loan is stated in terms of an interest rate, points, and other fees. A "point" is a fee that equals 1 percent of the loan amount. Points are usually paid to the lender, mortgage broker, or both, at the settlement or upon the completion of the escrow. Often, you can pay fewer points in exchange for a higher interest rate or more points for a lower rate. Ask your lender or mortgage broker about points and other fees.

A document called the Truth in Lending Disclosure Statement will show you the "Annual Percentage Rate" ("APR") and other payment information for the loan you have applied for. The APR takes into account not only the interest rate, but also the points, mortgage broker fees and certain other fees that you have to pay. Ask for the APR before you apply to help you shop for the loan that is best for you. Also ask if your loan will have a charge or a fee for paying all or part of the loan before payment is due ("prepayment penalty"). You may be able to negotiate the terms of the prepayment penalty.

◆ **Lender-Required Settlement Costs.** Your lender may require you to obtain certain settlement services, such as a new survey, mortgage insurance or title insurance. It may also order and charge you for other settlement-related services, such as the appraisal or credit report. A lender may also charge other fees, such as fees for loan processing, document preparation, underwriting, flood certification or an application fee. You may wish to ask for an estimate of fees and settlement costs before choosing a lender. Some lenders offer "no cost" or "no point" loans but normally cover these fees or costs by charging a higher interest rate.

◆ **Comparing Loan Costs.** Comparing APRs may be an effective way to shop for a loan. However, you must compare similar loan products for the same loan amount. For example, compare two 30-year fixed rate loans for $100,000. Loan A with an APR of 8.35% is less costly than Loan B with an APR of 8.65% over the loan term. However, before you decide on a loan, you should consider the up-front cash you will be required to pay for each of the two loans as well.

Another effective shopping technique is to compare identical loans with different up-front points and other fees. For example, if you are offered two 30-year fixed rate loans for $100,000 and at 8%, the monthly payments are the same, but the up-front costs are different:

Loan A - 2 points ($2,000) and lender required costs of $1,800 = $3,800 in costs.

Loan B - 2-1/4 points ($2,250) and lender required costs of $1,200 = $3,450 in costs.

A comparison of the up front costs shows Loan B requires $350 less in up-front cash than Loan A. However, your individual situation (how long you plan to stay in your house) and your tax situation (points can usually be deducted for the tax year that you purchase a house) may affect your choice of loans.

✦ **Lock-ins.** "Locking in" your rate or points at the time of application or during the processing of your loan will keep the rate and/or points from changing until settlement or closing of the escrow process. Ask your lender if there is a fee to lock-in the rate and whether the fee reduces the amount you have to pay for points. Find out how long the lock-in is good, what happens if it expires, and whether the lock-in fee is refundable if your application is rejected.

✦ **Tax and Insurance Payments.** Your monthly mortgage payment will be used to repay the money you borrowed plus interest. Part of your monthly payment may be deposited into an "escrow account" (also known as a "reserve" or "impound" account) so your lender or servicer can pay your real estate taxes, property insurance, mortgage insurance and/or flood insurance. **Ask your lender or mortgage broker if you will be required to set up an escrow or impound account for taxes and insurance payments.**

✦ **Transfer of Your Loan.** While you may start the loan process with a lender or mortgage broker, you could find that after settlement another company may be collecting the payments on your loan. Collecting loan payments is often known as "servicing" the loan. Your lender or broker will disclose whether it expects to service your loan or to transfer the servicing to someone else.

✦ **Mortgage Insurance.** Private mortgage insurance and government mortgage insurance protect the lender against default and enable the lender to make a loan which the lender considers a higher risk. Lenders often require mortgage insurance for loans where the downpayment is less than 20% of the sales price. You may be billed monthly, annually, by an initial lump sum, or some combination of these practices for your mortgage insurance premium. Ask your lender if mortgage insurance is required and how much it will cost. Mortgage insurance should not be confused with mortgage life, credit life or disability insurance, which are designed to pay off a mortgage in the event of the borrower's death or disability.

You may also be offered "lender paid" mortgage insurance ("LPMI"). Under LPMI plans, the lender purchases the mortgage insurance and pays the premiums to the insurer. The lender will increase your interest rate to pay for the premiums - but LPMI may reduce your settlement costs. You cannot cancel LPMI or government mortgage insurance during the life of your loan. However, it may be possible to cancel private mortgage insurance at some point, such as when your loan balance is reduced to a certain amount. Before you commit to paying for mortgage insurance, find out the specific requirements for cancellation.

✦ **Flood Hazard Areas.** Most lenders will not lend you money to buy a home in a flood hazard area unless you pay for flood insurance. Some government loan programs will not allow you to purchase a home that is located in a flood hazard area. Your lender may charge you a fee to check for flood hazards. You should be notified if flood insurance is required. If a change in flood insurance maps brings your home within a flood hazard area after your loan is made, your lender or servicer may require you to buy flood insurance at that time.

E. Selecting a Settlement Agent

Settlement practices vary from locality to locality, and even within the same county or city. Settlements may be conducted by lenders, title insurance companies, escrow companies, real estate brokers or attorneys for the buyer or seller. You may save money by shopping for the settlement agent.

In some parts of the country (particularly western states), settlement may be conducted by an escrow agent. The parties sign an escrow agreement which requires them to provide certain documents and funds to the agent. Unlike other types of settlement, the parties do not meet around a table to sign documents. Ask how your settlement will be handled.

F. Securing Title Services

Title insurance is usually required by the lender to protect the lender against loss resulting from claims by others against your new home. In some states, attorneys offer title insurance as part of their services in examining title and providing a title opinion. The attorney's fee may include the title insurance premium. In other states, a title insurance company or title agent directly provides the title insurance.

• **Owner's Policy.** A lender's title insurance policy **does not protect you.** Similarly, the prior owner's policy does not protect you. If you want to protect yourself from claims by others against your new home, you will need an owner's policy. When a claim does occur, it can be financially devastating to an owner who is uninsured. If you buy an owner's policy, it is usually much less expensive if you buy it at the same time and with the same insurer as the lender's policy.

• **Choice of Title Insurer.** Under RESPA, the seller may not require you, as a condition of the sale, to purchase title insurance from any particular title company. Generally, your lender will require title insurance from a company that is acceptable to it. In most cases you can shop for and choose a company that meets the lender's standards.

• **Review Initial Title Report.** In many areas, a few days or weeks before the settlement or closing of the escrow, the title insurance company will issue a "Commitment to Insure" or preliminary report or "binder" containing a summary of any defects in title which have been identified by the title search, as well as any exceptions from the title insurance policy's coverage. The commitment is usually sent to the lender for use until the title insurance policy is issued at or after the settlement. You can arrange to have a copy sent to you (or to your attorney) so that you can object if there are matters affecting the title which you did not agree to accept when you signed the agreement of sale.

• **Coverage & Cost Savings.** To save money on title insurance, compare rates among various title insurance companies. Ask what services and limitations on coverage are provided under each policy so that you can decide whether coverage purchased at a higher rate may be better for your needs. However, in many states, title insurance premium rates are established by the state and may not be negotiable. If you are buying a home which has changed hands within the last several years, ask your title company about a "reissue rate," which would be cheaper. If you are buying a newly constructed home, make certain your title insurance covers claims by contractors. These claims are known as "mechanics' liens" in some parts of the country.

◆ **Survey.** Lenders or title insurance companies often require a survey to mark the boundaries of the property. A survey is a drawing of the property showing the perimeter boundaries and marking the location of the house and other improvements. You may be able to avoid the cost of a complete survey if you can locate the person who previously surveyed the property and request an update. Check with your lender or title insurance company on whether an updated survey is acceptable.

G. RESPA Disclosures

One of the purposes of RESPA is to help consumers become better shoppers for settlement services. RESPA requires that borrowers receive disclosures at various times. Some disclosures spell out the costs associated with the settlement, outline lender servicing and escrow account practices and describe business relationships between settlement service providers.

◆ **Good Faith Estimate of Settlement Costs.** RESPA requires that, when you apply for a loan, the lender or mortgage broker give you a Good Faith Estimate of settlement service charges you will likely have to pay. If you do not get this Good Faith Estimate when you apply, the lender or mortgage broker must mail or deliver it to you within the next three business days.

Be aware that the amounts listed on the Good Faith Estimate are only estimates. Actual costs may vary. Changing market conditions can affect prices. Remember that the lender's estimate is not a guarantee. **Keep your Good Faith Estimate so you can compare it with the final settlement costs and ask the lender questions about any changes.**

◆ **Servicing Disclosure Statement.** RESPA requires the lender or mortgage broker to tell you in writing, when you apply for a loan or within the next three business days, whether it expects that someone else will be servicing your loan (collecting your payments).

◆ **Affiliated Business Arrangements.** Sometimes, several businesses that offer settlement services are owned or controlled by a common corporate parent. These businesses are known as "affiliates." When a lender, real estate broker, or other participant in your settlement refers you to an affiliate for a settlement service (such as when a real estate broker refers you to a mortgage broker affiliate), RESPA requires the referring party to give you an Affiliated Business Arrangement Disclosure. This form will remind you that you are generally not required, with certain exceptions, to use the affiliate and are free to shop for other providers.

◆ **HUD-1 Settlement Statement.** One business day before the settlement, you have the right to inspect the HUD-1 Settlement Statement. This statement itemizes the services provided to you and the fees charged to you. This form is filled out by the settlement agent who will conduct the settlement. Be sure you have the name, address, and telephone number of the settlement agent if you wish to inspect this form. The fully completed HUD-1 Settlement Statement generally must be delivered or mailed to you at or before the settlement. In cases where there is no settlement meeting, the escrow agent will mail you the HUD-1 after settlement, and you have no right to inspect it one day before settlement.

♦ **Escrow Account Operation & Disclosures.** Your lender may require you to establish an escrow or impound account to assure that your taxes and insurance premiums are paid on time. If so, you will probably have to pay an initial amount at the settlement to start the account and an additional amount with each month's regular payment. Your escrow account payments may include a "cushion" or an extra amount to ensure that the lender has enough money to make the payments when due. RESPA limits the amount of the cushion to a maximum of two months of escrow payments.

At the settlement or within the next 45 days, the person servicing your loan must give you an initial escrow account statement. That form will show all of the payments which are expected to be deposited into the escrow account and all of the disbursements which are expected to be made from the escrow account during the year ahead. Your lender or servicer will review the escrow account annually and send you a disclosure each year which shows the prior year's activity and any adjustments necessary in the escrow payments that you will make in the forthcoming year.

H. Processing Your Loan Application

There are several federal laws which provide you with protection during the processing of your loan. The Equal Credit Opportunity Act ("ECOA"), the Fair Housing Act, and the Fair Credit Reporting Act ("FCRA") prohibit discrimination and provide you with the right to certain credit information.

♦ **No Discrimination.** ECOA prohibits lenders from discriminating against credit applicants on the basis of race, color, religion, national origin, sex, marital status, age, the fact that all or part of the applicant's income comes from any public assistance program, or the fact that the applicant has exercised any right under any federal consumer credit protection law. To help government agencies monitor ECOA compliance, your lender or mortgage broker must request certain information regarding your race, sex, marital status and age when taking your loan application.

The Fair Housing Act also prohibits discrimination in residential real estate transactions on the basis of race, color, religion, sex, handicap, familial status or national origin. This prohibition applies to both the sale of a home to you and the decision by a lender to give you a loan to help pay for that home. Finally, your locality or state may also have a law which prohibits discrimination.

Frequently, there are differences in the types and amounts of settlement costs charged to the borrower - for example, some borrowers are charged greater fees for mortgages depending on their credit worthiness. These differences may be justified or they may be unlawfully discriminatory. It is important that you examine your settlement documents closely, especially lines 808-811 on the HUD-1 Settlement Statement, and do not hesitate to compare your settlement costs with those of your friends and neighbors.

If you feel you have been discriminated against by a lender or anyone else in the home buying process, you may file a private legal action against that person or complain to a state, local or federal administrative agency. You may want to talk to an attorney; or you may want to ask the federal agency that enforces ECOA (the Board of Governors of the Federal Reserve System) or the Fair Housing Act (HUD) about your rights under these laws.

◆ **Prompt Action/Notification of Action Taken.** Your lender or mortgage broker must act on your application and inform you of the action taken no later than 30 days after it receives your **completed** application. Your application will not be considered complete, and the 30 day period will not begin, until you provide to your lender or mortgage broker all of the material and information requested.

◆ **Statement of Reasons for Denial.** If your application is denied, ECOA requires your lender or mortgage broker to give you a statement of the specific reasons why it denied your application or tell you how you can obtain such a statement. The notice will also tell you which federal agency to contact if you think the lender or mortgage broker has illegally discriminated against you.

◆ **Obtaining Your Credit Report.** The Fair Credit Reporting Act ("FCRA") requires a lender or mortgage broker that denies your loan application to tell you whether it based its decision on information contained in your credit report. If that information was a reason for the denial, the notice will tell you where you can get a free copy of the credit report. You have the right to dispute the accuracy or completeness of any information in your credit report. If you dispute any information, the credit reporting agency that prepared the report must investigate free of charge and notify you of the results of the investigation.

◆ **Obtaining Your Appraisal.** The lender needs to know if the value of your home is enough to secure the loan. To get this information, the lender typically hires an appraiser, who gives a professional opinion about the value of your home. ECOA requires your lender or mortgage broker to tell you that you have a right to get a copy of the appraisal report. The notice will also tell you how and when you can ask for a copy.

I. RESPA Protection Against Illegal Referral Fees

RESPA was enacted because Congress felt that consumers needed protection from "...unnecessarily high settlement charges caused by certain abusive practices that have developed in some areas of the country." Some of the practices Congress was concerned about are discussed below. Most professionals in the settlement business provide good service and do not engage in these practices.

◆ **Prohibited Fees.** It is illegal under RESPA for anyone to pay or receive a fee, kickback or anything of value because they agree to refer settlement service business to a particular person or organization. For example, your mortgage lender may not pay your real estate broker $250 for referring you to the lender. It is also illegal for anyone to accept a fee or part of a fee for services if that person has not actually performed settlement services for the fee. For example, a lender may not add to a third party's fee, such as an appraisal fee, and keep the difference.

◆ **Permitted Payments.** RESPA does not prevent title companies, mortgage brokers, appraisers, attorneys, settlement/closing agents and others, who actually perform a service in connection with the mortgage loan or the settlement, from being paid for the reasonable value of their work. If a participant in your settlement appears to be taking a fee without having done any work, you should advise that person or company of the RESPA referral fee prohibitions. You may also speak with your attorney or complain to a regulator listed in the Appendix to this Booklet.

◆ **Penalties.** It is a crime for someone to pay or receive an illegal referral fee. The penalty can be a fine, imprisonment or both. You may be entitled to recover three times the amount of the charge for any settlement service by bringing a private lawsuit. If you are successful, the court may also award you court costs and your attorney's fees.

J. Your Right to File Complaints

◆ **Private Lawsuits.** If you have a problem, the best place to have it fixed is at its source (the lender, settlement agent, broker, etc.). If that approach fails and you think you have suffered because of a violation of RESPA, ECOA or any other law, you may be entitled to sue in a federal or state court. This is a matter you should discuss with your attorney.

◆ **Government Agencies.** Most settlement service providers are supervised by a governmental agency at the local, state and/or federal level, some of which are listed in the Appendix to this Booklet. Your state's Attorney General may have a consumer affairs division. If you feel that a provider of settlement services has violated RESPA or any other law, you can complain to that agency or association. You may also send a copy of your complaint to the HUD Office of Consumer & Regulatory Affairs. The address is listed in the Appendix.

◆ **Servicing Errors.** If you have a question any time during the life of your loan, RESPA requires the company collecting your loan payments (your "servicer") to respond to you. Write to your servicer and call it a "qualified written request under Section 6 of RESPA." A "qualified written request" should be a separate letter and not mailed with the payment coupon. Describe the problem and include your name and account number. The servicer must investigate and make appropriate corrections within 60 business days.

III. YOUR SETTLEMENT COSTS

A. Specific Settlement Costs

This part of the Booklet discusses the settlement services which you may be required to get and pay for and which are itemized in Section L of the HUD-1 Settlement Statement. You also will find a sample of the HUD-1 form to help you to understand the settlement transaction.

When shopping for settlement services, you can use this section as a guide, noting on it the possible services required by various lenders and the different fees quoted by service providers. Settlement costs can increase the cost of your loan, so compare carefully.

700. SALES/BROKER'S COMMISSION: This is the total dollar amount of the real estate broker's sales commission, which is usually paid by the seller. This commission is typically a percentage of the selling price of the home.

L. SETTLEMENT CHARGES	PAID FROM BORROWER'S FUNDS AT SETTLEMENT	PAID FROM SELLER'S FUNDS AT SETTLEMENT
700. TOTAL SALES/BROKER'S COMMISSION based on price $ @ % =		
Division of Commission (line 700) as follows:		
701. $ to		
702. $ to		
703. Commission paid at Settlement		
704.		

800. ITEMS PAYABLE IN CONNECTION WITH LOAN: These are the fees that lenders charge to process, approve and make the mortgage loan:

801. Loan Origination: This fee is usually known as a loan origination fee but sometimes is called a "point" or "points." It covers the lender's administrative costs in processing the loan. Often expressed as a percentage of the loan, the fee will vary among lenders. Generally, the buyer pays the fee, unless otherwise negotiated.

802. Loan Discount: Also often called "points" or "discount points," a loan discount is a one-time charge imposed by the lender or broker to lower the rate at which the lender or broker would otherwise offer the loan to you. Each "point" is equal to one percent of the mortgage amount. For example, if a lender charges two points on a $80,000 loan this amounts to a charge of $1,600.

803. Appraisal Fee: This charge pays for an appraisal report made by an appraiser.

804. Credit Report Fee: This fee covers the cost of a credit report, which shows your credit history. The lender uses the information in a credit report to help decide whether or not to approve your loan and how much money to lend you.

805. Lender's Inspection Fee: This charge covers inspections, often of newly constructed housing, made by employees of your lender or by an outside inspector. (Pest or other inspections made by companies other than the lender are discussed in line 1302.)

806. Mortgage Insurance Application Fee: This fee covers the processing of an application for mortgage insurance.

807. Assumption Fee: This is a fee which is charged when a buyer "assumes" or takes over the duty to pay the seller's existing mortgage loan.

808. Mortgage Broker Fee: Fees paid to mortgage brokers would be listed here. A CLO fee would also be listed here.

800. ITEMS PAYABLE IN CONNECTION WITH LOAN			
801. Loan Origination Fee	%		
802. Loan Discount	%		
803. Appraisal Fee	to		
804. Credit Report	to		
805. Lender's Inspection Fee			
806. Mortgage Insurance Application Fee to			
807. Assumption Fee			
808. Mortgage Broker Fee			
809.			
810.			
811.			

900. ITEMS REQUIRED BY LENDER TO BE PAID IN ADVANCE: You may be required to prepay certain items at the time of settlement, such as accrued interest, mortgage insurance premiums and hazard insurance premiums.

901. Interest: Lenders usually require borrowers to pay the interest that accrues from the date of settlement to the first monthly payment.

902. Mortgage Insurance Premium: The lender may require you to pay your first year's mortgage insurance premium or a lump sum premium that covers the life of the loan, in advance, at the settlement.

903. Hazard Insurance Premium: Hazard insurance protects you and the lender against loss due to fire, windstorm, and natural hazards. Lenders often require the borrower to bring to the settlement a paid-up first year's policy or to pay for the first year's premium at settlement.

904. Flood Insurance: If the lender requires flood insurance, it is usually listed here.

900. ITEMS REQUIRED BY LENDER TO BE PAID IN ADVANCE			
901. Interest from to @ $ /day			
902. Mortgage Insurance Premium for months to			
903. Hazard Insurance Premium for years to			
904. years to			
905.			

1000-1008. ESCROW ACCOUNT DEPOSITS: These lines identify the payment of taxes and/or insurance and other items that must be made at settlement to set up an escrow account. The lender is not allowed to collect more than a certain amount. The individual item deposits may overstate the amount that can be collected. The aggregate adjustment makes the correction in the amount on line 1008. It will be zero or a negative amount.

1000. RESERVES DEPOSITED WITH LENDER			
1001. Hazard Insurance	months @ $	per month	
1002. Mortgage insurance	months @ $	per month	
1003. City property taxes	months @ $	per month	
1004. County property taxes	months @ $	per month	
1005. Annual assessments	months @ $	per month	
1006.	months @ $	per month	
1007.	months @ $	per month	
1008. Aggregate Adjustment			

1100. TITLE CHARGES: Title charges may cover a variety of services performed by title companies and others. Your particular settlement may not include all of the items below or may include others not listed.

1101. Settlement or Closing Fee: This fee is paid to the settlement agent or escrow holder. Responsibility for payment of this fee should be negotiated between the seller and the buyer.

1102-1104. Abstract of Title Search, Title Examination, Title Insurance Binder: The charges on these lines cover the costs of the title search and examination.

1105. Document Preparation: This is a separate fee that some lenders or title companies charge to cover their costs of preparation of final legal papers, such as a mortgage, deed of trust, note or deed.

1106. Notary Fee: This fee is charged for the cost of having a person who is licensed as a notary public swear to the fact that the persons named in the documents did, in fact, sign them.

1100. TITLE CHARGES			
1101. Settlement or closing fee	to		
1102. Abstract or title search	to		
1103. Title examination	to		
1104. Title insurance binder	to		
1105. Document preparation	to		
1106. Notary fees	to		
1107. Attorney's fees	to		
(includes above item numbers;	)		
1108. Title insurance	to		
(includes above item numbers;	)		
1109. Lender's coverage	$		
1110. Owner's coverage	$		
1111.			
1112.			
1113.			

1107. Attorney's Fees: You may be required to pay for legal services provided to the lender, such as an examination of the title binder. Occasionally, the seller will agree in the agreement of sale to pay part of this fee. The cost of your attorney and/or the seller's attorney may also appear here. If an attorney's involvement is required by the lender, the fee will appear on this part of the form, or on lines 1111, 1112 or 1113.

1108. Title Insurance: The total cost of owner's and lender's title insurance is shown here.

1109. Lender's Title Insurance: The cost of the lender's policy is shown here.

1110. Owner's (Buyer's) Title Insurance: The cost of the owner's policy is shown here.

1200. GOVERNMENT RECORDING AND TRANSFER CHARGES: These fees may be paid by you or by the seller, depending upon your agreement of sale with the seller. The buyer usually pays the fees for legally recording the new deed and mortgage (line 1201). Transfer taxes, which in some localities are collected whenever property changes hands or a mortgage loan is made, can be quite large and are set by state and/or local governments. City, county and/or state tax stamps may have to be purchased as well (lines 1202 and 1203).

1200. GOVERNMENT RECORDING AND TRANSFER CHARGES		
1201. Recording fees: Deed $; Mortgage $; Releases $		
1202. City/county tax/stamps: Deed $; Mortgage $		
1203. State tax/stamps: Deed $; Mortgage $		
1204.		
1205.		

1300. ADDITIONAL SETTLEMENT CHARGES:

1301. Survey: The lender may require that a surveyor conduct a property survey. This is a protection to the buyer as well. Usually the buyer pays the surveyor's fee, but sometimes this may be paid by the seller.

1302. Pest and Other Inspections: This fee is to cover inspections for termites or other pest infestation of your home.

1303-1305. Lead-Based Paint Inspections: This fee is to cover inspections or evaluations for lead-based paint hazard risk assessments and may be on any blank line in the 1300 series.

1300. ADDITIONAL SETTLEMENT CHARGES		
1301. Survey to		
1302. Pest inspection to		
1303		
1304.		
1305.		

1400. TOTAL SETTLEMENT CHARGES: The sum of all fees in the borrower's column entitled "Paid from Borrower's Funds at Settlement" is placed here. This figure is then transferred to line 103 of Section J, "Settlement charges to borrower" in the **Summary of Borrower's Transaction** on page 1 of the HUD-1 Settlement Statement and added to the purchase price. The sum of all of the settlement fees paid by the seller are transferred to line 502 of Section K, **Summary of Seller's Transaction** on page 1 of the HUD-1 Settlement Statement.

1400. TOTAL SETTLEMENT CHARGES		
(enter on lines 103, Section J and 502, Section K)		

Paid Outside Of Closing ("POC"): Some fees may be listed on the HUD-1 to the left of the borrower's column and marked "P.O.C." Fees such as those for credit reports and appraisals are usually paid by the borrower before closing/settlement. They are additional costs to you. Other fees such as those paid by the lender to a mortgage broker or other settlement service providers may be paid after closing/settlement. These fees are usually included in the interest rate or other settlement charge. They are not an additional cost to you. These types of fees will not be added into the total on line 1400.

B. Calculating the Amount You Need at Settlement

The first page of the HUD-1 Settlement Statement summarizes all the costs and adjustments for the borrower and seller. Section J is the summary of the borrower's transaction and Section K is the summary of the seller's side of the transaction. You may receive a copy of the seller's side, but it is not required.

Section 100 summarizes the borrower's costs, such as the contract cost of the house, any personal property being purchased, and the total settlement charges owed by the borrower from Section L.

Beginning at line 106, adjustments are made for items (such as taxes, assessments, fuel) that the seller has previously paid. If you will benefit from these items after settlement, you will usually repay the seller for that portion of the cost.

Here is an example for you to use in making your own calculations:

J. SUMMARY OF BORROWER'S TRANSACTION	
100. GROSS AMOUNT DUE FROM BORROWER	
101. Contract sales price	100,000.00
102. Personal property	
103. Settlement charges to borrower (line 1400)	4,000.00
104.	
105.	
Adjustments for items paid by seller in advance	
106. City/town taxes to	
107. County taxes to	
108. Assessments 6/30 to 7/31 (owner's assn.)	40.00
109. **Fuel Oil** 25 gals. @ $1.00/gal.	25.00
110.	
111.	
112.	
120. GROSS AMOUNT DUE FROM BORROWER	104,065.00

Assume in this example, the cost of the house is $100,000 and the borrower's total settlement charges brought from Line 1400 of Section L are $4,000. Assume that the settlement date is July 1. Here the borrower has agreed to pay the seller for the $40 Home Owner's Association dues that have been paid for the month of July and for the 25 gallons of fuel oil left in the tank. This is added for a gross amount due from the borrower of $104,065.

200. AMOUNTS PAID BY OR IN BEHALF OF BORROWER	
201. Deposit of earnest money	2,000.00
202. Principal amount of new loan(s)	80,000.00
203. Existing loan(s) taken subject to	
204.	
205.	
206.	
207.	
208.	
209.	
Adjustments for items unpaid by seller	
210. City/town taxes to	
211. County taxes 1/1 to 6/30 $1,200/yr.	600.00
212. Assessments 1/1 to 6/30 $ 200/yr.	100.00
213.	
214.	
215.	
216.	
217.	
218.	
219.	
220. TOTAL PAID BY/FOR BORROWER	82,700.00

Section 200 lists the amount paid by the borrower or on behalf of the borrower. This will include the deposit of earnest money you put down with the agreement of sale, the loan(s) you are getting and any loan you may be assuming.

Beginning at line 210, adjustments are made for items that the seller owes (such as taxes, assessments) but for which you as the borrower will pay after settlement. The seller will usually pay you or credit you this portion at settlement.

In this example, assume the borrower paid an earnest deposit of $2,000 and is getting a loan for $80,000. A tax of $1,200 and an assessment of $200 are due at the end of the year. The seller will pay the borrower for six months or one-half of this amount. Line 220 shows the total $82,700 to be paid by or for the borrower.

Section 300 reflects the difference between the gross amount due from the borrower and the total amount paid by/for the borrower. Generally, line 303 will show the amount of cash the borrower must bring to settlement.

300. CASH AT SETTLEMENT FROM/TO BORROWER	
301. Gross Amount due from borrower (line 120)	104,065.00
302. Less amounts paid by/for borrower (line 220)	(82,700.00)
303. CASH (☒ FROM) (☐ TO) BORROWER	21,365.00

In this example, the borrower must bring $21,365.00 to settlement.

C. Adjustments to Costs Shared by Buyer and Seller

At settlement it is usually necessary to make an adjustment between buyer and seller for property taxes and other expenses. The adjustments between buyer and seller are shown in Sections J and K of the HUD-1 Settlement Statement. In the example given above, the taxes, which are payable annually, had not yet been paid when the settlement occurs on July 1. The borrower will have to pay a whole year's taxes on the following December 1. However, the seller lived in the house for the first six months of the year. Thus, one half of the year's taxes are to be paid by the seller. Accordingly, lines 211 and 511 on the HUD-1 Settlement Statement would read as follows:

211. County taxes	1/1/97	to	6/30/97	600.00
511. County taxes	1/1/97	to	6/30/97	600.00

The borrower is given credit for this amount at the settlement and the seller will pay this amount or count it as a deduction from sums payable to the seller.

Similar adjustments are made for homeowner association dues, special assessments, and fuel and other utilities, although the billing periods for these may not always be on an annual basis. Be sure you work out these cost sharing arrangements or "prorations" with the seller before the settlement. You may wish to notify utility companies of the change in ownership and ask for a special reading on the day of settlement, with the bill for pre-settlement charges to be mailed to the seller at his or her new address or to the settlement agent. This will eliminate much confusion that can result if you are billed for utilities used when the seller owned the property.

D. HUD-1 SETTLEMENT STATEMENT

A. U.S. DEPARTMENT OF HOUSING AND URBAN DEVELOPMENT

SETTLEMENT STATEMENT

C. NOTE: *This form is furnished to give you a statement of actual settlement cos were paid outside the closing; they are shown here for informatio*

D. NAME OF BORROWER:

E. NAME OF SELLER:

F. NAME OF LENDER:

G. PROPERTY LOCATION:

H. NAME OF SETTLEMENT AGENT:

I. SETTLEMENT DATE:

J. SUMMARY OF BORROWER'S TRANSACTION	
100. GROSS AMOUNT DUE FROM BORROWER	
101. Contract sales price	
102. Personal property	
103. Settlement charges to borrower (line 1400)	
104.	
105.	
Adjustments for items paid by seller in advance	
106. City/town taxes to	
107. County taxes to	
108. Assessments to	
109.	
110.	
111.	
112.	
120. GROSS AMOUNT DUE FROM BORROWER	
200. AMOUNTS PAID BY OR IN BEHALF OF BORROWER	
201. Deposit of earnest money	
202. Principal amount of new loan(s)	
203. Existing loan(s) taken subject to	
204.	
205.	
206.	
207.	
208.	
209.	
Adjustments for items unpaid by seller	
210. City/town taxes to	
211. County taxes to	
212. Assessments to	
213.	
214.	
215.	
216.	
217.	
218.	
219.	
220. TOTAL PAID BY/FOR BORROWER	
300. CASH AT SETTLEMENT FROM/TO BORROWER	
301. Gross amount due from borrower (line 120)	
302. Less amounts paid by/for borrower (line 220)	
303. CASH (☐ FROM) (☐ TO) BORROWER	

B. TYPE OF LOAN

1. ☐ FHA 2. ☐ FmHA 3. ☐ CONV. UNINS.
4. ☐ VA 5. ☐ CONV. INS.
6. FILE NUMBER 7. LOAN NUMBER

8. MORTGAGE INSURANCE CASE NUMBER

Amounts paid to and by the settlement agent are shown. Items marked "(p.o.c.)" purposes and are not included in the totals.

ADDRESS OF BORROWER:

ADDRESS OF SELLER:

ADDRESS OF LENDER:

ADDRESS OF SETTLEMENT AGENT:

PLACE OF SETTLEMENT:

K. SUMMARY OF SELLER'S TRANSACTION	
400. GROSS AMOUNT DUE TO SELLER	
401. Contract sales price	
402. Personal property	
403.	
404.	
405.	
Adjustments for items paid by seller in advance	
406. City/town taxes to	
407. County taxes to	
408. Assessments to	
409.	
410.	
411.	
412.	
420. GROSS AMOUNT DUE TO SELLER	
500. REDUCTIONS IN AMOUNT DUE TO SELLER	
501. Excess deposit (see instructions)	
502. Settlement charges to seller (line 1400)	
503. Existing loan(s) taken subject to	
504. Payoff of first mortgage loan	
505. Payoff of second mortgage loan	
506.	
507.	
508.	
509.	
Adjustments for items unpaid by seller	
510. City/town taxes to	
511. County taxes to	
512. Assessments to	
513.	
514.	
515.	
516.	
517.	
518.	
519.	
520. TOTAL REDUCTION AMOUNT DUE SELLER	
600. CASH AT SETTLEMENT FROM/TO SELLER	
601. Gross amount due to seller (line 420)	
602. Less reductions in amount due seller (line 520)	
603. CASH (☐ TO) (☐ FROM) SELLER	

HUD-1 Settlement Statement - page 2

L. SETTLEMENT CHARGES

700. TOTAL SALES/BROKER'S COMMISSION

	based on price	$		@

Division of Commission (line 700) as follows:

701.	$	to	
702.	$	to	
703.	Commission paid at Settlement		
704.			

800. ITEMS PAYABLE IN CONNECTION WITH LOAN

801.	Loan Origination Fee	%	
802.	Loan Discount	%	
803.	Appraisal Fee	to	
804.	Credit Report	to	
805.	Lender's Inspection Fee		
806.	Mortgage Insurance Application Fee to		
807.	Assumption Fee		
808.			
809.			
810.			
811.			

900. ITEMS REQUIRED BY LENDER TO BE PAID IN ADVANCE

901.	Interest from	to	@ $	/ day
902.	Mortgage insurance Premium for	months to		
903.	Hazard Insurance Premium for	years to		
904.		years to		
905.				

1000. RESERVES DEPOSITED WITH LENDER

1001.	Hazard Insurance	months @ $
1002.	Mortgage Insurance	months @ $
1003.	City property taxes	months @ $
1004.	County property taxes	months @ $
1005.	Annual assessments	months @ $
1006.		months @ $
1007.		months @ $
1008.	Aggregate Adjustment	months @ $

1100. TITLE CHARGES

1101.	Settlement or closing fee	to
1102.	Abstract or title search	to
1103.	Title examination	to
1104.	Title insurance binder	to
1105.	Document preparation	to
1106.	Notary fees	to
1107.	Attorney's fees	to
	(includes above item numbers);	
1108.	Title insurance	to
	(includes above item numbers);	
1109.	Lender's coverage	$
1110.	Owner's coverage	$
1111.		
1112.		
1113.		

1200. GOVERNMENT RECORDING AND TRANSFER CHARGES

1201.	Recording fees:	Deed $	; Mortgage $
1202.	City/county tax/stamps:	Deed $	; Mortgage $
1203.	State tax/stamps:	Deed $	; Mortgage $
1204.			
1205.			

1300. ADDITIONAL SETTLEMENT CHARGES

1301.	Survey	to
1302.	Pest inspection	to
1303.		
1304.		
1305.		

1400. TOTAL SETTLEMENT CHARGES *(enter on lines 103, Section J and 502, Section K)*

	PAID FROM BORROWER'S FUNDS AT SETTLEMENT	PAID FROM SELLER'S FUNDS AT SETTLEMENT
% =		
per month		
per month		
per month		
per month		
per month		
per month		
per month		
per month		
)		
)		
; Release $		

IV. APPENDIX

Consumer Information on Home Purchasing and Related Topics

U.S. Department of Housing and Urban Development

451 7th Street, SW
Washington, DC 20410
Web site: http://www.hud.gov

For information about FHA-insured home mortgage loans on one-to-four family dwellings call:
1-800 CALL FHA (800-225-5342)

For consumer counseling referrals call:
1-800-569-4287

For information regarding housing discrimination issues contact:
Office of Fair Housing and Equal Opportunity
(see above HUD address)
1-800-669-9777
Web site: http://www.hud.gov/fhe/fheo.html

For information about RESPA contact:
Office of Consumer and Regulatory Affairs
(see above HUD address)
Web site: http://www.hud.gov/fha/res/respa_hm.html

Other Agencies

For information about programs and pamphlets offered by the Department of Veterans Affairs, contact the nearest VA Regional Office.
Web site: http://www.va.gov/vas/loan

For information about rural housing loan programs contact:
Department of Agriculture
Rural Development/Rural Housing Services
Stop 0783
Washington, DC 20250
Web site: http://www.rurdev.usda.gov

For information about the Truth in Lending Act and the Equal Credit Opportunity Act contact:
Federal Reserve Board
20th Street and Constitution Avenue, NW
Washington, DC 20551
Web site: http://www.bog.frb.fed.us

 **U.S. Department of Housing and Urban Development
Office of Housing-Federal Housing Commission**

ITEM 5010 (9706)

GREATLAND ■ To Order Call: 800-530-9393

Mortgage Application—Form 1003

Uniform Residential Loan Application

This application is designed to be completed by the applicant(s) with the Lender's assistance. Applicants should complete this form as "Borrower" or "Co-Borrower," as applicable. Co-Borrower information must also be provided (and the appropriate box checked) when ☐ the income or assets of a person other than the Borrower (including the Borrower's spouse) will be used as a basis for loan qualification or ☐ the income or assets of the Borrower's spouse or other person who has community property rights pursuant to state law will not be used as a basis for loan qualification, but his or her liabilities must be considered because the spouse or other person has community property rights pursuant to applicable law and Borrower resides in a community property state, the security property is located in a community property state, or the Borrower is relying on other property located in a community property state as a basis for repayment of the loan.

If this is an application for joint credit, Borrower and Co-Borrower each agree that we intend to apply for joint credit (sign below):

Borrower   Co-Borrower

I. TYPE OF MORTGAGE AND TERMS OF LOAN

Mortgage Applied for:	☐ VA ☐ FHA	☐ Conventional ☐ USDA/Rural Housing Service	☐ Other (explain):		Agency Case Number	Lender Case Number
Amount $	Interest Rate %	No. of Months	Amortization Type:	☐ Fixed Rate ☐ GPM	☐ Other (explain): ☐ ARM (type):	

II. PROPERTY INFORMATION AND PURPOSE OF LOAN

Subject Property Address (street, city, state & ZIP)		No. of Units

Legal Description of Subject Property (attach description if necessary)	Year Built

Purpose of Loan	☐ Purchase ☐ Refinance	☐ Construction ☐ Construction-Permanent	☐ Other (explain):	Property will be: ☐ Primary Residence ☐ Secondary Residence ☐ Investment

Complete this line if construction or construction-permanent loan.

Year Lot Acquired	Original Cost $	Amount Existing Liens $	(a) Present Value of Lot $	(b) Cost of Improvements $	Total (a + b) $

Complete this line if this is a refinance loan.

Year Acquired	Original Cost $	Amount Existing Liens $	Purpose of Refinance	Describe Improvements ☐ made ☐ to be made Cost: $

Title will be held in what Name(s)	Manner in which Title will be held	Estate will be held in: ☐ Fee Simple
Source of Down Payment, Settlement Charges, and/or Subordinate Financing (explain)		☐ Leasehold (show expiration date)

III. BORROWER INFORMATION

	Borrower		Co-Borrower
Borrower's Name (include Jr. or Sr. if applicable)		Co-Borrower's Name (include Jr. or Sr. if applicable)	

Social Security Number	Home Phone (incl. area code)	DOB (mm/dd/yyyy)	Yrs. School	Social Security Number	Home Phone (incl. area code)	DOB (mm/dd/yyyy)	Yrs. School

☐ Married ☐ Separated	☐ Unmarried (include single, divorced, widowed)	Dependents (not listed by Co-Borrower) no. ages	☐ Married ☐ Separated	☐ Unmarried (include single, divorced, widowed)	Dependents (not listed by Borrower) no. ages
Present Address (street, city, state, ZIP) ☐ Own ☐ Rent ___ No. Yrs.			Present Address (street, city, state, ZIP) ☐ Own ☐ Rent ___ No. Yrs.		
Mailing Address, if different from Present Address			Mailing Address, if different from Present Address		

If residing at present address for less than two years, complete the following:

Former Address (street, city, state, ZIP) ☐ Own ☐ Rent ___ No. Yrs.	Former Address (street, city, state, ZIP) ☐ Own ☐ Rent ___ No. Yrs.

IV. EMPLOYMENT INFORMATION

	Borrower		Co-Borrower
Name & Address of Employer	☐ Self Employed	Yrs. on this job	Name & Address of Employer	☐ Self Employed	Yrs. on this job
		Yrs. employed in this line of work/profession			Yrs. employed in this line of work/profession
Position/Title/Type of Business	Business Phone (incl. area code)		Position/Title/Type of Business	Business Phone (incl. area code)	

If employed in current position for less than two years or if currently employed in more than one position, complete the following:

Name & Address of Employer	☐ Self Employed	Dates (from - to)	Name & Address of Employer	☐ Self Employed	Dates (from - to)
		Monthly Income $			Monthly Income $
Position/Title/Type of Business	Business Phone (incl. area code)		Position/Title/Type of Business	Business Phone (incl. area code)	
Name & Address of Employer	☐ Self Employed	Dates (from - to)	Name & Address of Employer	☐ Self Employed	Dates (from - to)
		Monthly Income $			Monthly Income $
Position/Title/Type of Business	Business Phone (incl. area code)		Position/Title/Type of Business	Business Phone (incl. area code)	

Freddie Mac Form 65 7/05
ITEM 7300 (0507)

(Page 1 of 4 pages)

Fannie Mae Form 1003 7/05
GREATLAND ■ To Order Call: 800-530-9393

— 245 —

V. MONTHLY INCOME AND COMBINED HOUSING EXPENSE INFORMATION

Gross Monthly Income	Borrower	Co-Borrower	Total	Combined Monthly Housing Expense	Present	Proposed
Base Empl. Income*	$	$	$	Rent	$	
Overtime				First Mortgage (P&I)		$
Bonuses				Other Financing (P&I)		
Commissions				Hazard Insurance		
Dividends/Interest				Real Estate Taxes		
Net Rental Income				Mortgage Insurance		
Other (before completing, see the notice in "describe other income," below)				Homeowner Assn. Dues		
				Other:		
Total	$	$	$	Total	$	$

* Self Employed Borrower(s) may be required to provide additional documentation such as tax returns and financial statements.

Describe Other Income

Notice: Alimony, child support, or separate maintenance income need not be revealed if the Borrower (B) or Co-Borrower (C) does not choose to have it considered for repaying this loan.

B/C		Monthly Amount
		$

VI. ASSETS AND LIABILITIES

This Statement and any applicable supporting schedules may be completed jointly by both married and unmarried Co-Borrowers if their assets and liabilities are sufficiently joined so that the Statement can be meaningfully and fairly presented on a combined basis; otherwise, separate Statements and Schedules are required. If the Co-Borrower section was completed about a non-applicant spouse or other person, this Statement and supporting schedules must be completed about that spouse or other person also.   Completed ☐ Jointly ☐ Not Jointly

ASSETS Description	Cash or Market Value	Liabilities and Pledged Assets. List the creditor's name, address, and account number for all outstanding debts, including automobile loans, revolving charge accounts, real estate loans, alimony, child support, stock pledges, etc. Use continuation sheet, if necessary. Indicate by (*) those liabilities, which will be satisfied upon sale of real estate owned or upon refinancing of the subject property.		
Cash deposit toward purchase held by:	$			
List checking and savings accounts below		**LIABILITIES**	**Monthly Payment & Months Left to Pay**	**Unpaid Balance**
Name and address of Bank, S&L, or Credit Union		Name and address of Company	$ Payment/Months	$
Acct. no.	$	Acct. no.		
Name and address of Bank, S&L, or Credit Union		Name and address of Company	$ Payment/Months	$
Acct. no.	$	Acct. no.		
Name and address of Bank, S&L, or Credit Union		Name and address of Company	$ Payment/Months	$
Acct. no.	$	Acct. no.		
Name and address of Bank, S&L, or Credit Union		Name and address of Company	$ Payment/Months	$
Acct. no.	$	Acct. no.		
Stocks & Bonds (Company name/ number & description)	$	Name and address of Company	$ Payment/Months	$
Life insurance net cash value	$	Acct. no.		
Face amount: $				
Subtotal Liquid Assets	$	Acct. no.		
Real estate owned (enter market value from schedule of real estate owned)	$	Name and address of Company	$ Payment/Months	$
Vested interest in retirement fund	$			
Net worth of business(es) owned (attach financial statement)	$	Acct. no.		
Automobiles owned (make and year)	$	Name and address of Company	$ Payment/Months	$
		Acct. no.		
Other Assets (itemize)	$	Alimony/Child Support/Separate Maintenance Payments Owed to:	$	
		Job-Related Expense (child care, union dues, etc)	$	
		Total Monthly Payments	$	
Total Assets a.	$	Net Worth (a minus b) ► $	**Total Liabilities b.**	$

Freddie Mac Form 65 7/05
ITEM 7300 (0507)

Fannie Mae Form 1003 7/05
GREATLAND ■ To Order Call: 800-530-9393

(Page 2 of 4 pages)

VI. ASSETS AND LIABILITIES (cont'd)

Schedule of Real Estate Owned (If additional properties are owned, use continuation sheet.)

Property Address (enter S if sold, PS if pending sale or R if rental being held for income) ▼	Type of Property	Present Market Value	Amount of Mortgages & Liens	Gross Rental Income	Mortgage Payments	Insurance, Maintenance, Taxes & Misc.	Net Rental Income
		$	$	$	$	$	$
	Totals	$	$	$	$	$	$

List any additional names under which credit has previously been received and indicate appropriate creditor name(s) and account number(s):

Alternate Name	Creditor Name	Account Number

VII. DETAILS OF TRANSACTION		VIII. DECLARATIONS				
a. Purchase price	$	If you answer "Yes" to any questions a through i, please use continuation sheet for explanation	Borrower		Co-Borrower	
			Yes	No	Yes	No
b. Alterations, improvements, repairs		a. Are there any outstanding judgments against you?				
c. Land (if acquired separately)		b. Have you been declared bankrupt within the past 7 years?				
d. Refinance (incl. debts to be paid off)		c. Have you had property foreclosed upon or given title or deed in lieu thereof in the last 7 years?				
e. Estimated prepaid items		d. Are you a party to a lawsuit?				
f. Estimated closing costs		e. Have you directly or indirectly been obligated on any loan which resulted in foreclosure, transfer of title in lieu of foreclosure, or judgment? (This would include such loans as home mortgage loans, SBA loans, home improvement loans, educational loans, manufactured (mobile) home loans, any mortgage, financial obligation, bond, or loan guarantee. If "Yes," provide details, including date, name, and address of Lender, FHA or VA case number, if any, and reasons for the action.)				
g. PMI, MIP, Funding Fee						
h. Discount (if Borrower will pay)						
i. Total costs (add items a through h)						
j. Subordinate financing						
k. Borrower's closing costs paid by Seller		f. Are you presently delinquent or in default on any Federal debt or any other loan, mortgage, financial obligation, bond, or loan guarantee? If "Yes," give details as described in the preceding question.				
l. Other Credits (explain)		g. Are you obligated to pay alimony, child support, or separate maintenance?				
		h. Is any part of the down payment borrowed?				
		i. Are you a co-maker or endorser on a note?				
		j. Are you a U.S. citizen?				
m. Loan amount (exclude PMI, MIP, Funding Fee financed)		k. Are you a permanent resident alien?				
		l. Do you intend to occupy the property as your primary residence? If "Yes," complete question m below.				
n. PMI, MIP, Funding Fee financed						
o. Loan amount (add m & n)		m. Have you had an ownership interest in a property in the last three years?				
		(1) What type of property did you own—principal residence (PR), second home (SH), or investment property (IP)?				
p. Cash from/to Borrower (subtract j, k, l & o from i)		(2) How did you hold title to the home—solely by yourself (S), jointly with your spouse (SP), or jointly with another person (O)?				

IX. ACKNOWLEDGEMENT AND AGREEMENT

Each of the undersigned specifically represents to Lender and to Lender's actual or potential agents, brokers, processors, attorneys, insurers, servicers, successors and assigns and agrees and acknowledges that: (1) the information provided in this application is true and correct as of the date set forth opposite my signature and that any intentional or negligent misrepresentation of this information contained in this application may result in civil liability, including monetary damages, to any person who may suffer any loss due to reliance upon any misrepresentation that I have made on this application, and/or in criminal penalties including, but not limited to, fine or imprisonment or both under the provisions of Title 18, United States Code, Sec. 1001, et seq.; (2) the loan requested pursuant to this application (the "Loan") will be secured by a mortgage or deed of trust on the property described in this application; (3) the property will not be used for any illegal or prohibited purpose or use; (4) all statements made in this application are made for the purpose of obtaining a residential mortgage loan; (5) the property will be occupied as indicated in this application; (6) the Lender, its servicers, successors or assigns may retain the original and/or an electronic record of this application, whether or not the Loan is approved; (7) the Lender and its agents, brokers, insurers, servicers, successors, and assigns may continuously rely on the information contained in the application, and I am obligated to amend and/or supplement the information provided in this application if any of the material facts that I have represented herein should change prior to closing of the Loan; (8) in the event that my payments on the Loan become delinquent, the Lender, its servicers, successors or assigns may, in addition to any other rights and remedies that it may have relating to such delinquency, report my name and account information to one or more consumer reporting agencies; (9) ownership of the Loan and/or administration of the Loan account may be transferred with such notice as may be required by law; (10) neither Lender nor its agents, brokers, insurers, servicers, successors or assigns has made any representation or warranty, express or implied, to me regarding the property or the condition or value of the property; and (11) my transmission of this application as an "electronic record" containing my "electronic signature," as those terms are defined in applicable federal and/or state laws (excluding audio and video recordings), or my facsimile transmission of this application containing a facsimile of my signature, shall be as effective, enforceable and valid as if a paper version of this application were delivered containing my original written signature.

Acknowledgement. Each of the undersigned hereby acknowledges that any owner of the Loan, its servicers, successors and assigns, may verify or reverify any information contained in this application or obtain any information or data relating to the Loan, for any legitimate business purpose through any source, including a source named in this application or a consumer reporting agency.

Borrower's Signature	Date	Co-Borrower's Signature	Date
X		X	

X. INFORMATION FOR GOVERNMENT MONITORING PURPOSES

The following information is requested by the Federal Government for certain types of loans related to a dwelling in order to monitor the lender's compliance with equal credit opportunity, fair housing and home mortgage disclosure laws. You are not required to furnish this information, but are encouraged to do so. The law provides that a lender may not discriminate either on the basis of this information, or on whether you choose to furnish it. If you furnish the information, please provide both ethnicity and race. For race, you may check more than one designation. If you do not furnish ethnicity, race, or sex, under Federal regulations, this lender is required to note the information on the basis of visual observation and surname if you have made this application in person. If you do not wish to furnish the information, please check the box below. (Lender must review the above material to assure that the disclosures satisfy all requirements to which the lender is subject under applicable state law for the particular type of loan applied for.)

BORROWER	I do not wish to furnish this information		CO-BORROWER	I do not wish to furnish this information	
Ethnicity:	Hispanic or Latino	Not Hispanic or Latino	Ethnicity:	Hispanic or Latino	Not Hispanic or Latino
Race:	American Indian or Alaska Native / Asian / Black or African American / Native Hawaiian or Other Pacific Islander / White		Race:	American Indian or Alaska Native / Asian / Black or African American / Native Hawaiian or Other Pacific Islander / White	
Sex:	Female	Male	Sex:	Female	Male

To be Completed by Interviewer	Interviewer's Name (print or type)	Name and Address of Interviewer's Employer
This application was taken by:		
☐ Face-to-face interview	Interviewer's Signature Date	
☐ Mail		
☐ Telephone	Interviewer's Phone Number (incl. area code)	
☐ Internet		

CONTINUATION SHEET/RESIDENTIAL LOAN APPLICATION

Use this continuation sheet if you need more space to complete the Residential Loan Application. Mark **B** for Borrower or **C** for Co-Borrower.	Borrower:	Agency Case Number:
	Co-Borrower:	Lender Case Number:

I/We fully understand that it is a Federal crime punishable by fine or imprisonment, or both, to knowingly make any false statements concerning any of the above facts as applicable under the provisions of Title 18, United States Code, Section 1001, et seq.

Borrower's Signature	Date	Co-Borrower's Signature	Date
X _____		X _____	

Freddie Mac Form 65 7/05

Fannie Mae Form 1003 7/05

ITEM 7500 (0507)

(Page 4 of 4 pages)

GREATLAND ■ To Order Call: 800-530-9393

Sample Good Faith Estimate

GOOD FAITH ESTIMATE OF BORROWER'S SETTLEMENT COSTS

APPLICANT ("We", "Us")	This Good Faith Estimate is being provided by
	a mortgage broker ("we"), and no lender has yet been obtained.

Date of this Estimate	Estimated Closing Date	Loan Officer

Loan Program

Term	; Rate	%; Origination Fee	%; Discount Fee	%

Purchase Price / Value $	Loan Amount $	Loan to Value	%

Property Address

The information provided below reflects estimates of the charges which you are likely to incur at the settlement of your loan. The fees listed are estimates - the actual charges may be more or less. Your transaction may not involve a fee for every item listed.

The numbers listed beside the estimates generally correspond to the numbered lines contained in the HUD-1 or HUD-1A settlement statement which you will be receiving at settlement. The HUD-1 or HUD-1A settlement statement will show you the actual cost for items paid at settlement.

800.	ITEMS PAYABLE IN CONNECTION WITH LOAN:			1006.		$
801.	Loan Origination Fee	%	$	1007.		$
802.	Loan Discount Fee	%	$	1000.		$
803.	Appraisal Fee		$	1100.	TITLE CHARGES:	
804.	Credit Report		$	1101.	Settlement Fee	$
805.	Lender's Inspection Fee		$	1102.	Abstract or Title Search	$
806.			$	1103.	Title Examination	$
807.	Assumption Fee		$	1104.	Title Insurance Binder	$
808.			$	1105.	Document Preparation Fee	$
809.			$	1106.	Notary Fee	$
810.			$	1107.	Attorney's Fee	$
811.			$	1108.	Title Insurance	$
812.			$	1111.		$
813.			$	1112.		$
814.			$	1113.		$
815.			$	1200.	GOVERNMENT RECORDING AND TRANSFER CHARGES:	
900.	ITEMS REQUIRED BY LENDER TO BE PAID IN ADVANCE:			1201.	Recording Fees	$
901.	Interest from				Deed $; Mortgage $;	
	to	at $	/day		Release $	
902.	Mortgage Insurance Premium		$	1202.	City / County Tax / Stamps	$
903.	Hazard Insurance Premium		$		Deed $; Mortgage $	
904.			$		Release $	
905.			$	1203.	State Tax / Stamps	$
1000.	RESERVES DEPOSITED WITH LENDER:				Deed $; Mortgage $	
1001.	Hazard Insurance Premium		$	1204.		$
	months at $	/month		1205.		$
1002.	Mortgage Insurance		$	1300.	ADDITIONAL SETTLEMENT CHARGES:	
	months at $	/month		1301.	Survey	$
1003.	City Property Taxes		$	1302.	Pest Inspection	$
	months at $	/month		1303.		$
1004.	County Property Taxes		$	1304.		$
	months at $	/month		1305.		$
1005.	Annual Assessments		$	1306.		$
	months at $	/month		1307.		$
				1400.	TOTAL ESTIMATED SETTLEMENT CHARGES:	$

EST. MONTHLY PMT.:	PPD. INT. & ESCROWS:	ANNUAL AMOUNT:	ANALYSIS OF ESTIMATED SETTLEMENT CHARGES:
P & I	Ppd. Interest		
R.E. Taxes	R.E. Taxes	R.E. Taxes	1400. Total Estimated Settlement Charges: $
Hazard Ins.	Hazard Ins.	Hazard Ins.	
Flood Ins.	Flood Ins.	Flood Ins.	Less: Prepaid Interest and Escrows $
Mtg. Ins.	Mtg. Ins.	Mtg. Ins.	
Other	Other	Other	= Other Estimated Settlement Charges: $
Total Pmt.	Total Ppds.		

THIS SECTION TO BE COMPLETED ONLY IF A PARTICULAR PROVIDER OF SERVICE IS REQUIRED. Listed below are providers of service which we require you use. The charges or ranges indicated in the Good Faith Estimate above are based upon the corresponding charge of the below designated providers.

Item No.	Name / Address				
Telephone		Relationship?	Yes	No	Nature of Relationship:
Item No.	Name / Address				
Telephone		Relationship?	Yes	No	Nature of Relationship:
Item No.	Name / Address				
Telephone		Relationship?	Yes	No	Nature of Relationship:

AGREEMENT: You acknowledge you have received a copy of the HUD Special Information Booklet, Settlement Costs, if your application is to purchase residential real property and the Lender will take a first lien on the property.

If for any reason the loan you have applied for does not close, and if permitted by applicable law, you agree to reimburse the mortgage broker for any and all costs incurred to process your application including but not limited to appraisal, survey and title insurance.

These estimates are provided pursuant to the Real Estate Settlement Procedures Act of 1974, as amended (RESPA). Additional information can be found in the HUD Special Information Booklet, which is to be provided to you by your mortgage broker or lender, if your application is to purchase residential real property and the lender will take a first lien on the property.

APPLICANT	DATE	APPLICANT	DATE
APPLICANT	DATE	APPLICANT	DATE
		AUTHORIZED OFFICIAL	

Sample Truth in Lending Disclosure

TRUTH-IN-LENDING DISCLOSURE FOR REAL ESTATE MORTGAGE LOANS (VARIABLE RATE OPTION)

NAME(S) / ADDRESS(ES) OF BORROWER(S) ("Borrower, you or your")	NAME / ADDRESS OF LENDER (CREDITOR) ("Lender, us or our")

PROPERTY ADDRESS

LOAN NUMBER	TRANSACTION DATE	
		☐ Preliminary ☐ Final

Words, numbers or phrases preceded by a ☐ are applicable only if the ☐ is marked.

ANNUAL PERCENTAGE RATE	FINANCE CHARGE	AMOUNT FINANCED	TOTAL OF PAYMENTS
The cost of your credit as a yearly rate.	The dollar amount the credit will cost you.	The amount of credit provided to you or on your behalf.	The amount you will have paid after you have made all payments as scheduled.
_____ %	$	$	$

YOUR PAYMENT SCHEDULE WILL BE:

Number of Payments	Amount of Payments	When Payments Are Due

VARIABLE RATE: ☐ Applicable   ☐ Not Applicable

The annual percentage rate may increase during the term of this transaction if the _____ average of the U.S. Treasury Bills with a maturity of _____ increases. Please refer to the Adjustable Rate Mortgage Documents for specific information concerning the variable rate provisions of this transaction.

The annual percentage rate may increase during the term of this transaction if the _____ increases. The rate may not increase more often than _____ and may not increase more than _____ % per adjustment. Any increase will take the form of _____ . For example,

☐ This transaction is subject to a variable rate feature and is secured by your principal dwelling. Variable rate disclosures have been provided at an earlier time.

PAYABLE ON DEMAND: ☐ This obligation is payable on demand   ☐ The disclosures are based on an assumed maturity of one year.

Filing / Recording Fee $ _____

You may obtain property insurance from anyone acceptable to the lender.

SECURITY: You are giving a security interest in the real property and any of the following items which are checked:
☐ Goods being purchased.   ☐ Funds on deposit with the lender.
☐ Other (Specify)   ☐ Collateral securing other loans with us may also secure this loan.

LATE CHARGE:

If you are more than _____ days late in making any payment, in addition to your payment, you will pay a late charge of:
☐ the lesser of   ☐ the greater of   ☐ an amount equal to   ☐ $ _____   or ☐ _____ % of the payment in default.

PREPAYMENT:

If you pay off early, you
☐ may ☐ will not have to pay a penalty.
☐ may ☐ will not be entitled to a refund of part of the finance charge.

ASSUMPTION:
If this loan is to purchase and is secured by your principal dwelling, and if checked here, ☐ someone buying your dwelling cannot assume the remainder of this purchase money mortgage loan on the original terms.
If this loan is to purchase and is secured by your principal dwelling, and if checked here, ☐ someone buying your dwelling may, subject to conditions, be allowed to assume the remainder of this purchase money mortgage loan.

See your contract documents for any additional information about nonpayment, default, any required repayment in full before the scheduled date, prepayment refunds and penalties and Creditor's policy regarding assumption of the obligation.   "e" means an estimate.

☐ Please refer to the "Good Faith Estimate" for a breakdown of fees, charges and amount financed.   ☐ Please refer to the Itemization of Amount Financed Statement.

SIGNATURES:

By signing you acknowledge receipt of a completed copy of this disclosure. You understand that this is not a contract and does not reflect all of the terms and conditions of the mortgage transaction to which the disclosures reflected on this form relate.

X _____   X _____
DATE   DATE

X _____   X _____
DATE   DATE

Sample HUD-1 Closing Statement

A. Settlement Statement

U.S. Department of Housing
and Urban Development

OMB No. 2502-0265

B. Type of Loan

1. ☐ FHA 2. ☐ FmHA 3. ☐ Conv. Unins.
4. ☐ VA 5. ☐ Conv. Ins.

6. File Number | 7. Loan Number | 8. Mortgage Insurance Case Number

C. Note: This form is furnished to give you a statement of actual settlement costs. Amounts paid to and by the settlement agent are shown. Items marked "(p.o.c.)" were paid outside the closing; they are shown here for information purposes and are not included in the totals.

D. Name and Address of Borrower	E. Name and Address of Seller	F. Name and Address of Lender

G. Property Location	H. Settlement Agent	
	Place of Settlement	I. Settlement Date

J. Summary of Borrower's Transaction		K. Summary of Seller's Transaction	
100. Gross Amount Due From Borrower		**400. Gross Amount Due To Seller**	
101. Contract sales price		401. Contract sales price	
102. Personal property		402. Personal property	
103. Settlement charges to borrower (line 1400)		403.	
104.		404.	
105.		405.	
Adjustments for items paid by seller in advance		**Adjustments for items paid by seller in advance**	
106. City/town taxes to		406. City/town taxes to	
107. County taxes to		407. County taxes to	
108. Assessments to		408. Assessments to	
109.		409.	
110.		410.	
111.		411.	
112.		412.	
120. Gross Amount Due From Borrower		**420. Gross Amount Due To Seller**	
200. Amounts Paid By or in Behalf of Borrower		**500. Reductions In Amount Due To Seller**	
201. Deposit or earnest money		501. Excess deposit (see instructions)	
202. Principal amount of new loan(s)		502. Settlement charges to seller (line 1400)	
203. Existing loan(s) taken subject to		503. Existing loan(s) taken subject to	
204.		504. Payoff of first mortgage loan	
205.		505. Payoff of second mortgage loan	
206.		506.	
207.		507.	
208.		508.	
209.		509.	
Adjustments for items unpaid by seller		**Adjustments for items unpaid by seller**	
210. City/town taxes to		510. City/town taxes to	
211. County taxes to		511. County taxes to	
212. Assessments to		512. Assessments to	
213.		513.	
214.		514.	
215.		515.	
216.		516.	
217.		517.	
218.		518.	
219.		519.	
220. Total Paid By/For Borrower		**520. Total Reduction Amount Due Seller**	
300. Cash At Settlement From/To Borrower		**600. Cash At Settlement To/From Seller**	
301. Gross Amount due from borrower (line 120)		601. Gross amount due to Seller (line 420)	
302. Less amounts paid by/for borrower (line 220) (	)	602. Less reductions in amt. due seller (line 520) (	)
303. Cash ☐ From ☐ To Borrower		**603. Cash** ☐ To ☐ From Seller	

Previous Edition Is Obsolete
ITEM 2384 (9301)

HUD-1 (3-86)
RESPA, HB 4305.2
GREATLAND ■
To Order Call: 800-530-9393 ☐ Fax: 616-791-1131

— 251 —

L. Settlement Charges

		Paid From Borrower's Funds at Settlement	Paid From Seller's Funds at Settlement
700. Total Sales/Broker's Commission based on price$ @ % =			
Division of Commission (line700) as follows:			
701. $ to			
702. $ to			
703. Commission paid at settlement			
704.			
800. Items Payable in Connection With Loan			
801. Loan Origination Fee %			
802. Loan Discount %			
803. Appraisal Fee to			
804. Credit Report to			
805. Lender's Inspection Fee			
806. Mortgage Insurance Application Fee to			
807. Assumption Fee			
808.			
809.			
810.			
811.			
812.			
813.			
814.			
815.			
900. Items Required By Lender To Be Paid in Advance			
901. Interest from to @$ /day			
902. Mortgage Insurance Premium for months to			
903. Hazard Insurance Premium for years to			
904. years to			
905.			
1000. Reserves Deposited With Lender			
1001. Hazard Insurance months @ $ per month			
1002. Mortgage Insurance months @ $ per month			
1003. City property taxes months @ $ per month			
1004. County property taxes months @ $ per month			
1005. Annual assessments months @ $ per month			
1006. months @ $ per month			
1007. months @ $ per month			
1008. months @ $ per month			
1100. Title Charges			
1101. Settlement or closing fee to			
1102. Abstract or title search to			
1103. Title examination to			
1104. Title Insurance binder to			
1105. Document preparation to			
1106. Notary fees to			
1107. Attorney's fees to			
(includes above item numbers:)			
1108. Title Insurance to			
(includes above item numbers:)			
1109. Lender's coverage $			
1110. Owner's coverage $			
1111.			
1112.			
1113.			
1200. Government Recording and Transfer Charges			
1201. Recording fees: Deed $; Mortgage $; Releases $			
1202. City/county tax/stamps: Deed$; Mortgage $			
1203. State tax/stamps: Deed $; Mortgage $			
1204.			
1205.			
1300. Additional Settlement Charges			
1301. Survey to			
1302. Pest inspection to			
1303.			
1304.			
1305.			
1400. Total Settlement Charges (enter on lines 103, Section J and 502, Section K)			

I have carefully reviewed the HUD-1 Settlement Statement and to the best of my knowledge and belief, it is a true and accurate statement of all receipts and disbursements made on my account or by me in this transaction. I further certify that I have received a copy of HUD-1 Settlement Statement.

_____   _____

Borrowers   Sellers

The HUD-1 Settlement Statement which I have prepared is a true and accurate account of this transaction. I have caused or will cause the funds to be disbursed in accordance with this statement.

_____   _____

Settlement Agent   Date

WARNING: It is a crime to knowingly make false statement to the United States on this or any other similar form. Penalties upon conviction can include a fine or imprisonment. Title 18 U.S. Code Section 1001 and Section 1010.

Homebuyer Checklist

Home Buyer Checklist
Provided by:
"Mortgage Myths"

Pre-inspection Items:	
Property Address:	
Realtor/Seller Contact: Phone:	
House Style:	Condo Townhouse Detached Semi-Detached Multi Unit Single Family Co-Op Other
Number of Stories:	
Asking Price:	$
Date Listed:	
Age of Home:	
Occupancy Date:	
Square Footage:	
Lot Size:	
Property Taxes:	$
Heat Type:	Gas Oil Propane Elect.
Air Conditioning:	Central Window None
Sanitary System:	Sewer Septic tank
Water Source:	Municipal Well
Number of Bedrooms:	
Number of Bathrooms:	
Finished Basement:	Yes No
Parking:	Garage Carport On Street None
Fireplace(s):	Gas Wood None
Pool:	In ground Above Ground
Deck	Yes No
Fence:	Yes No
Notes:	

The Neighborhood

Distance to Work:			
Distance to Schools:			
Neighborhood Makeup:	Adult	Family	
Closest Grocery Store:			
Nearest Shopping Ctr:			
Nearest Bank:			
Access to Highway:			
Public Transportation:	Yes	No	
Traffic Volume:	Busy	Moderate	Light
Condition of Street:	Good	Fair	Poor
Near Airport?:	Yes	No	
Near Railroad Tracks?:	Yes	No	
Near Factories?:	Yes	No	
First Impression:	Good	Fair	Poor

Positive Features:

Negative Features:

Notes:

Curb Appeal			
Type of Construction:	Brick	Vinyl	
	Wood	Pebbledash	
	Other		
Exterior Colors:			
Exterior Paint Condition:	Good	Fair	Poor
Driveway.		Yes	No
Condition of Driveway:	Good	Fair	Poor
Garage:		Yes	No
Condition of Garage:	Good	Fair	Poor
Condition of Yard:	Good	Fair	Poor
Any Large Trees:		Yes	No
Landscaping:	Good	Fair	Poor
Roof Condition:	Good	Fair	Poor
Number of Windows:			
Type of Windows:			
Outside Lighting:			
Direction Facing:	N	E	S	W
Front Door Condition:	Good	Fair	Poor
Notes:			

Inside the Home			
Smell	Clean	Musty	
	Air Freshener		
Cleanliness:	Good	Fair	Poor
Kitchen impression:	Good	Fair	Poor
Floor Type:			
Floor Condition:	Good	Fair	Poor
Cabinetry:	Good	Fair	Poor
Countertops:	Good	Fair	Poor
Appliances (if included)	Good	Fair	Poor
Sink Hardware:	Good	Fair	Poor
Lighting Fixtures:	Good	Fair	Poor
Ceiling condition:	Good	Fair	Poor
Kitchen Notes:			
Bathroom Impression:	Good	Fair	Poor
Floor Type:			
Floor Condition:	Good	Fair	Poor
Cabinetry:	Good	Fair	Poor
Sink Hardware:	Good	Fair	Poor
Tub/Shower Hardware:	Good	Fair	Poor
Lighting fixtures:	Good	Fair	Poor
Ceiling Condition:	Good	Fair	Poor
Bathroom Notes:			

Bedrooms

Bedroom #1

Condition:	Good	Fair	Poor
Room size:			
Closet size:			
Number of Windows:			
Number of Outlets:			
Floor Type:			
Floor Condition:	Good	Fair	Poor

Bedroom #1 Notes:

Bedroom #2

Condition:	Good	Fair	Poor
Room size:			
Closet size:			
Number of Windows:			
Number of Outlets:			
Floor Type:			
Floor Condition:	Good	Fair	Poor

Bedroom #2 Notes:

Bedroom 3

Condition:	Good	Fair	Poor
Room size:			
Closet size:			
Number of Windows:			
Number of Outlets:			
Floor Type:			
Floor Condition:	Good	Fair	Poor

Bedroom #3 Notes:

Important Things to Check

Inside:			
Doors & Windows:	Good	Fair	Poor
Pipes (Plumbing):	Good	Fair	Poor
Mold or Water Damage:	Yes	No	
Laundry Hookup:	Yes	No	
Signs of Insects or Mice:	Yes	No	
Smoke Detectors:	Yes	No	
Outside:			
Fence Condition:	Good	Fair	Poor
Pool Condition:	Good	Fair	Poor
Patio Condition:	Good	Fair	Poor
Deck Condition:	Good	Fair	Poor

Other Features & Overall Impression of Home:

Overall Rating *(1 to 10):*

Home Financing Checklist

MORTGAGE CHECKLIST

Ask your lender to help fill out this checklist.

	Mortgage A	Mortgage B
Mortgage amount	$	$

Basic Features for Comparison

	Mortgage A	Mortgage B
Fixed-rate annual percentage rate (the cost of your credit as a yearly rate, including both interest and other charges)		
ARM annual percentage rate		
Adjustment period		
Index used and current rate		
Margin		
Initial payment without discount		
Initial payment with discount (if any)		
How long will discount last?		
Interest-rate caps:		
periodic		
overall		
Payment caps		
Negative amortization		
Convertibility or prepayment privilege		
Initial fees and charges		

	Mortgage A	Mortgage B
Mortgage amount		

Monthly Payment Amounts

	Mortgage A	Mortgage B
What will my monthly payment be after 12 months if the index rate:		
stays the same		
goes up 2%		
goes down 2%		
What will my monthly payment be after 3 years if the index rate:		
stays the same		
goes up 2% per year		
goes down 2% per year		

Revised: 2005

Take into account any caps on your mortgage and remember that it may run 30 years.

Personal Qualification Form

Qualifying for a mortgage is simple! Use this form to determine your front and back ratios. Remember, lenders like to see your front ratio no greater than about 31%, and your back ratio no greater than 50% (may vary depending on program and LTV).

$ _____ Enter your gross MONTHLY income.

× 31%

= _____ This is your maximum suggested monthly payment, including principle, interest, taxes, and insurance (PITI).

$ _____ Enter your gross MONTHLY income.

× 19%

= _____ This is the maximum monthly allowable for other credit payments (car, credit card, etc.).

National/State Associations and Regulatory Agencies

For your reference, listed here are the various regulatory agencies and state and national organizations. For consumer complaints or to verify licensing, also check the major search engines and the Better Business Bureau. When proceeding with *any* major financial transaction, always do your research—and ask for references.

ALABAMA

Regulatory Agency
AL State Banking Dept
401 Adams Ave
Montgomery, AL 36130
Phone: 334-242-3452
Fax: 334-242-3500
www.bank.state.al.us

Mortgage Bankers Association
Mortgage Bankers Assn of Alabama
PO Box 230425
Montgomery, AL 36123-0425
Phone: (334) 260-8197
Fax: (334) 396-8880
www.mbaal.org

Mortgage Brokers Association
Alabama Mortgage Brokers Assn
108 Windsor Lane
Pelham, AL 35124
Phone: 866-845-2622
Fax: 866-906-2622
www.almba.org

ALASKA

Regulatory Agency
Alaska Division of Banking
Securities & Corporations
PO Box 110807
Juneau, AK 99811
Phone: 907-465-2521
Fax: 907-465-2549
www.dced.state.ak.us

Mortgage Bankers Association
Alaska Mortgage Bankers Assn
PO Box 92691
Anchorage, AK 99509-2691
Phone: (906) 762-5894
Fax: (907) 762-5899
www.akmba.org

Mortgage Brokers Association
Alaska Assn of Mortgage Brokers
224 N Yenlo, Suite 3B
Wasilla, AK 99654
Phone: 907-357-9640
Fax: 907-357-9644
www.akamb.org

CALIFORNIA

Regulatory Agency
Dept of Corporations
320 West 4th St., Ste 750
Los Angeles, CA 90013
Phone: 213-576-7500
Fax: 866-275-2677
www.corp.ca.gov

Mortgage Bankers Association
California Mortgage Bankers Assn
980 9th St, Ste 2120
Sacramento, CA 95814-2741
Phone: (916) 446-7100
Fax: (916) 446-7105
www.cmba.com

Mortgage Brokers Association
CA Assn of Mortgage Brokers
785 Orchard Drive, Suite 225
Folsom, CA 95630
Phone: 916-448-8236
Fax: 916-440-0237
www.cambweb.org

COLORADO

Regulatory Agency
Dept of Law
Colorado UCC Code
1525 Sherman St, 5th Fl
Denver, CO 80203
Phone: 303-866-4494
Fax: 303-866-5691
www.ago.state.co.us/ucc/ucclmai
n.cfm

Mortgage Bankers Association
Colorado Mortgage Lenders Assn
7000 E Belleview Ave, Ste 203
Greenwood Village, CO 80111-1622
Phone: (303) 773-9565
Fax: (303) 773-8746
www.cmla.com

Mortgage Brokers Association
CO Assn of Mortgage Brokers
7000 Broadway, Suite 320
Denver, CO 80221
Phone: 303-991-2240
Fax: 303 991 2241
www.camb.org

CONNECTICUT

Regulatory Agency
CT Dept of Banking
Consumer Credit Division
260 Constitution Plaza
Hartford, CT 6103
Phone: 860-240-8200
Fax: 860-240-8178
www.ct.gov/dob.site.default.asp

Mortgage Bankers Association
Connecticut Mortgage Bankers Assn
998 Farmington Ave, Ste 214
West Hartford, CT 06107-2184
Phone: (860) 232-9141
Fax: (860) 232-9434
www.cmba.org

Mortgage Brokers Association
CT Society of Mortgage Brokers
26 Broad Street
Milford, CT 6460
Phone: 203-874-3090
Fax: 203-783-4828
www.csmbct.com

DELAWARE

Regulatory Agency
Ofc of State Banking Comm.
555 E Loockerman St. Suite 210
Dover, DE 19901
Phone: 302-739-4235
Fax: 302-739-3609
http://banking.delaware.gov

Mortgage Bankers Association
No State Association
Contact Mortgage Bankers Association
Phone: 202-557-2700
www.mortgagebankers.org

Mortgage Brokers Association
No State Association
Contact National Association of
Mortgage Brokers
Phone: 703-342-5900
www.namb.org

FLORIDA

Regulatory Agency
Div of Securities & Finance
101 E Graines Street
Tallahassee, FL 32399
Phone: 850-410-9895
Fax: 850-410-9914
www.flofr.com/licensing

Mortgage Bankers Association
Mortgage Bankers Assn of Florida
PO Box 607826
Orlando, FL 32860
Phone: (407) 647-8839
Fax: (407) 629-2502
www.mbaf.org

Mortgage Brokers Association
Florida Assn of Mortgage Brokers
PO Box 6477
Tallahassee, FL 32314
Phone: 800-289-9983
Fax: 850-942-4654
www.famb.org

GEORGIA

Regulatory Agency
Dept of Banking & Finance
2990 Brandywine Road Ste 200
Atlanta, GA 30341
Phone: 770-986-1633
Fax: 770-986-1654

Mortgage Bankers Association
Mortgage Bankers Assn of Georgia
1239 2nd St
Macon, GA 31202-3121
Phone: (478) 743-8612
Fax: (478) 743-8278
www.mbag.org

Mortgage Brokers Association
Georgia Assn of Mortgage Brokers
4630 Clary Lakes Drive
Roswell, GA 30075
Phone: 770-993-5507
Fax: 770-643-9971
www.gamb.org

HAWAII

Regulatory Agency
Div of Financial Institutions
Department of Commerce
and Consumer Affairs
1010 Richards St., Rm 602-A
Honolulu, HI 96813
Phone: 808-586-2820
Fax: 808-586-2818
www.hawaii.gov/dcca/areas/dfi

Mortgage Bankers Association
Mortgage Bankers Assn of Hawaii
PO Box 4129
Honolulu, HI 96812-2801
Phone: (808) 528-7848
Fax: (808) 527-2801
www.MBA-HI.org

Mortgage Brokers Association
Hawaii Assn of Mortgage Brokers
PO Box 1074
Honolulu, HI 96808
Phone: 808-479-8960
www.hamb.org

IDAHO

Regulatory Agency
Department of Finance
State of Idaho
PO Box 83720,
Boise, ID 83720
Phone: 208-332-8002
Fax: 208-332-8097
http://finance.idaho.gov

Mortgage Bankers Association
Idaho Mortgage Lenders Assn
PO Box 7899,
Boise, ID 83707-1899
Phone: (208) 208-4726

Mortgage Brokers Association
Idaho Assn of Mortgage Brokers
PO Box 7981,
Boise, ID 83707
Phone: 208-321-9309
Fax: 208-321-4819
www.idahomortgagebrokers.org

ILLINOIS

Regulatory Agency
Ofc of Banks
Real Estate Residential Finance
310 S. Michigan Ave Ste 2130
Chicago, IL 60604
Phone: 312-793-1409
www.obre.state.il.us/legal.legal.
htm

Mortgage Bankers Association
Illinois Mortgage Bankers Assn
111 W Washington St, Ste 1320
Chicago, IL 60602-3459
Phone: (312) 236-6208
Fax: (312) 236-7117
www.imba.org

Mortgage Brokers Association
Illinois Assn of Mortgage Brokers
350 West 22nd Street
Lombard, IL 60148
Phone: 630-916-7720
Fax: 630-563-1784
www.iamb.org

INDIANA

Regulatory Agency
Dept of Financial Institutions
1024 State Office Building,
Indianapolis, IN 46204
Phone: 317-232-2955
www.in.gov/dfi

Mortgage Bankers Association
Indiana Mortgage Bankers Assn
1908 E 64th Street South Dr,
Indianapolis, IN 46220-2186
Phone: (317) 251-0682
Fax: (317) 259-4191
www.indianamba.org

Mortgage Brokers Association
Indiana Assn of Mortgage Brokers
5980 W 71st Street, Suite 200
Indianapolis, IN 46278
Phone: 317-964-1225
Fax: 317-964-1224
www.inamb.com

IOWA

Regulatory Agency
Iowa Division of Banking
200 East Grand Ave,Ste 300
Des Moines, IA 50309
Phone: 515-281-4014
Fax: 515-281-7688
www.idob.state.ia.us

Mortgage Bankers Association
Iowa Mortgage Assn
PO Box 6200
Johnston, IA 50131-6200
Phone: (515) 286-4300
Fax: (515) 280-4140
www.iowama.org

Mortgage Brokers Association
Iowa Assn of Mortgage Brokers
4949 Westown Pkwy, Ste 165-111
West DesMoines, IA 50266
Phone: 515-210-4675
Fax: 515-225-4885
www.iowamortgagebrokers.org

KANSAS

Regulatory Agency
Consumer Credit Commission
Jayhawk Tower
700 SW Jackson St,Ste1001
Topeka, KS 66603
Phone: 785-296-3151

Mortgage Bankers Association
Mortgage Bankers Assn of Greater Kansas
14904 W 87th Parkway
Lenexa, KS 66215
Phone: 913-894-1956
Fax: 913-397-8772
www.mbakc.com

Mortgage Brokers Association
Kansas Assn of Mortgage Brokers
14904 W 87th Parkway
Lenexa, KS 66215
Phone: 913-764-5600
Fax: 913-397-8772
www.kamb.org

KENTUCKY

Regulatory Agency
Dept of Financial Institutions
477 Versailles Road
Frankfort, KY 40601
Phone: 502-573-3390
Fax: 502-573-0086
www.kfi.ky.gov

Mortgage Bankers Association
Mortgage Bankers Assn of Kentucky
333 Whittington Pkwy
Louisville, KY 40222-4934
Phone: (502) 562-6450

Mortgage Brokers Association
Kentucky Mortgage Brokers Assn
PO Box 4584
Frankfort, KY 40604
Phone: 502-223-4840
www.kmba.net

LOUISIANA

Regulatory Agency
Ofc of Financial Institutions
PO Box 94095
Baton Rouge, LA 70804
Phone: 225-925-4660
Fax: 225-925-4548
www.ofi.state.la.us

Mortgage Bankers Association
Louisana Mortgage Lenders Assn
8550 Untited Plaza Blvd, Ste 1001
Baton Rouge, LA 70809-0200
Phone: (225) 922-4642
Fax: (225) 922-4011
www.lmla.com

Mortgage Brokers Association
Louisiana Mortgage Lenders Assn
8550 United Plaza Blvd, Ste 1001
Baton Rouge, LA 70809
Phone: 225-922-4642
Fax: 225-922-4611
www.lmla.com

MAINE

Regulatory Agency
Bureau of Financial Institutions
36 State House Station
Augusta, ME 04333
Phone: 207-624-8570
Fax: 207-624-8590
www.maine.gov/pfr/financialin
stitutions.index.shtml

Mortgage Bankers Association
Mortgage Bankers Assn of Maine
489 Congress St
Portland, ME 04101-3401
Phone: (207) 791-8412
Fax: (207) 774-5693
www.mortgagemaine.com

Mortgage Brokers Association
Maine Assn of Mortgage Brokers
PO Box 1053
Bath, ME 4530
www.mainemortgagebrokers.org

MARYLAND

Regulatory Agency
Maryland Division
of Financial Regulation
500 North Calvert St., Rm 402
Baltimore, MD 21202
Phone: 410-230-6100
Fax: 410-333-3866
www.dllr.state.md.us/finance

Mortgage Bankers Association
Maryland Mortgage Bankers Assn
PO Box 6293
Ellicott City, MD 21042-0293
Phone: (410) 465-6697
Fax: (617) 465-6699
www.mdmba.org

Mortgage Brokers Association
Maryland Assn of Mortgage Brokers
720 Light Street
Baltimore, MD 21230
Phone: 410-752-6262
Fax: 410-752-8295
www.mamb.org

MASSACHUSETTS

Regulatory Agency
MA Division of Banks
One South Station
Boston, MA 2110
Phone: 617-956-1500
Fax: 617-956-1599
www.mass.gov

Mortgage Bankers Association
Massachusetts Mortgage Bankers Assn
76 Canal St, Ste 301
Boston, MA 02114-2024
Phone: (617) 570-9114
Fax: (617) 570-9113
www.massmba.com

Mortgage Brokers Association
Massachusetts Mortgage Assn
607 North Ave, Building 14/2
Wakefield, MA 1880
Phone: 781-246-0601
Fax: 781-246-2625
www.massmort.org

MICHIGAN

Regulatory Agency
Office of Financial
& Insurance Svcs
PO Box 30224
Lansing, MI 48909
Phone: 517-373-3460
Fax: 517-335-0908
www.michigan.gov/cis

Mortgage Bankers Association
Michigan Mortgage Lenders Assn
PO Box 182520
Shelby Township, MI 48318-2520
Phone: (586) 226-2823
Fax: (248) 281-0307
www.mmla.net

Mortgage Brokers Association
Michigan Mortgage Brokers Assn
3300 Washtenaw Ave, Suite 220
Ann Arbor, MI 48104
Phone: 734-975-4426
Fax: 734-677-2407
www.mmbaonline.com

MINNESOTA

Regulatory Agency
Dept of Commerce
Div. of Financial Examinations
85 Seventh Place East, Ste 500
St Paul, MN 55101
Phone: 651-282-9855
www.state.mn.us

Mortgage Bankers Association
Mortgage Assn of Minnesota
1000 Westgate Dr, Ste 252
Saint Paul, MN 55114-1067
Phone: (651) 290-7474
Fax: (651) 290-2266
www.mortgageedu.com

Mortgage Brokers Association
Minnesota Assn of Mortgage Brokers
5200 Willson Road, Suite 300
Edina, MN 55424
Phone: 952-345-3240
Fax: 952-920-1533
www.mnamb.org

MISSISSIPPI

Regulatory Agency
Dept of Banking
& Consumer Finance
PO Drawer 23729
Jackson, MS 39225
Phone: 601-359-1031
Fax: 601-259-3557
www.dbcf.state.ms.us

Mortgage Bankers Association
Mortgage Bankers Assn of Mississippi
PO Box 55629
Jackson, MS 39296
Phone: (601) 605-6687
Fax: (601) 898-2456
www.msmba.org

Mortgage Brokers Association
Mississippi Assn of Mortgage Brokers
2107 Nicholson Avenue
Waveland, MS 39576
Phone: 866-844-6262
Fax: 601-926-1060
www.msamb.org

MISSOURI

Regulatory Agency
Mortgage Broker Section
Division of Finance
PO Box 716
Jefferson City, MO 65102
Phone: 573-751-3242
Fax: 573-751-9192
www.missouri-finance.org

Mortgage Bankers Association
Mortgage Bankers Assn of Missouri
101 E High St
Jefferson City, MO 65101-2989
Phone: (573) 634-4898
Fax: (573) 634-7429
www.mbamo.org

Mortgage Brokers Association
Missouri Assn of Mortgage Brokers
4700 S Lindbergh Blvd
St Louis, MO 63126
Phone: 314-909-9747
www.mamb.net

MONTANA

Regulatory Agency
MT Dept of Administration
Banking & Financial
Institutions Division
301 South Park, Suite 316
Helena, MT 59620
Phone: 406-841-2920
Fax: 406-841-2930
http://doa.mt.gov

Mortgage Bankers Association
Montana Bankers Assn
1 N Last Change Gulch
Helena, MT 59601
Phone: 406-443-4121
Fax: 406-443-7850
www.montantabankers.com

Mortgage Brokers Association
Montana Assn of Mortgage Brokers
PO Box 124
Helena, MT 59624
Phone: 406-227-5490
Fax: 406-227-5490
www.mtamb.com

NEBRASKA

Regulatory Agency
Nebraska Dept of
Banking & Finance
Commerce Court
1230 O Street, Suite 400
Lincoln, NE 68508
Phone: 402-471-2171
www.ndbf.org

Mortgage Bankers Association
Nebraska Mortgage Assn
6801 S 27th St
Lincoln, NE 68512-4823
Phone: (402) 323-1650
Fax: (402) 323-1530
www.nebraskamortgageassication.org

Mortgage Brokers Association
Nebraska Mortgage Assn
6801 S 27th St
Lincoln, NE 68512-4823
Phone: (402) 323-1650
Fax: (402) 323-1530
www.nebraskamortgageassication.org

NEVADA

Regulatory Agency
Mortgage Lending Division
3075 E Flamingo, # 104A
Las Vegas, NV 89121
Phone: 702-486-0780
Fax: 702-486-0785
www.mld.nv.gov

Mortgage Bankers Association
Mortgage Bankers Assn of Nevada
PO Box 60298
Las Vegas, NV 89160-0298
Phone: (702) 258-1842
Fax: (702) 453-4668
www.mbanv.org

Mortgage Brokers Association
Nevada Association of
Mortgage Professionals
6130 Elton Ave, # 224
Las Vegas, NV 89107
Phone: 702-216-0430
Fax: 702-216-0431
www.namp.us

NEW HAMPSHIRE

Regulatory Agency
Banking Dept
64b Old Suncook Rd
Concord, NH 3301
Phone: 603-271-3561
Fax: 603-271-1090
www.nh.gov

Mortgage Bankers Association
Mortgage Bankers & Brokers Assn
of New Hampshire
91 N State St, Ste 101
Concord, NH 03301-4300
Phone: (603) 228-4488
Fax: (603) 226-5885
www.mbba-nh.org

Mortgage Brokers Association
Mortgage Bankers & Brokers Assn
of New Hampshire
PO Box 0477
Waere, NH 3281
Phone: (000) 620 6001
Fax: Fax: (603) 529-5005
www.mbba-nh.org

NEW JERSEY

Regulatory Agency
Department of Banking
& Insurance / Div. of Banking
Ofc of Consumer Finance
PO Box 040
Trenton, NJ 08625
Phone: 609-292-5360
Fax: 609-292-5461
www.state.nj.us/dobi/index.shtml

Mortgage Bankers Association
Mortgage Bankers Assn of New Jersey
385 Morris Ave
Springfield, NJ 07081-1151
Phone: (973) 379-7447
Fax: (973) 379-5152
www.mbanj.com

Mortgage Brokers Association
New Jersey Assn of Mortgage Brokers
PO Box 309
Springfield, NJ 7081
Phone: 973-379-7447
Fax: 973-379-5152
www.njamb.org

NEW MEXICO

Regulatory Agency
Regulation & Licensing Dept
Financial Institutions Division
2550 Cerrillos Road, Third Floor
Santa Fe, NM 87505
Phone: 505-476-4885
Fax: 505-476-4670
www.rld.state.nm.us/index.html

Mortgage Bankers Association
New Mexico Mortgage Lenders Assn
PO Box 91058
Albuquerque, NM 87199-2700
Phone: (505) 821-2700
Fax: 505-823-9273
www.nmmla.org

Mortgage Brokers Association
New Mexico Assn of Mortgage Brokers
PO Box 3967
Albuquerque, NM 87190
Phone: 505-474-6864
Fax: 505-474-6963
www.nmamb.org

NEW YORK

Regulatory Agency
State of NY Banking Dept
Legal Financial Svcs Division
2 Rector Street, 21st Floor
New York, NY 10006
Phone: 212-618-6642
Fax: 212-618-6426
www.banking.state.ny.us

Mortgage Bankers Association
Mortgage Bankers Assn of New York
1055 Franklin Ave, Suite 304
Garden City, NY 11530
Phone: (212) 972-4790
Fax: (212) 687-4016
www.mbany.org

Mortgage Brokers Association
New York Assn of Mortgage Brokers
25 North Broadway
Tarrytown, NY 10591
Phone: 914-332-6233
Fax: 914-332-1541
www.nyamb.org

NORTH CAROLINA

Regulatory Agency
NC Commissioner of Banks
4309 Mail Service Center
Raleigh, NC 27699
Phone: 919-733-3016
Fax: 919-733-6918
www.nccob.org/NCCOB

Mortgage Bankers Association
Mortgage Bankers Assn of the Carolinas
PO Box 11721
Charlotte, NC 28220-1721
Phone: (704) 552-2860
Fax: (704) 552-7071
www.mbac.org

Mortgage Brokers Association
North Carolina Assn of
Mortgage Professionals
3901 Barrett Drive, Suite 202
Raleigh, NC 27609
Phone: 919-783-0767
Fax: 919-783-0967
www.ncmortgage.org

NORTH DAKOTA

Regulatory Agency
Dept of Banking
State Capitol
600 E Boulevard,
Bismarck, ND 58505
Phone: 701-328-9933
www.nd.gov/dfi

Mortgage Bankers Association
No State Association
Contact Mortgage Bankers Association
Phone: 202-557-2700
www.mortgagebankers.org

Mortgage Brokers Association
No State Association
Contact National Association of
Mortgage Brokers
Phone: 703-342-5900
www.namb.org

OHIO

Regulatory Agency
Dept of Commerce
Division of Financial Institutions
77 S high Street, 21st Floor
Columbus, OH 43266
Phone: 614-466-2221
www.com.state.oh.us

Mortgage Bankers Association
Ohio Mortgage Bankers Assn
30200 Detroit Rd,
Cleveland, OH 44145
Phone: (614) 221-9493
Fax: (614) 221-2335
www.ohiomba.org

Mortgage Brokers Association
Ohio Assn of Mortgage Brokers
5686 Dressler Road NW, Suite 150
North Canton, OH 44720
Phone: 330-497-7233
Fax: 330-497-6533
www.oamb.org

OKLAHOMA

Regulatory Agency
Dept of Consumer Credit
4545 Lincoln Blvd, Suite 104
Oklahoma City, OK 73105
Phone: 405-521-2653
Fax: 405-521-6740
www.ikdocc.state.ok.us

Mortgage Bankers Association
Oklahoma Mortgage Bankers Assn
101 N Broadway Ave, Ste 650
Oklahoma City, OK 73102-1091
Phone: (405) 270-1098
Fax: (405) 270-1091
www.okmba.org

Mortgage Brokers Association
Oklahoma Assn of Mortgage Brokers
PO Box 1334
Jenks, OK 74037
Phone: 918-760-4950
Fax:
www.okamb.com

OREGON

Regulatory Agency
Dept of Consumer and
Business Services
350 Winter Street NE, Rm 410
Salem, OR 97301
Phone: 503-947-7300
Fax: 503-947-7862
http://egov.oregon.gov/dcbs

Mortgage Bankers Association
Oregon Mortgage Lenders Assn
3727 SW Barnes Rd, PMB # 500
Portland, OR 97225
Phone: (503) 223-6622
Fax: (503) 223-1659
www.oregonmla.org

Mortgage Brokers Association
Oregon Assn of Mortgage Professionals
5285 SW Meadows Rd., Suite 320
Lake Oswego, OR 97035
Phone: 503-223-6262
Fax: 971-204-0209
www.oamb.com

PENNSYLVANIA

Regulatory Agency
Department of Banking
Bureau of Licensing
& Consumer Affairs
333 Market Street, 16th Floor
Harrisburg, PA 17101
Phone: 717-787-3717
Fax: 717-787-8773
www.banking.state.pa.us

Mortgage Bankers Association
Mortgage Bankers Assn of Pennsylvania
587 James Dr,
Harrisburg, PA 17112-2273
Phone: (717) 545-3975
Fax: (717) 545-9247
www.mba-pa.org

Mortgage Brokers Association
Pennsylvania Assn of Mortgage
Brokers
2690 Commerce Drive, Suite 100
Pennsylvania, PA 17110
Phone: 888-311-PAMB
Fax: 717-540-9499
www.pamb.org

RHODE ISLAND

Regulatory Agency
State of Rhode Island &
Providence Plantations
Dept of Business Regulation,
Div of Banking
233 Richmond Street, Suite 231
Providence, RI 2903
Phone: 401-277-2405
www.state.ri.us

Mortgage Bankers Association
Rhode Island Mortgage Bankers Assn
180 S Main St
Providence, RI 02903-2907
Phone: (401) 421-2338
Fax: (401) 421-2338
www.rimba.org

Mortgage Brokers Association
Rhode Island Mortgage Brokers Assn
180 South Main Street
Providence, RI 2903
Phone: 401-421-2338
Fax: 401-421-2338
www.rimba.org

SOUTH CAROLINA

Regulatory Agency
SC State Board
of Financial Instituitons
Consumer Finance Division
1015 Sumter Street, 3rd Floor
Columbia, SC 29201
Phone: 803-734-2020
Fax: 803-734-2025
www.llr.state.sc.us

Mortgage Bankers Association
Mortgage Bankers Assn of the Carolinas
PO Box 11721
Chatlotte, NC 28220-1721
Phone: (704) 552-2860
Fax: (704) 552-7071
www.mbac.org

Mortgage Brokers Association
South Carolina Mortgage Brokers Assn
1122 Lady Street, Suite 914
Columbia, SC 29201
Phone: 803-771-0416
Fax: 803-771-7207
www.scmba.org

SOUTH DAKOTA

Regulatory Agency
Division of Banking
State Capitol
500 East Capitol Ave
Pierre, SD 57501
Phone: 605-773-3421
www.state.sd.us/drr2/reg/bank
/BANK-HOM.htm

Mortgage Bankers Association
No State Association
Contact Mortgage Bankers Association
Phone: 202-557-2700
www.mortgagebankers.org

Mortgage Brokers Association
South Dakota Assn of
Mortgage Brokers
421 W. 18th St.,
Sioux Falls, SD 57105
Phone: 605-330-6033
Fax: 605-330-6032
www.sdamb.org

TENNESSEE

Regulatory Agency
State of Tennessee
Dept of Financial Institutions
502 John Sevier Building
Nashville, TN 37219
Phone: 615-741-2236
http://state.tn.us.tdfi

Mortgage Bankers Association
Tennessee Mortgage Bankers Assn
5543 Edmondson Pike # 136,
Nashville, TN 37211-5808
Phone: (931) 438-0238
Fax: (931) 433-6289
www.tnmba.org

Mortgage Brokers Association
Tennessee Assn of Mortgage Brokers
25 Century Blvd, Suite 602
Nashville, TN 37214
Phone: 615-695-5232
Fax: 615-695-5233
www.tnamb.org

TEXAS

Regulatory Agency
Texas Savings & Loan Dept
2601 North Lamar, Suite 201
Austin, TX 78705
Phone: 512-475-1350
Fax: 512-475-1360
www.sml.state.tx.us

Mortgage Bankers Association
Texas Mortgage Bankers Assn
823 Congress Ave, Ste 220
Austin, TX 78701-2668
Phone: (512) 480-8622
Fax: (512) 480-8621
www.texasmba.org

Mortgage Brokers Association
Texas Assn of Mortgage Brokers
14901 Quorum Drive, Suite 435
Dallas, TX 75254
Phone: 800-850-8262
Fax: 530-484-2906
www.tamb.org

UTAH

Regulatory Agency
State of Utah Dept of Financial
Institutions
PO Box 89,
Salt Lake City, UT 84110
Phone: 801-538-8830
Fax: 801-538-8894
www.dfi.state.ut.us/default.htm

Mortgage Bankers Association
Utah Mortgage Lenders Assn
60 S 600 E, Ste 200
Salt Lake City, UT 84102-1066
Phone: (801) 363-1353
Fax: (801) 363-1352
www.umla.org

Mortgage Brokers Association
Utah Assn of Mortgage Brokers
60 South 600 East, Suite 150
Salt Lake City, UT 84102
Phone: 801-364-6302
Fax: 801-364-8483
www.uamb.org

VERMONT

Regulatory Agency
Dept of Banking, Insurance,
Securities & Health Care Admin
89 Main Street, Drawer 20
Montpelier, VT 5620
Phone: 802-828-3301
www.bishca.state.vt.us

Mortgage Bankers Association
Vermont Mortgage Bankers Assn
PO Box 8503
Essex, VT 05451-8503
Phone: (802) 879-0334
Fax: (802) 879-2435
www.vermontmba.com

Mortgage Brokers Association
Vermont Assn of Mortgage Brokers
PO Box 315
West Dover, VT
Phone: 802-464-5512

VIRGINIA

Regulatory Agency
State of Virginia
Bureau of Financial Institutions
PO Box 640,
Richmond, VA 23218
Phone: 804-371-9657
Fax: 804-371-9704
www.scc.virginia.gov/division/
banking/index.htm

Mortgage Bankers Association
Tidewater Mortgage Bankers Assn
638 Independence Pkwy, Suite 100
Chesapeak, VA 23320
Phone: (757) 473-2160
Fax: (757) 473-9897
www.tmba.org

Mortgage Brokers Association
Virginia Assn of Mortgage Brokers
PO Box 71197
Richmond, VA 23255
Phone: 888-711-VAMB
Fax: 804-288-5559
www.vamb.org

WASHINGTON

Regulatory Agency
Dept of Financial Institutions
Division of Consumer
Services & Adminstration
210 11th Street SW, Room 300
Olympia, WA 98504
Phone: 360-902-8703
Fax: 306-664-2258
www.dfi.wa.gov

Mortgage Bankers Association
Washington Mortgage Lenders Assn
PO Box 141
Olympia, WA 98507-0104
Phone: (360) 943-9206
Fax: (360) 943-9545
www.wmla.com

Mortgage Brokers Association
Washington Assn of Mortgage Brokers
PO Box 2016
Edmonds, WA 98020
Phone: 866-425-7250
Fax: 425-771-9588
www.wamb.org

WEST VIRGINIA

Regulatory Agency
Division of Banking
1900 Kanawha Blvd, East
Building # 3, Room 311
Charleston, WV 25305
Phone: 304-558-2294
Fax: 304-558-0442
www.wvdob.org

Mortgage Bankers Association
No State Association
Contact Mortgage Bankers Association
Phone: 202-557-2700
www.mortgagebankers.org

Mortgage Brokers Association
No State Association
Contact National Association of
Mortgage Brokers
Phone: 703-342-5900
www.namb.org

WISCONSIN

Regulatory Agency
Dept of Financial Institutions
PO Box 7876
Madison, WI 53707
Phone: 608-261-7578
www.wdfi.org

Mortgage Bankers Association
Wisconsin Mortgage Bankers Assn
PO Box 1606
Madison, WI 53701-1606
Phone: (608) 255-4180
Fax: (608) 283-2589
www.wimba.org

Mortgage Brokers Association
Wisconsin Assn of Mortgage Brokers
16 North Carroll Street, Suite 900
Madison, WI 53703
Phone: 608-259-9262
Fax: 608-251-8192
www.wambrokers.com

WYOMING

Regulatory Agency
State of Wyoming Dept of Audit
Division of Banking-UCCC
122 West 25th Street, Herschler
Building - 3rd Floor
Cheyenne, WY 82002
Phone: 307-777-7797
Fax: 307-777-6605
http://audit.state.wy.us

Mortgage Bankers Association
No State Association
Contact Mortgage Bankers Association
Phone: 202-557-2700
www.mortgagebankers.org

Mortgage Brokers Association
No State Association
Contact National Association of
Mortgage Brokers
Phone: 703-342-5900
www.namb.org

Additional Resources

Homebuyer Education Classes

Homebuyer education classes are offered through many community colleges or local agencies. For a complete list of approved agencies, please go to www.HUD.gov or visit the resource web site at www.TheMortgageMyths.com.

Other Web Site Resources

Listed below are several web site resources that will assist in providing additional information on loans, programs, and property values.

FNMA (Fannie Mae)	www.FannieMae.com
FHLMC (Freddie Mac)	www.FreddieMac.com
GNMA (Ginnie Mac)	www.GinnieMae.gov
FHA	www.HUD.gov
Veterans Affairs (VA)	www.VA.gov
Zillow	www.Zillow.com (approximate home values)
Trulila	www.Trulila.com (search home values)
Redfin	www.Redfin.com (home values)
HouseValues.com	www.HouseValues.com (home values)
Bankrate.com	www.Bankrate.com (consumer information)
MGIC	www.MGIC.com (mortgage insurance info)

Terms You Need to Know

The mortgage industry has a language all its own. The following list is provided to help you navigate some of the strange terms you will hear:

Addendum Additional terms or changes in a contract or purchase agreement.

Adjustment period The length of time that determines how often the interest rate can change on an adjustable-rate mortgage.

Amortization Creative process of retiring debt through predetermined periodic payments.

APR Annual percentage rate. Calculation disclosed on the TIL that indicates the total cost of credit when all costs are taken into account.

ARM Adjustable-rate mortgage. A mortgage in which the rate can change.

AU Automated underwriting. System used by lenders to determine a borrower's eligibility for loan programs.

Cap The maximum adjustment allowed for an ARM loan.

Certificate of Eligibility Document issued by the VA that shows the amount of entitlement used and any remaining guaranty available.

Chattel Term used to describe personal property included in a real estate transaction.

CLTV Combined loan to value. The total LTV with all mortgages included.

Closing A ritual that takes place with all the parties to sign documents, disburse funds, and transfer the ownership of real estate.

Closing costs Costs incurred by borrowers, or paid on their behalf, incurred to close on a real estate transaction. Listed on the GFE and the HUD-1.

COFI Cost of Funds Index. An index sometimes used to determine rates or increases in rates or payments.

CPI Consumer Price Index. An index sometimes used to determine rates or increases in rates or payments.

DO Desktop Originator. AU system utilized by Fannie Mae to automatically approve loan applications.

EMD Earnest money deposit. Funds put up by a purchaser to show "good faith" intentions on performance of a sales agreement.

FHA Federal Housing Administration. Part of the Department of Housing and Urban Development.

FICO Fair Isaac & Company term to describe its proprietary credit scoring system used by lenders to determine risk.

FSBO For sale by owner. Term used when owners decide to sell their own property.

GFE Good Faith Estimate. A list of estimated costs involved in the loan transaction provided to the borrower prior to or within three days of application.

HELOC Home equity line of credit. Credit line established that is secured by a piece of real property.

HUD Department of Housing and Urban Development. Oversees FHA.

HUD-1 Settlement statement used at closing to disclose all costs and credits for borrowers and sellers involved in a real estate transaction.

Index An indicator that is used to calculate rates on some mortgage loan products, notably ARM loans. Changes on a regular basis.

K-1 Federal tax form that reports income for an individual who has an interest in a partnership or corporation.

Lien A claim against a property. A mortgage is a type of lien.

LP Loan Prospector. Automated underwriting system used by Freddie Mac to approve borrower loan applications.

LTV Loan-to-value ratio. For example, an 80% LTV on a $100,000 loan would be $80,000.

Margin An amount added to an index to calculate an adjustment for an ARM loan. The margin remains constant during the loan period.

MIP Mortgage insurance premium. Term used for insurance required for FHA-insured loans.

Mortgage A loan that is secured by real estate. States that are not trust states use a mortgage as the legal instrument to secure a lien against the property.

Note Legal instrument that describes the terms of the mortgage loan.

PITI Term used to describe a payment that includes principal, interest, taxes, and insurance.

PMI Private mortgage insurance. Insurance required on high-LTV conventional loans.

POC Paid outside closing. Costs that are paid in advance or by another party outside of the actual closing.

Prepaids Costs of a transaction listed on the GFE or HUD-1 that are paid in advance for the benefit of the borrower.

Reserves Amount of liquid assets that a borrower has left after paying all costs for the transaction.

RESPA Real Estate Settlement and Procedures Act. Federal law that requires lenders to disclose settlement costs (GFE and HUD-1) as well as the procedures for consumer disclosure.

TIL or TILA Truth in Lending Act. Federal law that requires lenders to follow certain guidelines for disclosing loan terms, including the APR.

Title The owner of record for a parcel of real estate.

Title Insurance Insurance that covers the lender and/or new owner of real estate against any title defects.

VA Department of Veterans Affairs. Insures loans made by lenders to eligible veterans.

VAFF VA Funding Fee. Fee paid for insuring VA loans.

VOD Verification of Deposit. Used by a lender to establish liquid assets.

VOE Verification of Employment. Used by a lender to establish employment information, including income.

VOM Verification of Mortgage. Used by a lender to establish mortgage balance and payment history if not on a credit report.

VOR Verification of Rent. Used by a lender to determine rental history and payments.

YSP Yield spread premium. An amount paid by a lender to a broker as compensation for origination and delivery services.

Index

ABCs of FHA Lending, The
    (Cummings), 66
ABN AMRO Mortgage Group, 25
Acquisti, Audrey:
    on interest rates, 41
    on preapproval, 120–127
    on reviewing documents before
        closing, 145
Acquisti, Dave:
    on large versus small lenders,
        25–26
    on refinancing, 163
Adjustable-rate mortgages (ARMs):
    basics of, 38, 44–46
    calculation method, 44
    changes in mortgage payments and,
        154–155
    consumer handbook on, 121,
        208–222
    FHA*Secure* program and, 172, 203
    as financial tool, 46–47
    versus fixed-rate, 43–47
Agbamu, Atare, 166–167
American Society of Home Inspectors
    (ASHI), 98
Amortization, 38
Annual Escrow Disbursement
    statement, 155
Annual percentage rate (APR), 40
Applications:
    forms for, 122–125, 245–250
    never signing blank, 10

Appraisals:
    conformity and neighborhood,
        95
    house cost and, 74–76
    house value and, 83–86
    types of, 84–85
Appreciation, of real estate values:
    booming areas and, 101–103
    buying maximum house to take
        advantage of, 61–63
    inflation and, 173–175
    investing and, 4–5
    versus stock gains, 33–35
    term of mortgage and, 49–50
Approval, for loan, *see also*
    Preapproval, for loan;
    Qualification, for loan
    bankruptcy and, 7–10, 63–65
    credit score and, 9, 43, 55–61
    divorce and, 63–65
    losing of, 125–127
    process and time frame, 119–121
    self-employment and, 133–135
Attorney, need for, 96–97
Auction process, for foreclosure
    property, 109–113
Automated Underwriting (AU), 137

"Bad" neighborhoods, loans for houses
    in, 7
Balloon note, seller financing and, 188
Bank of America, 25

273

Bankruptcy:
  to avoid foreclosure, 204
  loan qualification and, 7–10, 63–65
Banks, *see* Lenders
Bennett, Pam:
  on annual percentage rate, 40
  on credit, 8, 52
Biweekly payments, 183–185
Booming areas, cautions about,
    101–103
Break-even periods:
  rate of return on investments and,
    175–176
  refinancing costs and, 157–161
Buyer:
  lease-option plans and, 198
  money-making and, 114–115
  present when offer made to seller,
    89
  seller financing and, 185–188
Buyer's agent, 86–88, 89
Buying Your Home guide, 223–244

Capitalization appraisal, 85
Capozzoli, Jay, 120
Caps, on ARM rates, 44–45
Carroll, George, 128
Cash back at closing, avoiding, 29, 33
Certified Mortgage Consultant
    (CMC), 22
Certified Mortgage Planning
    Specialist (CMPS), 22
Chapter 13 bankruptcy:
  approval and, 63–65
  FHA loans and, 67
Chapter 7 bankruptcy:
  approval and, 65
  FHA loans and, 67
Citibank, 25
Citizenship, not needed for loan,
    11–12

Closing:
  costs of and GFE, 71–72, 160
  costs of and seller financing, 186
  reviewing documents at, 150–152
  reviewing documents before,
    144–146
  scheduling of, 139–140, 143–144
  time from approval to, 119–121
Closing Protection Letter, 143
Combination loans, 69
Commissions, real estate agents and,
    86–89
Comps, 84
Conditional loan approval, *see*
    Preapproval, for loan
Condominiums:
  advantages and disadvantages of
    owning, 91–92
  financing of, 90–91
Confidentiality, choice of lender and,
    27–29
Consideration, contract and, 103–104
Consolidation, of credit card accounts,
    51–52
  mortgage refinancing and, 161–164
Constructions loans, compared to
    refinancing, 172–173
Consumer credit, 7–8, 53. *See also*
    Credit score (FICO)
*Consumer Handbook on Adjustable
    Rate Mortgages*, 121, 209–222
Contracts:
  attorneys and, 96–97
  basic elements of, 103–104
  condominiums and, 91
  importance of writing accurate,
    82–83
  key details of, 105
  review of FSBO, 79–80
  withdrawal from, 106–107
Cost appraisals, 84

Covenants, restricted, 91–92
Credit cards.
    consolidating debt from, 51–52,
        161–164
    paying off before making extra
        mortgage payments, 185
    reducing debt to qualify for loans,
        195
Credit enhancement services, 55
Credit life insurance, 153–154
Credit score (FICO):
    basics of, 51–52
    components of, 56–58
    credit reports and, 52–55
    Fair Isaac website, 54
    loan approval and, 9, 43, 55–61
    steps to raise, 61
    working with imperfect, 7–10,
        50–55, 63–65

Debt, see also Credit cards
    -to-equity ratio, 125
    -to-income ratio, 179
Deed in lieu of foreclosure, 202,
    204
Delinquent accounts, credit score
    and, 51
Disclosures:
    accuracy of seller's, 92–95
    Buying Your Home guide, 223–244
    Consumer Handbook on Adjustable
        Rate Mortgages, 209–222
    loans and, 122–125
Divorce, credit and, 63–65, 127
Documents, see also Contracts;
        specific documents
    reviewing at closing, 150–152
    reviewing before closing, 121
Down payments:
    damaged credit and, 9
    gifts intended for, 181–183, 194

lease-option plans and, 197–200
nonconforming lenders and,
    194–195
size of, 18–20
subprime loans and, 54
working without, 16–18
Dual agents, 86, 88–89

Early-payment penalty, 50, 164–165
Emotion-based transaction, avoiding,
    100–101
Equifax, 52–53
Equity, in home:
    benefits of reinvesting, 5–6
    financial difficulties and, 201–202
    leverage and, 62–63
    lines of credit and, 172–173,
        177–179
    reverse mortgages and, 166–169
    term of mortgage and building of,
        47–50
Earnest money deposit (EMD),
    103–105
    loss of, 106–107
    return of, 106
Escrow accounts:
    refinancing and, 179–180
    for repairs, 135–136, 150
    sale of loan and, 169
    for taxes and insurance, 132–133,
        154–155
Eviction, from foreclosure property,
    112
Expense ratios, loan approval and,
    57–59
Experian, 52–53

Factual information, providing to
        lender, 9–10
Fair Housing Act, 137
Fair Isaac, see Credit score (FICO)

Falk, Joe:
  on professionals' certification and
    advice, 23–24
  on shopping for mortgage, 32
Faynor, Ruth:
  on approval process, 121
  on choice of lender, 28–29
  on closing, 140
  on standard documents, 123
Federal Housing Administration
    (FHA):
  foreclosed properties of, 81
  loans and, 66–67
  LTV cash-out option and, 164
  mortgage insurance from, 70
  programs of, 189–190
  refinancing and, 171, 180
  reverse mortgages and, 167
  Secure program of, 172, 203
Federal Reserve Bank, 42–43
Ferguson, Ginny:
  on credit score, 54, 59–60
  on finding credit, 9
  on Vantage Score, 55
FHA, *see* Federal Housing
    Administration (FHA)
First-time buyers, 190
Fixed-rate mortgages (FRMs):
  versus ARMs, 43–47
  changes in mortgage payments and,
    154–155
  interest rate and, 38
Flipping Houses For Dummies
    (Roberts), 113
Floating interest rate, 128–129
Flood insurance, 152
Forbearance, 201–202, 203
Foreclosure, *see also* Foreclosure
    properties, investing in
  approval and, 65
  house hunting and, 81

process of, 107–109, 205
  working to avoid, 201, 203–204
Foreclosure Investing For Dummies
    (Roberts), 113
Foreclosure properties, investing in,
    see also Foreclosure
  advantages and disadvantages of,
    111–112
  buying at auction, 109–111
  estimating amount to bid for,
    112–113
  financing and, 24
  repair costs and, 136
  title searches and, 143
Foreign nationals, loans to, 11–12
Form 1003 (Uniform Residential Loan
    Application), 10, 122–123, 125
  sample form, 123, 245–248
For sale by owner (FSBO), 77–80
Friends, as lenders, 26–29
Fully-indexed rate (FIR), 45

GFE, *see* Good Faith Estimate (GFE)
Gifts, for down payment:, 181–183, 194
Good Faith Estimate (GFE):
  cautions about, 71–72
  online lenders and, 32
  sample form, 124, 249
Government-insured loans, *see*
    Federal Housing Administration
    (FHA); Veterans Administration
    (VA)
Government-seized properties, 81

Habib, Barry, 22
Home buyer checklist, 253–258
Home equity line of credit:
  compared to refinancing, 172–173,
    177–179
  down payment and, 20
Home equity loan, 177–178

Home financing check list, 259
Home inspectors, 97–100. See also
    Inspection of property
Homeowners insurance:
    amount needed, 152–153
    escrow and, 132–133
Homestead exemption, 176
Home warranties, 146–149
House hunting:
    emotions and, 100–101
    preapproval before, 12–16
    price range and, 80–82
    property checklist for, 94
Housing expense ratio, 57–58
HUD-1 (Uniform Settlement
    Statement), 144–146
    reviewing at closing, 150–151
    sample form, 251–252

Income approach appraisal, 85
Income taxes, see Taxes, income
Inflation, appreciation of home value
    and, 173–175
Information piracy, size of lender and,
    25
Inquiries, on credit report, 52
Inspection of property, see also
    Repairs
    by buyer, before closing, 99,
        149–150
    foreclosure property, 109–111
    by professional, 97–100
Insurance, see also Private mortgage
    insurance (PMI)
    changes in mortgage payments and,
        154–155, 169
    credit life, 153–154
    escrow accounts for, 132–133,
        179–180
    flood, 152
    homeowners, 132–133, 152–153

sale of loan and, 169
    title, 108, 112, 140–143, 188
Interest rates:
    closing and prepaid, 143–144
    credit score and, 56–58
    Federal Reserve and, 42–43
    goal of finding lowest, 37–42
    locking in, 128–131
    other elements of mortgage pricing
        and, 37–42
    PMI and, 69
    prepayment penalties and, 164
    refinancing at higher, 161–164
    refinancing savings calculation,
        157–161
Internet:
    finding lenders on, 29–33
    interest rates and, 129
    realtors and, 74
    risk and, 90
    tips for using, 31–32
Investments, in property, see also
        Foreclosure properties,
        investing in
    break-even point and, 175–176
    buying rather than renting, 2–6
    condominiums, 90–92
    disclosures and, 93–94
    down payment and rate of return
        on, 20
    expandability of house size and, 96
    lease-options and, 197–200
    preapproval and, 16
    prepayment penalties and, 165
    profit and, 2–6, 33–35, 114–115
    rental properties and, 116–118
    repair costs and, 136
    term of mortgage and, 47–50
    title searches and, 143
IRA, borrowing down payment from,
    194

Junk fees:
  mortgage pricing and, 39–40
  watching for at closing, 145

Kleyla, Tim:
  on checking documents at closing,
    151
  on home inspection, 99
  on warranties, 147–148

Land contracts (lease-purchase plans),
    197, 199
Landlording, 116–118
Lease-option plans, 197–200
Lease-purchase plans (land contracts),
    197, 199
Lenders, *see also* Approval, for loan;
    Nonconforming lenders
  buying from inventory of, 81
  financial difficulties and working
    with, 200–205
  foreclosure auctions and, 110–111
  foreclosure process and, 107–109
  friends and local institutions as,
    26–29
  gifts for down payments and,
    181–183, 194
  on Internet, 29–33
  profiling and, 137
  size of, 24–26
Leverage:
  down payment and rate of
    investment return, 20
  equity and appreciation, 62–63
  term of mortgage and, 47–50
Licensing, of agents and brokers,
    21–24
Life insurance, 153–154
Limited income, stated assets
    (LISA) documentation program,
    193

Loan officers:
  regulation of, 21–24
  using agent's preferred, 73–75
Loans, *see also* Approval, for loan;
    Closing; Payments
  assistance in qualifying for, 7–10
  availability of special financing,
    66–67
  best ways to compare, 41–42
  checklist for, 259
  condominiums and, 90–91
  need for attorney and, 96–97
  paying biweekly, 183–185
  sale of, 169–170
  seller financing and, 180, 185–189
  term of, 47–50, 183–185
Loan servicers:
  sale of loan and, 169–170
  seller financing and, 189
Loan to value ratio (LTV) , refinancing
    and, 164, 178–179
Local lenders, 26–29, 74
Location:
  home appreciation and, 101–103
  importance of, 114–115
  loans for houses in "bad"
    neighborhoods, 7
  size of house and, 95–96
Longer versus shorter-term
    mortgages, 47–50
Lost interest, refinancing calculations
    and, 160
LTV (loan to value ratio), refinancing
    and, 164, 178–179
Luxury homes, renting of, 117
Lyons, Sarah, 169

Market:
  importance of knowing, 5–6
  length of property on, 82
Material facts, on applications, 87

Metaj, Aaron, 126
Mortgage brokers:
  licensing and regulation of, 21–24
  nonconforming lenders and,
    195–196
  safety and, 24–26
  special financing and, 66–67
Mortgage Brokers Association (MBA),
  21
Mortgage credit, 7–8, 53
Mortgage insurance, see Private
  mortgage insurance (PMI)
Mortgage Insurance Program (MIP),
  of FHA, 70
Mortgage pricing, 38–42
Murphy, Terri:
  on checking contracts, 82
  on FSBO properties, 78–79
  on house as investment, 61
My Community mortgage, 7, 8, 65

National Association of Mortgage
  Brokers (NAMB), 21–23
National associations and regulatory
  agencies, 269
Neighborhood, see Location
No-documentation loans, 134,
  192–194
No down payment mortgages,
  16–18
No income, no assets (NINA)
  documentation program, 193
No income documentation program,
  193
No income verification documentation
  program, 192
Noncitizens, loans to, 11–12
Nonconforming lenders, 190–196
  documentation methods of,
    192–194
  down payments and, 194–195

mortgage brokers and, 195–196
reducing debt to qualify with, 195
Non-payment assistance funds
  (DPAs), 18
Nonresident aliens, loans to, 11–12
No ratio documentation program,
  192–193

Online mortgages, see Internet
Oral agreements, 103
Origination fee, for mortgage,
  39–40
Out-of-state banks/brokers, 26
Overages, mortgage pricing and, 38

"Par" rate, 38–39
Payments:
  biweekly, 183–185
  changes in, 154–155
  dates of and closing, 143–144
  financial difficulties and, 200–205
  versus rent payments, 2–6
  sale of loan and, 169–170
Perfect credit history, 50–55
Personal profiling, 137
Personal property, defined, 82
Piggy-back loans, 17, 71
Points, on mortgage, 38–40, 41
Preapproval, for loan, 12–16
  advantages of, 14–15
  conditional, 119–121
  losing of, 125–127
  varying lender criteria and,
    131–132
Preferred partners, 73–75
Prepaid interest, 143
Prepayment penalty, 50, 164–165
Prequalification, for loan, 12–16
  form for, 15, 260
  worksheet for, 58
Privacy, choice of lender and, 27–29

Private mortgage insurance (PMI):
  advantages of, 68–70
  credit history and, 8
  down payment and, 18, 19
  refinancing and, 160, 163
  sale of loan and, 169
Processing fee, for mortgage, 39–40
Profiling, by lenders, 137
Property:
  condition at closing, 149–150
  importance of location of, 114–115
  inspection by professional, 97–100
Property taxes, *see* Taxes, property
Public notice, of foreclosure, 108
Public record postings, 7–8, 54
Purchase agreement:
  basic elements of, 103–104
  key details of, 105
  withdrawal from, 106–107
Purchase price:
  house hunting within price range,
    80–82
  size of house and, 95–96
  value of stretching yourself for,
    61–63
  what's included in, 82–83

Qualification, for loan, *see also*
    Approval, for loan;
    Prequalification, for loan
  differs from approval, 56–57
  nonconforming lenders and,
    192–194
  personal qualification form, 260
  refinancing and, 170–172
  rental properties and, 117

Real estate agents:
  preferred partners of, 73–75
  sales agreements and, 104
  working for seller, 74, 86–89

Real property, defined, 82
Rebates, mortgage pricing and,
    38–40
Referrals:
  importance of, 21–24
  from real estate agents and loan
    officers, 73–75
Refinancing:
  calculating benefits of, 157–161
  compared to home equity lines of
    credit, 172–173, 177–179
  floating interest rate and, 129
  at higher interest rates, 161–164
  qualifying for, 170–172
Regulation, of brokers and lenders,
    21–24
Renting:
  of investment property, 116–118
  versus buying decision, 2–6
Repairs:
  appraisals and, 83–86
  escrow accounts for, 135–136
  refinancing and, 170–172
Restrictive covenants, condominiums
    and, 91–92
Retirement income, reverse
    mortgages and, 166–169
Reverse mortgages, 166–169
Reverse Mortgages for Dummies
    (Lyons), 169
Risk, purchase price and, 61–63
Roberts, Ralph:
  on avoiding fraud, 10
  on down payments, 18
  on finding good agent, 15–16
Rodriguez, Dave, 126

Safety, size of lender and, 24–26
Sale of loans, 169–170
Sale of property, money-making and,
    114–115

Sales agreement, *see* Purchase
    agreement
Sales comparison appraisal method,
    84
Second mortgages:
    consolidation of debt and, 161–164
    down payment and, 17
    financial difficulties and, 204
    PMI and, 69, 70
    self-employed borrowers and,
    134
Self-employment, loan approval and,
    133–135
Sellers:
    accuracy of disclosures by, 92–95
    down payment and, 17
    financing by, 180, 185–189
    FSBO savings and, 77–80
    home warranty of, 146–149
    PMI and, 69
    preapproval and, 14
    presentation of offer to, 89
    real estate agents' obligations to, 74,
    86–87, 89
    self-employed borrowers and,
    134–135
Settlement, *see* Closing
Settlement Costs and You booklet,
    121
Shorter versus longer-term mortgages,
    47–50
Short sale, 202, 204
State associations and regulatory
    agencies, 260–268
Stated income, stated assets
    documentation program (SISA),
    192, 193
Stated income, verified assets
    documentation program, 192
Stocks, versus real estate as
    investment, 33–35

Subprime loans, 7–8, 10
    alternatives to, 67
    categories of borrowers, 8–9
    credit history and, 53–54

Take backs, by seller, 17
Taxes, income:
    mortgage interest's impact on, 3–4,
    35
    PMI and, 70
    profit on sale of home and, 5–6, 35
    reverse mortgages and, 168
    self-employed borrowers and, 134
Taxes, property:
    changes in mortgage payments and,
    154–155
    escrow accounts for, 132–133,
    179–180
    income tax deduction and, 3, 35
    sale of loan and, 169
Tenants, income from, 116–118
Term of mortgage:
    benefits of longer versus shorter,
    47–50
    biweekly payments and, 183–185
Third-party fees, mortgage pricing
    and, 39–40
30-year bonds, 42
Tierce, Amy:
    on earnest money deposit, 106
    on good faith estimate, 72
    on interest rates, 41
    on Internet lending, 30–31, 90
    on mortgage insurance, 19
    on preapproval, 125
    on private mortgage insurance, 68
    on regulation of certification, 21–22
Title insurance:
    finding of, 142–143
    foreclosure properties and, 108, 112
    to protect buyer, 141

Title insurance: (*continued*)
  to protect lender, 140–141
  seller financing and, 188
Torch, Paco:
  on credit, 54–55
  on good faith estimate, 72
  on handling financial difficulties, 202–203
  on preapproval, 127
Total expense ratio, 57–59
TransUnion, 52–53
Truth-in-Lending Disclosure statement, sample form, 122, 124, 250
2% rule, for refinancing, 157–158

Underwriting fee, for mortgage, 39–40
Uniform Residential Loan Application (Form 1003), 10, 122–123, 125
  sample form, 123, 245–248
Uniform Settlement Statement (HUD-1), 144–146
  reviewing at closing, 150–151
  sample form, 251–252
Upset price, at foreclosure auction, 110
U.S. citizenship, loan qualification and, 11–12
Utilization ratio, on credit cards, 51

VA, *see* Veterans Administration (VA)
Vacation homes, condominiums as, 92
Value of home:
  appraisals and, 83–86
  determining of, 96

important when house hunting, 80–82
inflation and, 173–175
Vantage Score, 55
Verbal offers, 103
Veterans Administration (VA):
  foreclosure properties of, 81
  loans and, 16–18, 190, 196

Walk-through inspection, 99, 149–150
Warranty policies, 146–149
Wealth creation, *see* Investments, in property
Weinstein, Eric:
  on house hunting, 81
  on loans to non-citizens, 11–12
  on trust, 16
Wells Fargo, 25
When Your Home is on the Line booklet, 121
Wooding, Tim:
  on credentials, 22–23
  on credit scoring, 60
  on Internet lending, 31–33
  on locking in rates, 130
  on refinancing to obtain cash, 177
Wooten, Lorenzo, 7–8
Written contract, *see* Contracts; Documents

Yamato, Patrice:
  on ARMs, 45
  on closing, 139–140
  on credentials, 22, 23
Yield spread premium (YSP), 38

Zero-down mortgages, 16–18